Inventing Nanjing Road

Inventing Nanjing Road

Commercial Culture in Shanghai, 1900-1945

Edited by
Sherman Cochran

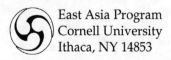

East Asia Program
Cornell University
Ithaca, NY 14853

The Cornell East Asia Series is published by the Cornell University East Asia Program and has no formal affiliation with Cornell University Press. We are a small, non-profit press, publishing reasonably-priced books on a variety of scholarly topics relating to East Asia as a service to the academic community and the general public. We accept standing orders which provide for automatic billing and shipping of each title in the series upon publication.

If after review by internal and external readers a manuscript is accepted for publication, it is published on the basis of camera-ready copy provided by the volume author. Each author is thus responsible for any necessary copy-editing and for manuscript formatting.

Submission inquiries should be addressed to Editorial Board, East Asia Program, Cornell University, Ithaca, New York 14853-7601.

Number 103 in the Cornell East Asia Series.
© 1999 by Sherman Cochran. All rights reserved
ISSN 1050-2955
ISBN 1-885445-63-6 hc
ISBN 1-885445-03-2 pb
Printed in the United States of America
14 13 12 11 10 09 08 07 06 05 04   9 8 7 6 5 4 3 2

COVER DESIGN BY KAREN K. SMITH

⊗The paper in this book meets the requirements for permanence of ISO 9706:1994.

To the memory of
Janis Lee Cochran

Contents

Introduction

Part I
Importing Western-style Commercial Culture into Shanghai

Part II
Inventing Shanghai-style Commercial Culture

Part III
The Fate of Shanghai's Commercial Culture in Wartime

Afterword

Nanjing Road, Broadway, and the Roots of International Corporate Commerce

Illustrations

Tables

Acknowledgments

This book has resulted from a series of conferences sponsored by the Luce Foundation for Asian Studies, and I am grateful to the foundation for its support and to Dr. Terry Lautz for skillfully and sensitively representing the foundation. The sponsorship came in the form of a Luce Collaborative Research Grant which was awarded jointly to Cornell University and the Shanghai Academy of Social Sciences (SASS). The conferences were held at both institutions, and at each conference scholars from both institutions participated. In holding the grant, it was my privilege to work with two fellow principal investigators who are both distinguished economic historians. Professor Zhang Zhongli, the president of SASS, and Professor Ding Richu, the leader of SASS's Institute for Economic Research. I wish to thank them and SASS's other participants in the SASS-Cornell Luce project, especially Professors Shen Zuwei, Du Xuncheng, Huang Hanmin, Pan Junxiang, Zhang Zhongmin, Xu Dingxin, Lu Xinglong, and Zhong Xiangcai who all made presentations in conferences at both SASS and Cornell. For making these conferences run smoothly, all credit goes to administrators at both institutions, notably Mr. Li Yihai and the Office of International Exchange at SASS and Ms. Laurie Damiani and the East Asia Program at Cornell.

The Luce Foundation grant was intended to produce collaboration between American and Chinese scholars, and I am pleased to report that it has achieved its objective. Unexpectedly it has produced other kinds of collaboration too. Since the Luce Foundation simultaneously awarded grants for SASS's collaboration with both the University of California at Berkeley and Cornell, Professors Frederic Wakeman and Wen-hsin Yeh of Berkeley and I teamed up and combined our efforts in Luce conferences held in Shanghai, Berkeley, and Ithaca. I have benefited from close cooperation with my Berkeley colleagues, and I want to thank Professor Yeh for participating in all three of the Luce conferences in Ithaca and for hosting my visits to Berkeley.

In another form of institutional collaboration, young scholars at various American colleges and universities attended the Luce conferences at Cornell. Many were still in graduate school or had just then taken their first teaching jobs. They came to the first conference in the series as observers, but before the series was over, several of them gave presentations, and ultimately no less than five—Carrie Waara (University of Michigan Ph.D.), Carlton Benson (University of California at Berkeley Ph.D.), Hanchao Lu (University of California at Los Angeles Ph.D.), Poshek Fu (Stanford University Ph.D.), and Susan Glosser (University of California at Berkeley Ph.D.)—have contributed essays to the present volume. It was exciting to hear about their new research and fresh ideas at the conferences, and it has been edifying to see them refine their interpretations since then.

Discussants were crucial to the success of the conferences, and our discussants were perceptive and helpful. They were Professors Marie-Clàire Bergere, Parks Coble, Jeffrey Cody, Robert Gardella, William Kirby, Thomas Lyons, Susan Naquin, Mark Selden, Vivienne Shue, Wen-hsin Yeh, and Madeleine Zelin.

On its way to publication this book has benefited from several people's efforts. An anonymous reader provided extremely useful comments and suggestions for all of the contributors. Dr. Liren Zheng solved a wide range of problems, especially concerning translations. Mr. Paul Festa closely read and rigorously edited the entire manuscript. Ms. Melissa Bernath made the index. Mr. James Barbat expertly formatted the text. Ms. Karen Smith presided over the editorial process. Mr. Lincoln Yung supported Cornell's Project on Business in Shanghai with gifts that have subsidized publication of this book. I am grateful to all of these people for their contributions.

If I may end on a personal note, I believe that I am acting on behalf of others as well as myself in dedicating this book to the memory of my wife Jan. For many years prior to her recent death, Jan used her beautifully accented Mandarin to befriend Chinese colleagues in Shanghai, and she came to understand the city's commercial culture by exploring not only Nanjing Road but also seemingly obscure and fascinatingly idiosyncratic shops and markets. In Ithaca, she graciously hosted participants at Cornell's Luce conferences on Shanghai and prepared elegant Chinese meals which put our Chinese guests at ease and made their visits memorable. As one observed with a smile of satisfaction, "Long after the conference discussions are forgotten, Jan's food will be remembered." For these and for many other reasons, it is appropriate to honor Jan in this book's dedication. I only wish that the dedication were to her rather than to our memory of her.

Introduction

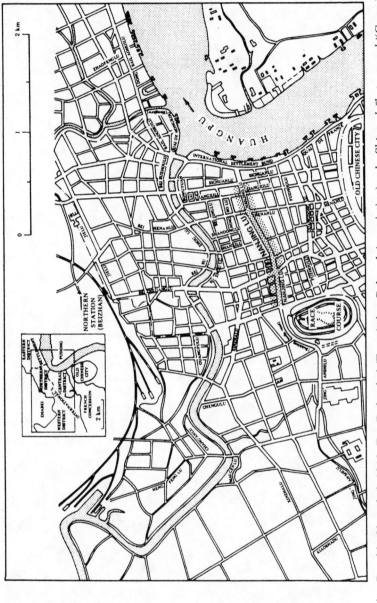

Nanjing Road in Shanghai, 1919. Tōa Dobūnkai (East Asian Cultural Association), ed., *Shina shōbetsu zenshi*(Complete list of the Provinces of China), vol. 15 (Tokyo, 1920) from Marie-Claire Bergère, *The Golden Age of the Chinese Bourgeoisie 1911- 1937* (Cambridge University Press, 1989), 101.

Commercial Culture in Shanghai, 1900-1945: Imported or Invented? Cut Short or Sustained?

Sherman Cochran

The essays in this book are about the construction of commercial culture in Shanghai during the first half of the twentieth century. The contributors have not given definitions of commercial culture in each essay, but they have tacitly agreed to a working definition that distinguishes commercial culture from the more familiar notions of high, popular, and mass culture. Unlike high culture, commercial culture is thoroughly secular; it lacks strong moral and religious overtones. Unlike popular culture, commercial culture is distinctly urban; it originates in cities, not the countryside. And unlike mass culture, commercial culture has locally oriented means of expression, not fully standardized mass media.

In retrospect, the construction of commercial culture in Shanghai marks a pivotal point between China's past and China's present. In China's late imperial past—even before extensive contact with the West—the country already had an indigenous "consumer society" insofar as its consumers had available to them a wide array of brand names during the Ming (1368-1644) and Qing (1644-1912) dynasties.[1] And in contemporary China of the 1980s and '90s, urban Chinese are beginning to establish a "consumer culture" according to social scientists' current observations of consumers' individual and collective behavior.[2] Although historical and social scientific research on these topics is barely underway, it has generated hypotheses and conclusions which frame and hinge upon some of the questions addressed in this book. If China already had a consumer society before extensive contact with the West in the

---

1. Gary G. Hamilton and Chi-Kong Lai, "Consumerism without Capitalism: Consumption and Brand Names in Late Imperial China," in Henry J. Rutz and Benjamin S. Orlove, eds., *The Social Economy of Consumption* (Lanham, Maryland: University Press of America, 1989), 267.

2. Deborah S. Davis, "Urban Consumers and Consumer Culture in Contemporary China," a proposal for a conference held at Yale University, New Haven, Connecticut, January 9-12, 1997.

nineteenth century, what was new about Shanghai's commercial culture in the first half of the twentieth century? By the same token, if Shanghai already had a commercial culture during the first half of the twentieth century, what legacies has it bequeathed to the emerging (or reemerging?) consumer culture in today's China?

The contributors to this book all agree that during the early twentieth century Shanghai's commercial culture was centered in the private sector of the city's economy, especially in the "concession" areas under Western or Japanese rule. These concession areas originated following the British military victory over China in the Opium War of 1839-42 and the signing of the treaty of Nanjing in 1842 which for the first time granted the British the privilege of unrestricted trade and residence in Shanghai and four other Chinese ports (Guangzhou, Xiamen, Fuzhou, and Ningbo). In the wake of this Anglo-Chinese treaty, the United States, France, and other Western countries signed similar treaties with the government of China's Qing dynasty which made available to them uninhabited land for settlements at Shanghai—the only one of the original five treaty ports that immediately began to grow and the one destined to become China's biggest city.

In the late nineteenth century, the British and other Westerners imported Western designs and materials to be used in building a new infrastructure for the International Settlement in Shanghai. Their insistence on making it Western and the relevance of this Western-centered approach to Shanghai's commercial culture were particularly apparent in the construction of Nanjing Road (Nanjing lu) which eventually became Shanghai's (and China's) single most central commercial place. As early as the 1850s British land developers opened this road to link the Huangpu River's west bank (known to Westerners as Shanghai's Bund and to Chinese as *waitan*) with their new race course, which they called a "park," and they named the new road "Park Lane" (Huayuan dao). In 1865, Western officials on the Shanghai Municipal Council in the city's foreign settlement gave Nanjing Road its current name (simultaneously naming all of the streets parallel to it after Chinese cities too).[3] By then Chinese had designated Nanjing Road as Shanghai's main street, referring to it in the vernacular as The Great Road (Da malu) and referring to streets running parallel to it and immediately south of it as Second Street (Er ma lu), Third Street (San ma lu), Fourth Street (Si ma lu), and Fifth Street (Wu ma lu), which were also known (and are still known) as Jiujiang Road, Hankou Road, Fuzhou Road, and Guangdong Road. In the late nineteenth century, the

---

3. Wu Guifang, *Shanghai fengwu zhi* (Scenery and stories of Shanghai) (Shanghai, 1982), 47-51.

Shanghai Municipal Council acknowledged and enhanced Nanjing Road's centrality by building their city hall on it (in 1864), installing gas lamps along it (in 1865), introducing electricity to it (by 1882), providing running water for it (by 1883), and carrying out other public works projects serving it.[4]

In the first years of the twentieth century, entrepreneurs in the private sector added new forms of transportation to funnel shoppers into Nanjing Road. In 1908, Shanghai's first streetcar company ran trolleys up and down a mile of tracks on it between the Bund and Tibet Road (Xizang lu), and in 1910 a steam-powered ferry began regularly delivering passengers from Pudong on the Huangpu River's east bank to a dock located on the west bank at the foot of Nanjing Road.[5]

The contributors to this volume have not debated the significance of the Western intrusion in China and the Western role in designing and building up Shanghai in the nineteenth century. In fact, they have all implicitly acknowledged the importance of Shanghai's Western-style infrastructure by citing Nanjing Road as the central location or point of origin for a wide variety of commercial enterprises: department stores (in Wellington Chan's essay), advertisers (in my essay), magazine and book stores (within the "Nanjing Road sphere" on a parallel street in Carrie Waara's essay), silk shops (in Carlton Benson's essay), housing developments (in Hanchao Lu's essay), cinemas (in Poshek Fu's essay), and manufacturers' associations (in Susan Glosser's essay). What they have debated or at least approached from different angles is the issue of whether foreign influence was decisive in the creation of Shanghai's commercial culture during the first half of the twentieth century. Between 1900 and 1937, was Shanghai's commercial culture imported from the West or invented locally? And between 1937 and 1945, was the history of this commercial culture cut short by Japanese military invasions and occupations of the city or was it sustained locally even in wartime? The following essays contain more than one answer to each of these questions, and they have been grouped according to where their authors stand on the issues.

---

4. Zheng Zu'an, "Jindai Shanghai dushi de xingcheng—yibasisannian zhi yijiuyisinian Shanghai chengshi fazhan shulue" (The formation of the modern city of Shanghai—the story of the development of Shanghai as a city, 1843-1914), in Wang Pengcheng, et al., eds., *Shanghai shi yanjiu* (Studies in Shanghai history) (Shanghai, 1984), 181.

5. Wu Shenyuan, *Shanghai zui zao de zhongzhong* (The first things to appear in Shanghai) (Shanghai, 1989), 49-50.

A. Nanjing Road in 1871 was lined with two-story modern-fronted shops which featured Chinese-style signboards (*zhao pai*). Cen Dechang, *Shanghai zujie lue shi* (A short history of Shanghai's International Settlement), (Shanghai, 1931), facing p. 280.

B. Nanjing Road in 1911 was still lined with similar shops and signboards and had acquired electric power lines and poles. G. L. Wilson, "Architecture, Interior Decoration, and Building in Shanghai: Twenty Years Ago and To-day," *China Journal*, 12.5 (May 1930): following 248. I am grateful to Jeffrey Cody for alerting me to this article.

C. Nanjing Road in 1930 was lined with taller concrete buildings which replaced wooden-fronted shops. Since 1908 trolleys had transported passengers to shops extending for a mile along Nanjing Road from the city's waterfront (on the Huangpu River) westward to Tibet Road. Ibid.

D. Nanjing Road (on the right) in 1945 was lined with numerous multi-storied concrete buildings including skyscrapers. This photograph was taken from Tibet Road looking east on the day that Japan ended its wartime occupation of Shanghai. AP/Wide World Photos.

Importing Western-style Commercial Culture into Shanghai

In the first two essays, Wellington Chan and I document the roles played in Shanghai's commercial culture by entrepreneurs from abroad. In his essay, Chan focuses on Cantonese owners of department stores who had gained experience in Australia or North America and had established headquarters in Hong Kong before they extended their operations to Shanghai and built the city's first department stores. These Cantonese "pioneers" (as Chan calls them) blazed a trail for commercial culture in Shanghai by introducing it as an alternative to the traditional approach used by local Chinese merchants. Chan notes that the local Shanghainese merchants had developed sophisticated techniques for selling goods during Shanghai's considerable history as a commercial center (dating from the Ming period), and he argues that their commitment to this old way of doing business prevented them from adopting Western commercial techniques (such as advertising in newspapers and displaying goods in open cases) despite the presence of Western-owned businesses which could have served as models for Chinese-owned businesses in Shanghai during the nineteenth century. As a result, even though Nanjing Road was built by the British and became lined with Western- and Chinese-owned shops during the nineteenth century, it still lacked vitality as a center for commercial culture as late as the 1910s according to Chan. Not until the Cantonese entrepreneurs Ma Yingbiao and the Guo brothers opened Shanghai's first department stores on Nanjing Road in 1917 and 1918 did this street "take off" (in Chan's phrase). In those two years, he suggests, the construction of two new Cantonese-owned Western-style department stores, Sincere's (Xianshi gongsi) and Wing On (Yong'an gongsi), was the catalyst that set off a building boom on Nanjing Road and attracted bigger crowds of consumers to this street than to any other in Shanghai (and, for that matter, in all of China).

While Chan concentrates on Cantonese entrepreneurs who had learned from Western businesses, I take as my subject the Shanghai branch of a Western-owned business, British-American Tobacco Company (BAT). Founded in 1902, BAT had its worldwide headquarters in New York and established itself in Shanghai in the same year—fifteen years earlier than the Cantonese-owned department stores did. Like them, it exported to Shanghai techniques based on experience with commercial culture abroad, and as a cigarette company, it concentrated in particular on advertising. But BAT's American managers, unlike Cantonese managers of Shanghai's department stores, felt that their use of imported techniques was not initially effective in Shanghai. Instead of achieving instant popularity, BAT's American-made advertising was at first ignored or made the butt of Chinese jokes and puns.

BAT's top managers were Americans—James B. Duke presided over its worldwide headquarters in New York and James A. Thomas was Duke's appointee as the manager of its headquarters for China in Shanghai—but they reacted to the initial ineffectiveness of their advertising by shifting responsibility for it from the United States to China. First they exported printing presses and other publishing technology to Shanghai, and then they recruited local Chinese painters to produce advertising and local Chinese commercial agents to help distribute it not only in Shanghai but throughout China. By these means, they projected a Chinese image which made BAT seem less foreign and intrusive and more familiar and acceptable in China.

These two essays in part I of the volume raise the question of whether Shanghai's commercial culture was imported or invented and thereby set the stage for part II. Chan's essay provides a valuable starting point for this volume because the author has set a date, 1917-18, for the "take-off" of commercial culture in Shanghai.[6] More significantly, he has supported his case for department stores as the catalysts of commercial culture by analyzing the business practices of several of these stores. While his essay shows that Cantonese imported Western-style commercial culture into Shanghai, mine shows that Westerners did too. But my conclusions suggest that even though BAT was a Western-owned company, it only succeeded at making its advertising popular in China by relying on the inventiveness of local Chinese.

Inventing Shanghai-style Commercial Culture

In part II, Carrie Waara, Carlton Benson, and Hanchao Lu all highlight the inventiveness of local Chinese entrepreneurs and artists as the source of Shanghai's new commercial culture. This inventiveness, as each author mentions, has been celebrated by Shanghainese as the "Shanghai style" (*Haipai*). Ironically, the term *Haipai* originated as a negative characterization —an epithet coined in the late nineteenth century by Chinese critics in the rival

---

6. It is worth noting that Chan refers to the "take off" rather than the "origin" of commercial culture, and neither he nor any other contributor to this volume has pinpointed a date when commercial culture originated in Shanghai. Hanchao Lu's essay in this volume and a recent essay by Rudolf Wagner on the history of publishing both suggest that the origins of Shanghai's commercial culture can be traced to the 1870s. More specifically, Wagner has argued that 1872, the year of the founding of the newspaper *Shenbao* and the publishing house Shenbaoguan, "in fact marks the beginning and first high point of Shanghai's modern print culture." Rudolf G. Wagner, "Commercialization of Chinese Culture: Ernest Major in Shanghai," a paper presented at the Symposium on the Urban Development of Modern Chinese Cities at Shanghai Academy of Social Sciences, Shanghai, August 22-23, 1996.

city of Beijing to pan the kind of opera and painting then being done in Shanghai. But in the early twentieth century, Shanghainese seized upon this designation and applied it to themselves with positive connotations. As Waara, Benson, and Lu all show, Shanghainese gave meaning to the term *Haipai* by imaginatively combining commerce and culture.

Carrie Waara's principal examples of Shanghai-style historical figures are local Chinese who published art magazines in Shanghai between the founding of the Chinese republic in 1911 and the Japanese military invasion of China in 1937. Compared to Benson and Lu, she has given more attention to her Chinese subjects' receptivity to Western thought especially in their "competitive nationalism" which caused them to join China's "struggle for a higher position in the hierarchy of nations" and in their willingness to accept Western and Japanese standards for judging the quality of the technical and industrial arts. But her major emphasis is on Chinese art publishers and the contributors to their magazines as inventors, not as slavish imitators of foreign models. They showed awareness of foreign designs and invoked foreign motifs, but they did so for the sake of constructing a Shanghai-style modern commercial culture—Shanghai-style modern applied arts and technology, Shanghai-style modern houses and decorations, Shanghai-style modern industrial innovations.

Besides inventing new representations of things, local Chinese artists and art publishers invented new representations of people, especially one type of person: the Shanghai-style modern woman. Waara quotes the Chinese writer Cao Juren as saying,"*Haipai* [Shanghai style] is like a modern girl," and she illustrates his point by citing covergirls from magazines of the 1920s and 1930s who all appear "confident, stylish and beautiful . . . the model of contemporary, urban propriety." These covergirls were more than duplicates of their counterparts on the covers of Western magazines. In Waara's view, they should be seen in relation to Chinese "classic beauties" (*shinu*), the figures in a genre of Chinese portrait painting that originated as early as the Ming dynasty and continued during the first half of the twentieth century. Thus were the representations of covergirls on Shanghai's magazines both modern and Shanghai-style.

Waara's general observations about the Shanghai style and specific references to the Shanghai-style modern woman complement Carlton Benson's treatment of these same subjects. Like Waara, Benson opens his essay by briefly tracing the rise of the Shanghai style from its lowly origins as a smear term in the late nineteenth century to its elevated status as a badge of pride ostentatiously worn by Shanghainese during the first half of the twentieth century. Within his essay, again like Waara, Benson devotes considerable attention to representations of modern Shanghai-style women, and he shows how these representations were used in advertisements to construct a Shanghai-style commercial culture. But Benson has developed these themes very differently than Waara has done. Whereas she has called attention to an alliance of artists and entrepreneurs by analyzing the artists' publications, he has shown an alliance between artists and entrepreneurs by concentrating more directly on the entrepreneurs' commercial practices.

In Benson's essay, Chinese entrepreneurs took advantage of oral art forms: a traditional storytelling genre called *tanci* and a type of short song known as *kaipian* which was traditionally used to open a storytelling performance. The entrepreneurs in this case were silk merchants and advertising agents, and they proved to be extraordinarily inventive at adapting these old forms to a new mass medium—radio. For example, the silk store manager Wang Zhongnian, a local merchant whose shops had been in Shanghai since the 1870s, seems to have had little difficulty mastering the art of producing timely radio commercials in *kaipian*, particularly after he moved his Lao Jiu He Silk and Foreign Goods Emporium to the heart of Shanghai's commercial district on Nanjing Road in 1928. In Benson's richly detailed account of the early 1930s, Wang deftly adjusted his promotional songs to shifts in the political winds. In Wang's most imaginative and subversive radio promotions, he outmaneuvered the New Life Movement, a political campaign in which the Nationalist government of Chiang Kai-shek used the mobilizational methods of modern fascism to restore traditional Confucian values. Since the government called for patriotism, Wang echoed its patriotic rhetoric, but whereas the government tried to achieve militaristic austerity, Wang cunningly commanded consumers and especially women to fulfill their obligations as patriots by buying Chinese-made silk and satin. In their *kaipian*, Wang's storytellers promoted fashion-consciousness, zealous consumerism, and other attitudes which, Benson argues, undermined the austere anti-materialism of the New Life Movement. In Benson's words, "Wang Zhongnian urged women to fulfill their patriotic duty by practicing customs that were in many ways inimical to New Life ideals."

As this rivalry between Shanghainese merchants and China's government was played out, Benson shows, the merchants proved to be far from defenseless. The techniques of silk merchant Wang Zhongnian were adopted by his local Chinese rivals, and he and other merchants extended their reach by employing advertising agents who, ironically, promoted consumerism in *kaipian* commercials for Wang and other entrepreneurs at the very same time that they promoted anti-consumerism in *kaipian* commercials for Chiang Kai-shek's New Life Movement. In the end, Benson concludes, Shanghainese merchants created "a commercial culture that could inspire and swamp an official campaign."

Benson's emphasis on the inventiveness of local Shanghainese is reinforced by Lu Hanchao's essay. Even as Benson traces the history of a distinctive form of Shanghainese local storytelling, so Lu traces the history of a distinctive form of Shanghainese local architecture. Even as Benson focuses on the twentieth-century commercial practices of local silk merchants whose shops had been located in Shanghai since the nineteenth century, so Lu focuses on the twentieth-century commercial practices in Shanghai's modern real estate market whose origins he finds in the nineteenth century. And like both Benson and Waara, Lu explicitly attributes the growth of commercial culture in China to modern Shanghainese and their development of the Shanghai style.

The "stone-framed wooden door" house (*shikumen*) is the cultural form analyzed by Lu. According to his chronology, it was first built in the 1870s and it owed one of its key original features—construction in rows—to Western influence. But even at the outset it was not wholly Western; its interior design was derived from Chinese sources, particularly the Chinese courtyard house (*siheyuan*). Over time, local Chinese made all major subsequent renovations, notably the replacement of the original U-shaped stone-framed wooden door houses with single bay alleyway houses (*lilong*) which resembled the stone-framed wooden door houses but were built on a smaller scale, shrinking to one-fourth the size of the originals by the 1930s.

According to Lu, Shanghai's housing market paralleled the development of the stone-framed wooden door house in following a similar two-phase pattern: it originated with Westerners and then passed largely into the hands of local Shanghainese. Lu maintains that throughout Chinese history there had been no modern real estate market (in which commercial-minded developers built consumer-oriented, similar-looking houses) until Westerners created one at Shanghai in 1860. But once this market came into existence, local Chinese immediately entered it and eventually flocked into it in large numbers. As Lu emphasizes, these local Chinese real estate agents in Shanghai were not confined to "great real estate investors" (who numbered over 3,000 by the late 1940s) and other land owners. Far more numerous were "second landlords" who subletted to "third tenants." Whether landowners or subletters, Chinese entrepreneurs handling real estate proliferated as Shanghai's population jumped from approximately 1 million in 1900 to 3 million in 1930 and 5.5 million in 1949 and as more and more stone-framed wooden door houses were built and then were subdivided to the point where single rooms or even parts of single rooms accommodated entire families. In an extraordinary triumph for an architectural form, stone-framed wooden door houses spread from their original location around Nanjing Road in the 1870s throughout Shanghai in the early twentieth century. By the 1940s, alleyway houses constituted no less than

72 percent of the city's residences, and of these alleyway houses, three-quarters were stone-framed wooden door houses.

The history of this architectural form and its promoters, Lu concludes, shows the extent to which local Chinese participated in the construction of Shanghai's commercial culture. In this case, Western influence "may have served as the first motive power (in the sense of getting the ball rolling) but the later development and innovation were almost entirely Chinese." These Chinese creators of China's commercial culture were, more specifically, modern Shanghainese: "Shanghai has long been regarded as the epitome of China's commercial culture. . . . It is legitimate to name such a culture after a city, hence the term Haipai (the Shanghai school or the Shanghai type)."

Taken together, the essays by Waara, Benson, and Lu make the case for the inventiveness of local Shanghainese and for their success at constructing a strong, pervasive and durable commercial culture in Shanghai during the early twentieth century. Benson has demonstrated its ability to fend off the Nationalist government, Lu has traced its spread into the roots of urban society, and Waara has surveyed its promotion of a new lifestyle throughout the 1920s and 1930s. But could it survive a military invasion and foreign occupation? It was put to this test during the Sino-Japanese War of 1937-45.

The Fate of Shanghai's Commercial Culture in Wartime

Like the other contributors to this volume, Poshek Fu and Susan Glosser have written essays that bear upon the issue of whether Shanghai's commercial culture was imported or invented. Both have singled out commodities imported from the West—film in Fu's case and milk in Glosser's case—and both have analyzed how local Chinese entrepreneurs promoted these commodities in Shanghai's commercial culture. But compared to the other contributors, Fu and Glosser have devoted less attention to whether Shanghai's commercial culture was imported or invented and more attention to the duration of its survival in the course of the Sino-Japanese War of 1937-45. On this latter issue, both agree that Shanghai's commercial culture survived during the late 1930s, but each provides a somewhat different assessment of its fate during the early 1940s.

In Poshek Fu's essay, he looks closely at the period 1937-41 when Shanghai was known as a "solitary island" (*gudao*) because the Japanese had occupied the surrounding area and the portion of the city previously under the jurisdiction of the Chinese government, leaving the Western concessions as the only part of Shanghai not under Japanese control. In the "solitary island" of the concession areas, Fu argues, Chinese filmmakers were unable to sustain their success more than two or three years.

Led by Shanghainese entrepreneur Zhang Shankun, they initially took advantage of Shanghai's commercial culture in a few spectacular films at the beginning of the war in 1938-39 but failed to find a formula for extending their commercial success in 1940 and 1941. Already experienced at advertising before entering the film industry, Zhang began making films on the eve of the war in the mid-1930s and soon became known for his "show-biz style" as Fu calls it. To promote his first wartime big budget success, *Diaochan*, Zhang used several advertising weapons: posters in the display windows of every department store on Nanjing Road, splashy advertisements in the city's newspapers, and an opening on Nanjing Road in the posh Grand Theatre which had never before shown a Chinese-made film, only Hollywood imports.

Buoyed by the success of *Diaochan* in 1938, the next year Zhang released a costume melodrama, *Hua Mulan Joins the Army*, based on the traditional story of a woman warrior who disguised herself as a man and led her father's troops into battle against foreign invaders during the Tang dynasty (617-907 A.D.). Zhang chose a timely topic because, as Fu observes, "The story beautifully captured the agony and ambivalence of the occupation experience, interweaving a patriotic theme with a romantic narrative intended to increase its box-office power." To increase its box-office power still more, Zhang advertised it even more extravagantly than he did *Diaochan*. Besides putting up posters, running newspaper advertisements, and arranging a grand opening, he recruited Chen Yunshang, a Cantonese actress from Hong Kong, to play the title role, and he mounted a campaign to make her (as Fu puts it) "into a Shanghai pop icon." Zhang's publicity portrayed her as both a modern Chinese beauty and a nationalistic Chinese patriot, and, as Fu shows, Zhang popularized this image through fan magazines, tabloid stories, gossip columns, star photos, life-sized posters, and personal appearances at the biggest department stores along Nanjing Road as well as in Shanghai's most glamorous night clubs.

After priming his potential audience with this publicity, Zhang arranged to have the first showing of *Hua Mulan Joins the Army* coincide with the grand opening of the theater in which it premiered, and he then enjoyed a handsome return on his investments in publicity. Opening on February 16, 1939 (New Year's Day on the Chinese lunar calendar), it ran for 85 days to packed houses and continued to draw crowds in later runs. Popular with film critics as well as viewing audiences, it became, in Fu's evaluation, "a wartime classic."

And yet, despite the commercial success of these and other films in 1938 and 1939, Zhang and other filmmakers began to falter as early as 1940. They did not fail for lack of trying; in fact, they produced over 200 feature films between 1937 and 1941—more than in any other four-year period prior to 1949. Instead they failed, Fu concludes, for lack of a formula that would have allowed them to duplicate Zhang Shankun's success with *Hua Mulan Joins the Army*. For all of their successes in commercial culture—including "the marketing genius of Zhang Shankun and the patriotic persona of Chen Yunshang"—they failed to overcome "the political predicament."

Although Fu challenges the standard interpretation of film history by maintaining that Shanghai continued to be a center for filmmaking between 1937 and 1941, he cites evidence of political and economic deterioration that raises doubts about whether any Chinese entrepreneur could have achieved commercial success in the early 1940s. If already suffering in 1940 and 1941, could local Chinese entrepreneurs possibly have sustained and taken advantage of Shanghai's commercial culture after the Japanese occupation of the entire city in December 1941?

In her essay, Susan Glosser gives a strikingly affirmative answer to this question. Like Fu, Glosser analyzes Chinese entrepreneurs' efforts in Shanghai to retain their market during the war, but unlike Fu, she finds that the entrepreneurs in her study did not succumb to deteriorating business conditions in the early 1940s. As producers of milk, they complained about wartime shortages and inflation (just as Chinese filmmakers and other entrepreneurs did), but they sustained the growth of their enterprises even after the Japanese occupied all of Shanghai between December 1941 and the end of the war in August 1945. In support of this claim, Glosser cites the case of the leading Chinese milk producer in Shanghai, T. M. Yu, who had 120 head of cattle before the war broke out in 1937, raised the number to 130 producing 1,200 pounds of milk per day by August 1943, and raised the number again to 144 producing 1,700 pounds per day by January 1944. Other Chinese entrepreneurs in the milk industry also generally retained and enlarged their dairies during the last years of the war, and after judiciously weighing the evidence, Glosser concludes, "Although the occupation strained the industry, it did not ruin it."

Glosser attributes the remarkable resilience of the milk industry to its Chinese entrepreneurs' successes at promoting their product in Shanghai's commercial culture and at negotiating favorable deals with Japanese officials in the city during the war. As promoters, they did not advertise in spectacular displays of patriotism like the ones staged by filmmakers. Instead they continued during the war (as in the prewar period) to run more sober promotional campaigns identifying milk with Western modernity and science. In their publicity, Glosser observes, "Milk was the epitome of what it meant to be scientific and modern." Although their advertisements for milk were not devoid of patriotism, they expressed themselves on the subject subtly, as in the promotional publication *Milk and Its Products* which urged Chinese consumers to drink milk for the sake of becoming scientific people and reminded them that "an unscientific people will find itself behind the times and conquered."

In their relations with the Japanese, Chinese entrepreneurs also made the case for milk as a modern and scientific product, and they did not take explicitly patriotic stands against the Japanese or let patriotism prevent them from selling to Japanese consumers during the war. Their negotiating style is concretely documented here (on the basis of Glosser's archival research) in a series of exchanges between the Chinese president of the Shanghai Dairy Association, T. M. Yu, and a Japanese official in the Shanghai Municipal Council's Commodity Control Division, O. Hirano. Despite their inability to use each other's native language, the two men established considerable rapport by communicating in English. During the early 1940s, Yu's official requests for permission to raise prices, secure electric power, and obtain raw materials won Hirano's endorsements, and in August 1945, even after Japan had lost the war and recalled Hirano, Yu and the Shanghai Dairy Association gave him a farewell party and expressed their gratitude by presenting him with a gift.

Did these Chinese entrepreneurs' styles of advertising and negotiating make them traitorous wartime collaborators with the enemy? Glosser addresses this sensitive question by evaluating their contributions to commercial culture, and she reaches conclusions about them that contrast sharply with Fu's conclusions about filmmakers' contributions to wartime commercial culture. Whereas Fu characterizes the filmmaker Zhang Shankun's patriotic portrayal of the actress Chen Yunshang as "mere fabrication," Glosser maintains that the milk makers' promises of health and vigor "cannot be dismissed as the simple products of cynical advertising." Even though T. M. Yu and other Chinese entrepreneurs in the milk industry did not make sensational appeals to popular patriotism during the war, Glosser insists that they believed in "the efficacy of the link between commercial success and national strength." The depth of this conviction did not mean that they were incapable of duplicity—as in their claims that they devoted themselves to feeding the Chinese needy when in fact they were supplying Japanese customers—but it raises the possibility that Shanghai's commercial culture was not devoid of moral concerns during the war.

Other Times and Places

This introduction has framed the following essays around issues on which the contributors have disagreed or have offered interpretations that seem at variance with each other. While the differences in the contributors' approaches are thought provoking, it is also worth noting that they seem to be in agreement on the broad questions raised earlier about the pivotal place of Shanghai's commercial culture in Chinese history. On the question of whether Shanghai's commercial culture was new compared to China's earlier "consumer society," the contributors have generally given an affirmative answer. They have acknowledged that pretwentieth-century Chinese cultural forms (of painting, storytelling, and architecture) persisted in the twentieth century, but they have concluded that these old forms were transformed when entrepreneurs adapted them in new markets (as for real estate) and new media (as in calendar-posters, magazines, radio, and film).

On the question of relevance to contemporary China, the contributors have not drawn explicit connections between past and present, but they have documented Chinese marketing techniques and commercial representations in the early twentieth century that might well serve as appropriate historical baselines for evaluating contemporary Chinese business practices and commercial art in the late twentieth century. Even though these marketing techniques and commercial images were all used before 1945, they are arguably more closely parallel to contemporary Chinese marketing techniques and commercial images than the ones produced in Mao's China (1949-1976) or in the West of the 1990s. To gain historical perspective on contemporary Chinese marketing techniques, for example, it is helpful to compare them with the techniques used by early twentieth-century Chinese entrepreneurs running department stores, silk shops, and dairies in the early twentieth century as described in the following essays. And to cast images of the contemporary Chinese woman in a historical light, it is worth taking a look at the presocialist modern Shanghai-style woman who is depicted in the following essays as a pin-up on a calendar poster, a covergirl on a magazine, a shopper in a radio commercial, and a patriotic movie star in a film.

All except the final essay in this volume are set in China with no more than passing references to other countries (or even other Chinese cities outside Shanghai). Nonetheless, the contributors have taken inspiration from William Taylor, the author of the one explicitly comparative essay in this book, and hope to benefit from exchanges of ideas with those interested in the history of commercial culture outside China as well as within it. We have deliberately modeled our title for this book after the title of a book in American history edited by Taylor, *Inventing Times Square* (1991),[7] and we are delighted that Taylor has added an afterword to our book that compares Shanghai with New York. His essay sets an example for us and for specialists on commercial culture elsewhere in the world by implicitly challenging us all to think globally and to make cross-cultural comparisons. Without question the subject of commercial culture begs for worldwide comparisons because, as pointed out

---

7. William R. Taylor, ed., *Inventing Times Square: Commerce and Culture at the Crossroads of the World* (New York, 1991).

by one of the contributors to *Inventing Times Square*, "consumption as a global ideal [is] the most universal ideal in human history."[8]

---

8. Eric Lampard, "Introductory Essay," in Taylor, ed., *Inventing Times Square*, 35.

Part I
Importing Western-style Commercial Culture into Shanghai

Selling Goods and Promoting a New Commercial Culture: the Four Premier Department Stores on Nanjing Road, 1917-1937

Wellington K.K. Chan

I

In China, the rise of commercial culture as an ideal to be sought after is strictly a twentieth century phenomenon. To be sure, there were many aspects of commercial culture in late imperial China. Many merchant groups, formed around various locality, commodity and profession-based guilds, played a prominent role in their communities, including, for example, those for the salt merchants in Yangzhou, bankers from Shanxi and Cohong merchants in Guangzhou.[1] The distinctive feature of their presence was their wealth which in turn affected a life style that was very different from the life style of a general population of subsistence peasants. Thus there was a long tradition of conspicuous consumption by many of the wealthy merchant elite. For example, two of the greatest Chinese novels of the late imperial period, *The Golden Lotus* and *The Dream of the Red Chamber*, provide a vivid glimpse of this aspect of commercial culture, for their central characters as well as their authors draw their income and life style from the world of commerce. Ximeng Qing of *The Golden Lotus* was a full-time merchant who enjoyed excellent connections with officialdom. As for the Jia family of *The Dream of the Red Chamber*, its fabulous wealth came from a combination of large landholdings, delegated businesses, official titles, and imperial commissions on state

---

1. The most recent study in Chinese and published in ten volumes is *Zhongguo shida shangbang*, ed. Zhang Haipeng (Hong Kong: Zhonghua shujie, 1995). The standard works on guilds are Ho Ping-ti, *Zhongguo huiguan shilun* (Taipei: Xuesheng Press, 1966); Negishi Tadashi, *Chugoku no girudo* (Tokyo: Nihon Hyoronsyahan, 1953); and Hosea Ballou Morse, *The Gilds of China: with an Account of the Gild Merchants or Cohong of Canton* (London: Longman, 1919).

industries. Indeed the lavish life style amidst a setting of abundant materialism, as described in *The Dream of the Red Chamber,* has given rise to the expression, "Grannie Liu pays a visit to the Jia family estate, the Daguan yuan."[2] It signifies, in a kind of tongue-in-cheek fashion, the rustic bumpkin who is totally befuddled by his or her first encounter with the opulent life style of the rich.

Throughout traditional China, such a display of materialistic excesses was often castigated by the official Confucian ideology. Even though there was a clear understanding that an active and prosperous political economy was a primary concern of the state, Chinese officials continued to repeat the formulaic observance that the merchant's profession represented *moye* (nonessential occupation). Commercial culture remained suspect while those elements which emphasized consumption-driven materialism were tolerated only in certain commercial enclaves such as Suzhou and Shanghai.

Around 1900, several elements came together to effect changes in perspective on commercial culture. The first element was China's political weakness vis-a-vis the West during this period. It led many influential reformers, from senior officials like Li Hongzhang to influential scholars like Liang Qichao, to promote modern commerce and industry as a means to gain wealth and power for the state. Liang, whose influential writing as late as 1896 was still denigrating merchants for being "subversive, manipulative and monopolistic," changed his attitude rather dramatically so that by 1902, he was effusively lauding the same Chinese merchants for being "industrious, frugal and entrepreneurial." Liang argued that his age was a Darwinian age in which only the fittest would emerge victorious; his aim was to raise support for his compatriot merchants in their "commercial warfare" (*shangzhan*) against their Western counterparts. To the extent that that struggle succeeded, China would become stronger and closer to modernity. In this roundabout way, Chinese merchants and their activities which formed part of the commercial culture were given a re-evaluation of staus and social meaning.[3]

A second element that promoted a positive attitude towards commercial culture was the growing prominence of the Western controlled settlements in Shanghai and Hong Kong during the second half of the nineteenth century. The leadership role Western merchants played in the community as well as their collective wealth, symbolized by their firms' grand edifices along the

---

2. *The Story of the Stone: a Chinese Novel by Cao Xueqin in Five Volumes,* Vol. 1, "The Golden Years," tr. by David Hawkes (Harmondsworth, England: Penguin Books, 1973), 150-166; esp. 157-160.

3. Cf. Wellington K.K. Chan, *Merchants, Mandarins and Modern Enterprise in Late Ch'ing China* (Cambridge, Mass.: Harvard University Press, 1977), 29-33, 39.

Bund in Shanghai, elevated the social status of their profession. The changes they brought with them, however, were not limited to Western-style buildings, but also extended to other material objects of two main types: wide boulevards, piped-in water, gas-lit street lamps, electricity and the telephone that qualitatively transformed the nature of municipal amenities, and new articles of daily necessities that included soap, face towels, machine-made sewing needles, perfumery and cosmetics, knitted stockings, glasswares, oil lamps and mechanical clocks.

These new objects of Western material culture, most of which were the products of the West's recent technological breakthroughs, were introduced or imported in rising quantities to Shanghai and Hong Kong from the 1860s or the 1870s on.[4] When they were combined with the newly installed institutions and rules of municipal governance, the most stunning transformations to both the physical setting and urban living occurred. No less than the Confucian scholar and radical reformer, Kang Youwei, noted in his diary that he was greatly impressed by what he saw in the same two cities while visiting them during the 1890s. But not even his perspicacious observations could have prepared him for the fact that for the next hundred years, similar artifacts of Western material and consumer culture would do more to transform China's modernization than all of the West's political and military interventions put together.

By the late 1890s, Shanghai's population in the International Settlement was about 350,000, having overtaken the size of the Chinese city to the south.[5] It had also become much more prosperous as wealthy Chinese gravitated to live there. They did so not just as a haven from political strife, but more importantly in order to enjoy the better living conditions provided by more accessible shopping and greater range of theaters and other forms of entertainment.[6] For by 1900, most of the larger establishments selling fancy domestic goods, as well as the new imported items mentioned earlier, were all concentrated inside the International Settlement, near or on Nanjing Road. Older shops of prominence which had established themselves in the Chinese city had also moved to or opened up branches in the new area. As a result,

---

4. On the new articles and their rapid increases, see *Shanghai jindai baihuo gongsi shangye shi* (Shanghai: Shanghai Academy of Social Sciences Press, 1988), 4-5. Note, for example, that the import of Western-style machine-made needles rose 12 times, from 207,000 dozen in 1867 to 2,422,000 dozen in 1894.

5. *Shanghai gonggong zujie shigao* (Shanghai: Renmin chuban she, 1980), Tables on pp. 12-13. The standard work on Shanghai's changing population is Zou Yiren, *Jiu Shanghai renkou bianqian di yanjiu* (Shanghai: Renmin chubanshe, 1982).

6. Cf. *Shanghai yanjiu ziliao* (Shanghai: Shanghai shudian, 1984; original edition by Shanghai tongshe, 1936), 559, 566.

several smaller streets and lanes, or sections of larger ones, formed clusters of shops selling common lines of specialized goods, such as drapery, footwear, hats, as well as those, like millinery and hosiery, that catered exclusively to ladies' fashions.[7]

The third element that brought forth a new view about commercial culture is closely related to these new shifts in the physical layout and socioeconomic tempo of the foreign concessions. The new objects of material culture imported from the West, however, did not by themselves cause a re-evaluation of commercial culture. What led to it was the way these new objects were introduced and marketed. The initial inspiration came from Western merchants who, by aggressively forcing Chinese ports to open to their goods, introduced many structural and functional changes to the manner in which the Chinese market conducted business. As his book title, *The Commercial Revolution in Nineteenth-Century China: The Rise of Sino-Western Mercantile Capitalism*[8], suggests, Yen-p'ing Hao argues that these changes constituted a "commercial revolution." They ranged from the simple offering of credit and discounts on goods taken in by Chinese wholesalers to the much more complex introduction of new forms of corporate and financial institutions and services, new types of transportation, market information and insurance.

There were also new ways of marketing and retailing goods, such as holding public auctions after publicizing them through newspaper advertisements, running holiday sales, and sprucing up the shopping area with elegant displays of goods and friendly service. For by the early 1900s, there were several Western-owned and -run modern style department stores, including Hall & Holtz and Weeks & Company in Shanghai, and Lane Crawford in both Shanghai and Hong Kong.[9] And even though these stores catered almost exclusively to the Western clientele, observant Chinese retailers were aware of these practices. But in this one area of marketing, it appears that Chinese retail shopowners were quite reluctant to adopt any of these Western practices. When the change finally arrived, it came from a different group of Chinese merchants. And with it also came the cultivation of a new attitude towards goods, services and consumption.

---

7. Du Zhensheng, *Haipai shangye wenhua yanjiu* (Shanghai: Shanghai Academy of Social Sciences Press, 1995), 26-30; Yao Gonghe, *Shanghai xianhua* (Shanghai: Guji chubanshe, 1989; original ed. 1917), 27-29, 66-67; *Shanghai jindai baihuo gongsi*, 22, 29.

8. (Berkeley: University of California Press, 1986)

9. Nicholas R. Clifford, *Spoilt Children of Empire: Westerners in Shanghai and the Chinese Revolution of the 1920s* (Hanover, NH, and London: Middlebury College Press, 1991), 62.

II

A long distinguished tradition of doing retail business, coupled with the growing prosperity of Shanghai's International Settlement, most likely made the traditional retailers less prepared to look to Western models for adoption. After all, several had beginnings stretching back to the older Shanghai of the pre-treaty port era. Even then, in around 1840, Shanghai had an urban population of over 200,000, and within its walled city, there were some 30 merchant-run native place guilds (*huiguan*) and common trade associations (*gongsuo*), making it one of the 20 largest cities in the country. Indeed, since at least the late Ming period, it has become one of China's major commercial centers, so that those merchants who were able to establish themselves in Shanghai became some of the best, or proved they could compete successfully with the best, in traditional China.[10] Moreover, the old way of retailing was in several aspects quite contrary to the Western way. For example, Western shop owners advertised liberally in newspapers to announce new and existing stock and provided glowing descriptions to enhance customers' interest. On the other hand, until the mid-1910s, only a few of their Chinese counterparts would place similar ads in any newspapers. It appears there was general belief that such publicity would only debase the good name and the value of any high-quality product. Thus, the only commercial items regularly advertised in the local Chinese newspapers were theater announcements and the exaggerated claims on the therapeutic effects of various medicinal pills.[11] For the same reason, high-priced goods were not openly displayed, but kept in locked cabinets upstairs, access to which was limited to properly introduced and wealthy patrons. Finally, because all the larger "retail" establishments in the International Settlement continued to rely on wholesale goods for the bulk of their total sales, the pressure to overhaul retail practices along Western lines was further reduced.

Turning that climate around took risk and vision. One group of entrepreneurs who made the greatest impact was led by three pioneers, Ma Yingbiao, Guo Luo and his brother Guo Chuan, and several of their associates, including Liu Xiji, Li Minzhou, Cai Xing and Cai Chang. Between 1917 and 1936, they opened four large-scale modern department stores on Nanjing Road in Shanghai that became the four premier stores of that type in all of China: The Sincere Company, Ltd. (1917) by Ma, The Wing On

---

10. Linda C. Johnson, *Shanghai: From Market Town to Treaty Port, 1074-1858* (Stanford: Stanford University Press, 1995), 8-9, 96-101, 111-16, 119-21.

11. Yao Gonghe, p. 136. Also see Ping Jinye and Chen Ziqian, "Shanghai guanggao shihua," in *Shanghai difangshi ziliao*, No. 3 (1984), 132-41.

Company, Ltd. (1918) by the two Guo brothers, The Sun Sun Company, Ltd. (1926) by Liu and Li, and the Dah Sun Company, Ltd. (1936) by the two Cais. One other common element among them is that they all came from neighboring villages in Zhongshan County of Guangdong Province which, being next to Macau, exposed them and their families to generations of Western influence. Indeed, all had gone to either Australia or North America to seek a living before returning to China. Many other Zhongshanese who did not go overseas worked for Western firms as compradors, including some very prominent ones like Tang Tingshu (Tong Kong-sing), Xu Run and Zheng Guanying. Their common native place origin as well as similar work experience created a social network which not only offered them mutual support in Shanghai and Hong Kong but also sharpened their particular perspective on how consumer products should be presented and what role they should serve.

What general concerns motivated this group's pioneers and what could they do to help ratify them? They started out with a twin set of concerns: that China's political and economic position was extremely weak, and that Chinese merchants ran small businesses and lacked knowledge of the outside world's economy. Ma, in his preface to the *Twenty Fifth Anniversary Commemorative Issue of the Sincere Company*, thought that Chinese merchants were "too obstinate and set in the old ways," and that they "behaved like pedlars" when making business decisions. In their separate autobiographies, Guo Luo and Guo Chuan expressed very similar sentiments. Guo Chuan added that it was only after some Chinese, like himself, had gone overseas to make a living that they became aware of the existence of the large-scale business organization and strategies practised in the West. He was particularly impressed by the knowledge and training Western corporations provided for their salespeople, and he observed ruefully that by contrast, Chinese salespeople

usually have no training. When they serve customers, they would only answer what they are asked, and do not care if they make any sales. Furthermore, they dislike anyone who picks and chooses, their displeasure and surly looks clearly showing in their voices and facial expressions.[12]

---

12. *Xianshi gongsi ershiwu zhounian jinian ce* (Hong Kong, 1925), section on "Record," 1-2; Ma Yingbiao, "Jiating biji," (Unpublished ms.)(n.p.,n.d.); Guo Luo, *Huiyi lu* (n.p., n.d.), 6-7; Guo Chuan, *Yong'an jingshen zhi faren ji qi changcheng shilue* (n.p., preface, 1960), 24-25.

As for their prescriptions, on one level, what they offered was firm and quite straightforward. It was also rather similar to the *shangzhan* arguments advanced earlier by Liang Qichao and others: China would regain its national strength if Chinese businessmen would establish large-scale enterprises and modernize their organization and practices in order to compete successfully in the international market. But on the more personal level, they were much more tentative, especially as to how they themselves could contribute towards relieving those concerns. For they realized that they had little resources and no real political influence. What they had, however, were some strongly held ideas which they hoped to use to start a new kind of business.

Ma Yingbiao was the first among his group to have an opportunity to put his ideas to the test. And he quite openly acknowledged where his ideas came from and how they had influenced him. The official record of the company's early years reports it this way:

When Mr. Ma was in Sydney, Australia, he saw a fixed one-price department store. Its employees numbered several thousands, and its annual receipts from sales grossed in the millions and billions. When he examined its history, he learned that its owner had started as a pedlar. After he had set up the fixed, one-price store, it expanded so rapidly that in less than 30 years, its shopping floors covered several tens of *mou* [Chinese acres]. Goods from all over the world were displayed with exquisite elegance and glitter. At this time, Mr. Ma had already established the Wing Sang Company, and had frequent business relations with that department store. He was thus able to examine the pattern of its organization and the nature of its operations. He kept them in his mind, assuring himself that if he were to return to China, he would adopt and make use of them to blaze a trail of color and wonderment to the business community. Consequently, today's Sincere Company is modeled after that department store.[13]

---

13. *Xianshi gongsi ershiwu zhounian*, section on "Record," 1. Ma's account, based on his own recollections, exaggerated the size of the Sydney department store. Horderns, which was the largest of that era, had less than 1,000 employees and perhaps 2 acres of total floor space. At 6 *mou* to an acre, Ma's estimate would again have made the Sydney store at least 2-3 times larger. Finally, the annual receipts, too, must have been far smaller. I am grateful to Professor John Perkins of the University of New South Wales, Sydney, for providing these corrections.

The fixed, one-price department store model which had so inspired Ma was Sydney's largest and highly organized department store, Anthony Hordern & Company. In 1899, having returned to China several years earlier, Ma successfully persuaded eleven other fellow Zhongshanese to form a partnership with him in Hong Kong for a small, modern-style department store. Like him, they had returned to Hong Kong after having worked in or managed businesses in Australia. Ma turned the ideas he had borrowed from Anthony Hordern into four guiding principles: 1) to procure the best consumer goods available and to sell each of them at a fixed price; 2) to display all goods openly and tastefully, in elegant glass counters and carefully groomed surroundings; 3) to offer friendly and courteous service; and 4) to design a rationally planned and clearly articulated corporate organization.

In 1900, with rather modest capital of 25,000 Hong Kong dollars (HK$)[14] and 25 employees, Ma rented a 2-store front and two floors in mid-town Hong Kong and launched the Sincere Department Store. The store's paid-up capital, the number of clerks and salespersons, its physical size and even its location on Queen's Road, Central, Hong Kong, were all quite comparable with those larger retail stores on or around Shanghai's Nanjing Road discussed earlier. Both sold similar kinds of goods as well—imports, upscale fabrics, head and footwear, cosmetics, foodstuffs, household utensils and small appliances, arts and crafts, and the like—although the Shanghai ones were still using the old-fashioned name called *Yangguang zahuopu* (lit. Western and Guangdong miscellaneous goods shops).[15] But by keeping firm to Ma's ideas, the Sincere store in Hong Kong was a very different operation from any of the Shanghai counterparts. First, during the first three years, the store had several mishaps; some through natural causes, like the typhoon which blew off part of the store's roof; others because he had to fight hard to keep to his principles, including his insistence to abide by the fixed, one-price items, to issue receipts for every transaction, and to provide elegant display of various items for sale. Second, his refusal to allow any haggling over prices and his methodical tracking of inventory through written receipts and detailed bookkeeping scared off many traditional brokers who were too set in their ways . Finally, there was the rather lavish spending on a large number of glass counters, on elegant displays and for creating a pleasing ambiance in the shopping area, so much so that they cost most of his working capital when the store was opened for business.[16]

---

14. The Hong Kong dollar was worth half of the U.S. dollar.
15. *Shanghai jindai baihuo gongsi*, pp. 12, 21, 27.
16. *Xianshi gongsi ershiwu zhounian*, section on "Record," 1-2.

The Sincere department store's first three years were therefore very difficult years. But Ma's perseverance paid off. The business turned profitable from the fourth year on. Profits mounted up quickly; and as earnings were plowed back and new investors joined in, Ma reorganized the partnership into a corporation under Hong Kong's British law, moved to larger quarters, then by 1910, opened a newer and bigger store with its own capital in Guangzhou. By this time, the Guo brothers, having learned of Ma's successes, had also returned to Hong Kong from Australia and, with the help of other returned Zhongshanese, set up their own partnership to launch a similar kind of department store which they named Wing On (or Yong'an in Mandarin Chinese). Success followed quickly, for the Guos seem to have learned from Ma's mistakes, so that Wing On was able to follow Sincere very closely in time with similar steps of corporate reorganization and expansion.[17]

One measure of their remarkable success is that by around 1912, both companies had accumulated very sizeable paid-up capital of about HK$600,000 each. Such a fast-paced growth, from Sincere's HK$25,000 in 1900 and Wing On's HK$160,000 in 1907, would have been quite extraordinary under any circumstances. For China in 1912, it meant that they had far outpaced not only those large retail shops in Shanghai, but also all other Chinese-owned commercial enterprises that conducted most of their business at the retail level. Yet, within half a dozen years—by 1917 for Sincere and 1918 for Wing On—they outdid themselves again by successfully raising HK$2 million each for their newest project, which was to open two very large department stores on Nanjing Road in Shanghai. They accomplished this by registering themselves as public companies with the British authorities in Hong Kong and Shanghai, thus allowing them to openly solicit public subscription of their company stock. Of the HK$2 million that each company successfully raised in this way, about 25 percent came from internal self-financing, from retained earnings of their Hong Kong and Guangzhou operations, as well as from the distributed dividends of the original shareholders. Practically all the rest came from several thousand small contributors who were fellow Zhongshanese either living abroad or, having returned, residing in Zhongshan, Hong Kong or Shanghai. It was also the largest public subscription of capital up to that time for commercial projects.[18]

---

17. *Xianggang Yong'an gongsi ershiwu zhounian* (Hong Kong, preface, 1932), section on "History."

18. The comparable figures in paid-up capital for another major Chinese-owned company, the Nanyang Tobacco Company, were 100,000 Chinese yuan (Ch.Y) in 1912, Ch.Y 978,000 in 1916, and Ch.Y 2,700,000 in 1918. This company, however, combined both factory production and retailing while all the stock was owned by Jian Zhaonan and his family.

Elsewhere I have analyzed the strengths of Wing On's and Sincere's organization, the founders' personalities and their team spirit as reasons for their success.[19] However, there is one other reason that needs to be discussed, and that was their ability to create, and then exploit, a new market. They did this by presenting a full array of high quality and attractive consumer products in a readily accessible fashion, and fostering cultural values that supported the desire for their acquisition and use.

The success of their Hong Kong and Guangzhou stores proved to Ma and the Guo brothers that there were consumers out in the marketplace who were willing and able to buy such goods, especially if they were able to create a pleasing ambiance to attract these potential consumers' interest, so that more of them would come into their stores and be treated with attentive and courteous service. Their next move to build even larger department stores on Shanghai's Nanjing Road then followed logically. For they realized that the pool of potential customers in Hong Kong and Guangzhou was quite limited, especially when compared to Shanghai's. By this time, in the mid-1910s, Shanghai had become China's chief metropolis with the largest number of national and international wealthy businessmen, gentry-officials and other potential consumers of department store goods. Furthermore, because Western influence was most dominant there, Shanghai also claimed to have the latest fashion and cultural fads, the newest movie theaters, the largest circulation of Chinese newspapers, journals and other forms of public media, as well as the most cosmopolitan spirit. If they had to look for a place in all of China where their new ideas about consumer products and how they should be presented for sale and might have the greatest chance of being accepted, Shanghai would be the best choice.[20] Finally, Ma and the Guo brothers, with their Hong Kong, Guangdong, and Australian backgrounds, felt quite at home in Shanghai's International Settlement, because they would be operating under British law and because of the presence of long established Guangdongese merchants and politicians already there.

Between 1900 and 1929, the Ch.Y and the HK$ were worth about the same, while their exchange rates with the US$ were also quite consistent, at about ChY 2 (or HK$2) for each US$1. Only the years from 1917 to 1920 saw the ChY worth much higher, at about ChY 1.20 for each US$1. On Nanyang Tobacco's capitalization, see Sherman Cochran, *Big Business in China: Sino-Foreign Rivalry in the Cigarette Industry, 1890-1930* (Cambridge: Harvard University Press, 1980), 79, 101.

19. Wellington K.K. Chan, "Personal Styles, Cultural Values and Management: The Sincere and Wing On Companies in Shanghai and Hong Kong, 1900-1941," in *Business History Review*, Vol.70, No.2 (1996), 141-166.

20. Du Zhensheng, 30-31.

III

Around 1915, when Ma Yingbiao, followed soon afterwards by Guo Luo, went to Shanghai to explore the feasibility of setting up their largest stores there, Nanjing Road proper—nearly 2 miles in length between the Bund along the waterfront on its eastern end and Tibet (Xizang) Road on the western end—had not yet become China's mecca for shopping and fashion. But the general area was growing rapidly, especially after the introduction of Shanghai's first trolleys which, by 1908, were running the full length of Nanjing Road. The area, anchored as it was on its eastern end and along the Bund by dozens of Western financial, commerical and governmental establishments, had already attracted many Chinese businesses of all types, while in 1915 its western end seemed to be marked off by the opening there of China's largest amusement park, the New World (Xinshijie). In between the two ends, sections of Nanjing Road, especially those between Henan and Fujian Roads, had developed clusters of the large retail shops discussed earlier. Close by, in several smaller streets around the intersection between Nanjing and Jinling Roads, there were many commercial houses specializing in wholesaling. Then, just a short distance to the south, along sections of Fuzhou Road, clusters of literary and artistic establishments had sprung up since the late nineteenth century. They included art galleries, print shops, stationeries, some specializing in different kinds of rice papers, antique shops and bookstores, as well as more modern offices and printing presses of the Commercial Press and Shanghai's oldest Chinese newspaper, *Shenbao*. There was no mistaking that the entire area, with several intersections along Nanjing Road serving as hubs, was bubbling with commercial and cultural activities.[21]

But there were also sections of the street that were relatively undeveloped as, for example, the section to the west around its intersection with Zhejiang Road. And it was this area, amid dozens of small neighborhood stores and roadside eateries, that Ma and, several months later, Guo as well, chose to locate their future stores. They did so partly out of necessity, for the size of land they needed, between 1 1/2 and 2 acres each, was simply not available (or if available, prohibitively expensive) in the more developed part of this compact area. But they also selected their locations only after careful analysis of the neighborhood, traffic patterns and future potentials. Thus, Guo Luo made his choice only after he had two of his men, one standing on the north

---

21. Du Zhensheng, 32-33. Strictly speaking, Nanjing Road starting from 1865 had been extending westward to about double its original length. This is the section known today as Nanjing xi (Western Nanjing) Road. During this period, however, this section was not yet commercialized.

1.1. The Sincere Company opened in 1917 and is shown here in the 1920s at the corner of Nanjing Road and Zhejiang Road. *So–this is Shanghai* (Shanghai, 193?), [14].

side, the other on the south side, of the Nanjing Road directly in front of the selected site so that they could report back to him the number of people walking by on each side of the street during several given times of a normal work day. He then decided on the south side because not only did it have more pedestrians, it was also more accessible to the high income residents from the French Concession area nearby.[22] Earlier on, Ma, too, had apparently made similar surveys of the traffic flow around his site.[23]

Nanjing Road took off soon thereafter. As Sincere and then Wing On opened their doors ten months apart during 1917 and 1918, many other commercial establishments, spurred on by the massive multi-story buildings each was constructing, were also moving in. By 1918, the *Shanghai Commercial Register* reported that there were 341 commercial establishments

---

22. *Shanghai Yong'an gongsi di chansheng, fazhan wo gaizao* (Shanghai: Renmin chupenshe, 1981), 13-14.

23. Mai Guoliang, "Xiangshan jiren chuanban di sidaigongsi," *Zhongshan wenshi*, No. 17 (1989), 86-88.

on Nanjing Road. In the following year, when a traffic survey was taken to find out how many pedestrians and vehicles passed through the intersection of Nanjing Road and the Bund each day, the result was rather astounding. It counted 145,000 pedestrians, 66,100 rickshaws, 7,700 carts, 5,100 automobiles, 3,200 horse-driven carriages, 1,560 streetcars, over 10,000 bicycles, and an uncounted number of motorized carts and trucks.[24] Since the combined population of the International Settlement and the French Concession at the time was about 1 million, that intersection was unquestionably the busiest in Shanghai. By around 1920, Nanjing Road had arrived.

The arrival of Sincere and Wing On was the critical event that turned Nanjing Road into China's shopping mecca. On its opening day, Sincere's four floors of shopping areas, 300-plus salesmen and over 10,000 items of consumer goods, the majority of which came from Europe, Japan and North America, attracted an unprecedented number of more than 10,000 shoppers. It was then followed by Wing On's opening, which was even bigger and grander in all respects: five floors of shopping areas making up 10,000 square meters of floor space, 400 sales assistants displaying an even greater array of goods. It also counted more shoppers, in part because for fourteen consecutive days prior to the opening, it blanketed the local Chinese newspapers with full-page ads about its gala inaugural. This type of advertisement, both in terms of purpose and scale, was the first of its kind. It again demonstrates the Guo brothers' fresh approach and daring vision in presenting their goods. And Wing On's customers rewarded them by buying up more than Ch.Y 10,000 of goods each day, so much so that the company's initial inventory was more than half depleted just after the first 20 days of opening. Guo Luo had expected it to last a whole season. Indeed, Wing On's receipts from its daily sales amounted to what a medium-sized traditional retail shop normally grossed in one full year.[25]

Two more department stores followed the pattern initiated by Sincere and Wing On—in terms of organization, size, the range of goods and services, and the style of selling them. Liu Xiji, the initial organizer of Sun Sun (Xinxin in Mandarin Chinese) & Company, opened the next one on Nanjing Road in 1926. A former senior manager of Shanghai's Sincere Company and a long time associate of Ma Yingbiao with ties going back to their sojourn days in Australia, Liu broke with Ma after they disagreed over the way dividends and bonuses were distributed between the Hong Kong and Shanghai operations.

24. Du Zhensheng, 34.

25. *Shanghai Yong'an gongsi*, 16-18; *Shanghai jindai baihuo gongsi*, 103-05.

With the help of fellow Zhongshanese—led by one returnee from Australia, Li Minzhou, and two Hong Kong bankers Li Yutang and Li Xingqu—the new company raised Ch.Y 3 million so as to have a similarly impressive building and shopping area as the first two. However, the lack of cooperation among its senior directors and managers, as well as its inability to find sufficient working capital, crimped their style and expansion.

Sun Sun was also hurt by starting at a time of market turbulence and labor unrest in Shanghai. Repeated patriotic campaigns to boycott Western and Japanese goods forced all three department stores, which prided themselves on their slogan as "universal providers," to make adjustments. Wing On, with its usual deftness, took advantage of its top reputation to sign up the greatest number—over 70 by around 1930—of exclusive contracts with the stronger and better domestic manufacturers. Then, by providing the latter with samples of the latest fashions from overseas and by sending its own technicians and designers to assist them, Wing On also worked out a very effective system of cooperation with their suppliers. The result was mutually beneficial, for Chinese manufacturers would produce better quality and more stylish goods which, in turn, would yield higher sales at Wing On's shopping counters. On the other hand, Sun Sun having far less experience, prestige and contact, had a more difficult time in finding good domestic suppliers. The quality and variety of their goods suffered almost from the very beginning, and as a result, Sun Sun never quite recovered from the image of being a less upscale operation with goods commanding lower prices than those at either Wing On or Sincere.[26]

The last of the four premier department stores on Nanjing Road, The Dah Sun (Daxin in Mandarin Chinese) & Company opened its doors quite late, in 1936, when Nanjing Road's halcyon days had already passed. When planning for it was first attempted in about 1930, however, Nanjing Road's reputation as China's premier center for high fashion and conspicuous consumption was at its height. And given Wing On's and Sincere's continuing success, there was considerable appeal for other well-connected entrepreneurs to start yet another premier department store to compete with them. The Dah Sun team, led by Cai Xing and Cai Chang, had impressive credentials. Besides being Zhongshanese, both Cais had long experience in the department store business. Cai Xing had teamed up with Ma Yingbiao since their Sydney days, and for several years, had served as chairman of the Board of Directors of the Sincere Company. Cai Chang and his brother Cai Cong, on the other hand, had

---

26. For Sun Sun, cf. Li Chengji, "Xianfu Li Gong Minzhou yu Shanghai Xinxin [Sun Sun] gongsi," *Zhuanji wenxue* Vol. 35 No.5 (1979), 98-108; on the issue of the movement for domestic manufactured goods and its impact, cf. *Shanghai jindai baihuo gongsi*, 145-49.

been operating Dah Sun as a smaller department store in Hong Kong and in Guangzhou since the 1910s.

The decision to expand their operation to Shanghai and onto Nanjing Road was made only after they formed the alliance with Cai Xing, whose Sincere connection made him knowledgeable about the Shanghai market, and after they were able to enlarge their capital to HK$6 million, they realized that in order to compete successfully as a major department store on Nanjing Road, they had to be able to offer the kinds of enticements that the other three premier department stores were providing so skillfully. Thus, Dah Sun too had to look for a prime location to build its own building. They found it on the intersection of Nanjing and Tibet Roads, and when they turned the site into a 10-story Western-style building, it became the tallest of the four stores. To attract consumer interest and excitement, it introduced several new features not found in the other stores. For example, it installed the first escalator in Shanghai to service the first three floors of the shopping area, it boasted the first extensive below-street-level basement shopping arcade, and it was also the first store to have all its shopping floors centrally heated in the winter.

All this, strictly speaking, was not new. Back in the early 1910s, both Sincere and Wing On were the first retail stores to install elevators in their Hong Kong and Guangzhou buildings to attract shoppers' curiosity. Wing On's Shanghai store then put in the first neon lights, while Sun Sun's firsts were air-conditioning its building and setting up an in-house broadcasting station, called the Crystal Station, to play music and to announce sales and specials. Nonetheless, Dah Sun's aggressive style and new look during the first few years, as well as its good relationship with Shanghai's political elite, propelled it to an early success, and gave it a reputation as being second in rank to Wing On.[27]

IV

When the Sincere and Wing On department stores started their operation on Shanghai's Nanjing Road selling all manner of consumer goods—from daily necessities in foodstuffs, in piece goods and clothing, in appliances and household items, to luxury items such as jewelry, cosmetics and upscale imports, etc.—they did not invent a new desire for material things or create some new ideal of acquisitiveness. The yearnings for possession and consumption were strongly embedded in traditional Chinese culture even if

---

27. Li Chengji, "Shanghai sidabaihuo gongsi," *Zhuanji wenxue* Vol. 49, No. 5 (1986), 45-50; and Tu Shiping, *Shanghaishi daguan* (Shanghai: Zhongguo tushu bianyi guan, 1948) 81-84.

they were ideologically frowned upon. It might even be argued that these yearnings are part of a universal ideal shared by people everywhere throughout history.[28] What they, and following them many other retailers, accomplished on Nanjing Road during the next decade or two was to promote these basic wants as legitimate ideals and to make them far more accessible. In the process, they helped provide new contents, meanings, and perspectives in forming a modern Chinese commercial culture. And while other parts of China might express the various parts of their commercial culture somewhat differently, as each region would be influenced by its own history and local traditions, Nanjing Road's fashions, as well as its quality of goods and of service, set the standards for the entire nation.

There seems to have been several common themes which all four department stores practiced in trying to articulate a new commercial culture that they knew they had a stake in propagating. First was the unabashedly open acknowledgment of Western models which they followed in cultivating legitimacy and acceptance of the new commercial culture. The arrival of Sincere and Wing On in Shanghai during the middle years of the 1910s coincided with a period when the Western presence there symbolized modernity much more than oppression. The boycott against American goods, first begun by Shanghai merchants, took place in 1905 and memories about it had dimmed. China's humiliations at the Treaty of Versailles and the series of national campaigns against foreign goods had yet to come. Thus, Ma Yingbiao and Guo Luo were able to project themselves as harbingers of cultural and material progress when they closely identified their corporate entities and their practices with Western models. And nowhere was this more obvious than in the physical form they used to present themselves to the public.

Both Ma Yingbiao and Guo Luo went to great lengths to design and construct the two buildings which would provide space for shopping and for corporate headquarters on Nanjing Road. Sincere's 5-story structure, topped by a 3-story clock tower, was nicely matched by Wing On's 6-story structure and an equally impressive tower on its roof. Not only did they dwarf all other buildings in the neighborhood, they also looked decidedly different from all the other Chinese commercial buildings in the general area. For while the latter were arranged in rows of 2- and 3- story buildings with just touches of Western architectural influences, the Sincere and Wing On buildings were pure Western monuments, in the same Beaux Arts style which was then popular with Western commercial and public establishments along the Bund in Shanghai and in Hong Kong's central district. Thus, Wing On's 1918

---

28. Cf. William R. Taylor, ed., *Inventing Times Square: Commerce and Culture at the Crossroads of the World* (New York, 1991) for a similar conclusion.

building, with its distinct lintels, Italianate columns, and French mansard roof, looked strikingly similar to the Jardine House building which was completed just 10 years earlier in Hong Kong by the British architecture firm Palmer and Turner.[29] Although existing sources on Wing On are silent as to who the architect was, it is likely that the Guo brothers turned to the same architects to make their building look closely like the building housing Jardine, Matheson & Company, the premier British firm in Hong Kong. Moreover, commissioning a grand edifice for the shopping floors of a modern department store was in the tradition not only of Anthony Hordern in Sydney, but also of Rowland H. Macy in New York and of Aristide Boucicaut in Paris. As these Western counterparts intended their building monuments to be veritable cathedrals of material culture, the managers of the four premier department stores in Shanghai also made similar symbolism out of their own buildings to exalt their own institutions and practices.

Second, closely related to the grand physical form was the use of space for the display of all types of goods in rich abundance. There was a relentless search for marketing strategies to enhance the appeal of goods displayed and to expose them to the greatest number of potential customers. And most of these strategies centered around enticements through attractive window or glass case displays, carefully crafted ads, seasonal sales, lead items at below cost, and most important of all, courteous service. This is reflected in the several examples discussed above.[30] They also became a rationale for the many subsidiary businesses each company expanded into from their early days. This involved having the upper floors of their buildings, and in some cases adjacent buildings, turned into hotels, restaurants, night clubs and, for most of their rooftops, entertainment gardens. All these establishments provided added opportunities to attract more potential customers to their shopping floors and arcades.

A third theme dealt with the subtle cultivation of a new ideal: that of acquiring and consuming material goods tastefully as an intrinsic part of

---

29. For a comparative viewing, see their respective photographs reprinted in the following two volumes: *The Thistle and the Jade: A Celebration of 150 Years of Jardine, Matheson & Company*, ed. by Maggie Keswick (London: Octopus Book Ltd., 1982), 200-201; and He Wenxiang, *Xianggang jiazushi* (Hong Kong: Mingbao chubanshe,1992), 247.

30. Some of these changes, e.g., use of ads, display windows, fixed pricing, sales, etc., are discussed by Yuan Zijiang, "Ershiwunian lai Zhongguo shangye zhi bianqian," in *Xianshi gongsi ershiwu zhounian*, 91-98. On comparable strategies, some of which occurred in America only a decade or less before they were practiced in Hong Kong or Shanghai, see William Leach, *Land of Desire: Merchants, Power, and the Rise of a New American Culture* (New York: Pantheon Books, 1993). I am indebted to Sherman Cochran for bringing this fascinating study to my attention.

modern living and a validation of one's high social standing. Thus, there was all the meticulous concern with how goods were displayed and presented as well as the claims that the goods themselves were the best and latest in design and fashion that could be acquired anywhere. When Wing On's merchandisers were not in London, Paris or New York tracking down the latest fashion items and signing up exclusive rights to sell in China, they would be consulting with their own designers in Wing On's textile mills and dyeing factories to bring to their own sales counters the newest and the largest selection of cotton fabrics based on colors, patterns and grades. The large glass window and counter displays were also clear expressions of this new cultural ideal: that it was proper, and indeed, something to be publicly trumpeted, to be seen buying and wearing these high quality and high priced material goods. This led to the use of newspaper and magazine ads using culturally refined poetic expressions to introduce the fine characteristics of various goods and to include photographs and artistic sketches to give a pleasing visual image. Finally, there was the use of brand names to attract loyalty and accent the social status of their users. To drive home that healthful modern living was intrinsic to this material culture, the department stores presented a full array of cosmetics, toiletries, as well as simple items of daily necessities like toothpastes, tooth brushes, face and bath towels as symbols of personal and public hygiene. They were done in ads but also in commissioned articles by well-known writers and artists in newspapers and journals. Indeed, the use of the latter, culminating in Wing On publishing its own monthly magazine from the late 1930s to the late 1940s, shows a conscious effort not only to educate the public about the new ideal of material consumption, but also to influence the thinking of the cultural elite. By the promotion of these and other similar themes, these modern department stores on Nanjing Road succeeded not only in increasing vastly the sales of consumer goods but also in creating and validating a new commercial culture for twentieth-century China.

Transnational Origins of Advertising in Early Twentieth-Century China

Sherman Cochran

> Sure of itself, [America] bullies other civilizations, as a traveling salesman in a brown derby conquers the wisdom of China and tacks advertisements of cigarettes over arches for centuries dedicated to the sayings of Confucius.
>
> Sinclair Lewis, *Main Street* (1920)[1]

Does Chinese commercial culture have foreign origins which are traceable to the West and specifically to New York City's Times Square? An affirmative answer is implied in the title of a recently published collection of essays, *Inventing Times Square: Commerce and Culture at the Crossroads of the World* (1991), which was edited by William Taylor, the author of the final essay in this present volume.[2] The contributors to *Inventing Times Square*, all specialists on American history and culture, have focused on the topic described in the book's title. The following essay pursues the possibility mentioned in the book's subtitle by tracing the path of a Western-owned business, British-American Tobacco Company, as it carried commercial culture from New York at "the Crossroads of the World" overseas to China.

Did Americans "invent" Chinese commercial culture and disseminate it throughout China? What role did Chinese play in the production and distribution of Chinese commercial culture? These questions are worth asking about the history of British-American Tobacco Company because, as will be

---

1. I am grateful to Mark Lytle for calling my attention to this passage.

2. William R. Taylor, ed., *Inventing Times Square: Commerce and Culture at the Crossroads of the World* (New York, 1991).

shown here, this business played a prominent role in Chinese commercial culture as China's leading Western-owned advertiser in the early twentieth century.

Producing Chinese Commercial Culture

British-American Tobacco Company (BAT) was almost literally based in Times Square because it had its worldwide headquarters in New York at 111 Fifth Avenue. Founded in 1902, BAT was jointly owned by James B. Duke's American Tobacco Company (holder of two-thirds of BAT's stock) and the British-owned Imperial Tobacco Company (holder of the remaining one-third). BAT's owners assigned it responsibility for marketing cigarettes throughout the world outside the United States and Britain.

By the time of BAT's founding in 1902, Duke had already become famous for his use of advertising in American Tobacco Company's conquest of the American cigarette market. As *Collier's* reported in 1907, Duke set the standard for "devising new and startling methods which dismayed his competitors." Since the late nineteenth century, according to this magazine, Duke had "always [been] willing to spend a proportion of his profits [on advertising] which seemed appalling to more conservative manufacturers."[3] In the first years of the twentieth century, he instructed James A. Thomas, the American managing director of BAT's headquarters for China, to apply the same aggressive advertising techniques there that Duke had used in the United States[4] and Thomas wasted no time carrying out Duke's orders, but at first Thomas had disappointing results.

The rejection of American-made advertisements. In 1902, BAT set up its headquarters for China on Nanjing Road[5] in Shanghai and began exporting cigarettes to China. To promote these cigarettes, it initially adopted advertising that had been designed for use in the West and exported this advertising unaltered to China. For example, in China BAT put up advertising posters depicting American landscapes, American historical figures such as George Washington and Abraham Lincoln, and most numerous of all, American women as pin-ups.[6]

According to both Western and Chinese observers in China, this American- or Western-oriented advertising was jarring and confusing to Chinese

---

3. Quoted by Patrick G. Porter, "Origins of the American Tobacco Company," *Business History Review*, 43.1 (1969): 64-65.

4. James A. Thomas, *A Pioneer Tobacco Merchant in the Orient* (Durham, North Carolina, 1928), 10-23 and 36.

5. Ernest O. Hauser, *Shanghai: City for Sale* (New York, 1940), 101.

6. Wu Hao, Zhuo Botang, Huang Ying, and Lu Wanwen, *Duhui modeng: yuefenpai 1910-1930* (Calendar Posters of the Modern Chinese Woman) (Hong Kong, 1994), 9 and 161.

consumers. After witnessing BAT's advertising campaign in Yunnan province in 1910, the British consul-general there became convinced that it had bewildered local Chinese, and he speculated about how they had perceived the figures in BAT's posters:

> The average Yunnan Chinaman must have peculiar ideas regarding the persons represented on these posters—a picturesque pirate, a European lady, décolletée, of strange figure with yellow hair, and a fantastically dressed European man kicking at a ball, something like the dragon on a Chinese flag biting at a sun.[7]

Other Westerners in both China and the United States complained that scantily clad Western women in the risqué advertisements used by Western companies in China (such as the "European lady, décolletée," mentioned in the quotation above) were ruining America's reputation with the Chinese people.[8]

Whether or not this kind of advertising damaged America's reputation, it failed to establish BAT's reputation as the company's American managers had intended. At best, Chinese consumers seemed indifferent to BAT's American-oriented advertisements, and at worst they derisively characterized the scenes in the posters as "foreign pictures" (*yang hua'er*) and "hairy person pictures" (*maozi bian*)—"hairy person" being a smear term for Westerners in the Chinese vernacular.[9]

Importing American printing technology. Disappointed with this initial reception, BAT's management decided to produce advertising locally in China so that it could be designed to suit Chinese taste. As early as 1905, James Thomas began to import up-to-date American technology for making advertising. He installed three printing presses in Shanghai, and in 1908 he added seven more, all of which were capable of producing eye-catching images in polychrome. In 1915 he opened a school in lithography to teach workers to

---

7. FO 371/864, no. 8889, O'Brien-Butler to FO, February 4, 1910, Great Britain, Records of the British Foreign Office, Public Records Office, Kew Gardens, England.

8. John K. Winkler, *Tobacco Tycoon: The Story of James Buchanan Duke* (New York, 1942), 199-200.

9. Sun Chia-chi, "Cigarette Cards," trans. by Robert Christensen, *Echo of Things Chinese*, 6.4 (January 1977): 67; Zhang Yanfeng, *Lao yuefenpai guanggao hua* (Old calendar posters: advertising paintings) in *Han sheng zazhi* (Echo magazine) 61 (1994): I, 64-65; Wu Hao, 161.

use newly acquired printing machinery, and thereafter he continued to build up BAT's advertising establishment.[10]

According to Carl Crow, an advertising agent in early twentieth century China not employed by BAT, it had in Shanghai "the largest color-printing plant in the world and one of the finest."[11] To keep the new presses rolling, by the late 1910s BAT had an annual advertising budget for China of about 1.8 million yuan (a figure nearly half as large as the entire annual education budget of the Beijing government which was nominally the national government of the Republic of China between 1912 and 1927).[12]

Inventing Chinese images. BAT's imported technology gave it the capacity to reproduce commercial art in color and on a massive scale, but what was to be reproduced? The company's American managers resolved to make the images in their advertising "Chinese," and for this purpose, they turned to Chinese artists.

Of BAT's first Chinese commercial artists, Zhou Muqiao became the most influential because he set two major precedents: he was the first to produce for mass distribution a new form of Chinese commercial art, the calendar-poster advertising painting; and he was the first to create a new image of women within this form. Other Chinese artists had made calendar-poster advertising paintings (*yuefenpai guanggao hua*) (a term coined in 1896 to describe advertisements that merchants handed out on a local basis in Shanghai at the time),[13] but Zhou drafted the very first calendar-poster advertising painting ever reproduced by a business on a large scale for widespread distribution. He painted it for the China and the West Drug Store (Zhongxi da yaofang), a

---

10. Chen Zhen, comp., *Zhongguo jindai gongye shi ziliao di'er ji* (Historical materials on modern Chinese industry, second collection) (Beijing, 1958), 125; Zhang Yanfeng, I, 65 and 67, and II, 59 and 66; The British-American Tobacco Company, Ltd., *The Record in China of the British-American Tobacco Company, Limited* (Shanghai, 1925), 22.

11. Carl Crow, *Foreign Devils in the Flowery Kingdom* (New York, 1940), 58.

12. Julean H. Arnold, et. al, *Commercial Handbook of China*, U.S. Department of Commerce, Miscellaneous Series No. 84 (Washington, D.C., 1920), 393. On Chinese governments' education budgets, see Andrew D. Nathan, *Peking Politics, 1918-1923: Factionalism and the Failure of Constitutionalism* (Berkeley, 1976), 70; and Yip Ka-che, "Warlordism and Educational Finances, 1916-1927," in Joshua A. Fogel and William T. Rowe, eds., *Perspectives on a Changing China: Essays in Honor of Professor C. Martin Wilbur on the Occasion of His Retirement* (Boulder, 1979), 186-189.

13. According to meticulous research by the Chinese scholar Wang Shucun, the Hongfulai lusong dapiaochang, a lottery company, was the first to use this term. In 1896, it promoted the sale of lottery tickets by giving away a free premium which it called a "Sino-Western calendar poster" (*Zhongxi yuefenpai*)(Wu Hao, 9).

Chinese-owned firm, and he was probably recruited by BAT because of his success with it.[14]

Zhou composed this first calendar-poster advertising painting along the same lines as his earlier paintings. He had begun as a painter of Chinese New Year's pictures (*nian hua*), a genre of popular art which had existed for a thousand years (dating from the Song dynasty), and he had grown up in the city of Suzhou, the major center for New Year's painters in the vicinity of Shanghai,[15] where he had studied with Wu Youru (? - 1893), the most celebrated painter of New Year's pictures at the time. In making his calendar-poster advertising paintings, Zhou showed his indebtedness to this early training in his use of calligraphy and traditional painting techniques and in his appropriation of New Year's pictures' motifs such as ribbons adorning the upper borders of his calendar-poster advertising paintings.

After Zhou accepted a position in BAT's art department, he continued to borrow from existing genres of Chinese art, but he began to revise some images, especially of women. Previously, in the early 1890s, he had published magazine illustrations of Chinese "classic beauties" (*shinü hua*) and had portrayed them as frail and even sickly, thereby retaining the link that Chinese artists had earlier forged between a woman's beauty and her "spring longing," youthful lovesickness, and premature death.[16] His tendency to depict beautiful Chinese women as weak and dying had been evident in a series of illustrations that he had published in the magazine *Fleeting Shadow Pavillion* (*Feiyingge*) in the early 1890s. For example, his sketch of Lin Daiyu, the ill-fated female protagonist of the eighteenth-century novel *The Dream of the Red Chamber* (Honglou meng), shows her on the verge of collapse and leaning on a cane (see illustration 2.1). After Zhou began painting calendar posters for BAT, he continued to present classic Chinese beauties, including a series of characters from *The Dream of the Red Chamber* under the title "Five Beauties Reciting Mournful Poems in Xiaoxiang Villa" (Xiaoxiangguan beiti wumei yin),[17] but he also began making portraits of Chinese women in contemporary costumes.

In his calendar posters for BAT, Zhou identified the beauty of contemporary Chinese women less with past archetypes (like the sickly Lin Daiyu in illustration 2.1) and more with changes in current fashions. In BAT's

14. Zhang Yanfeng, I, 89.

15. The three major centers for producing New Year's pictures in China were Taohuawu at Suzhou and Yangliuqing and Weixian, both in North China.

16. Judith T. Zeitlin, "Making the Invisible Visible: Images of Desire and Constructions of the Female Body in Ming and Qing Literature, Medicine, and Art," a paper prepared for the symposium on Chinese Art of the Ming and Ch'ing Dynasties at the Art Institute of Chicago, July 26-28, 1996.

17. Zhang Yanfeng, I, 64-65; Wu Hao, 160.

2.1. Zhou Muqiao's sketch of the classic Chinese beauty Lin Daiyu. This illustration was published in the magazine *Fleeting Shadow Pavillion* before Zhou joined BAT. Zhou Muqiao, *Dayalou huabao sijuan* (four volumes of precious paintings from the Daya Gallery)(Shanghai, 1923), vol. 2, facing p. 25.

2.2. Zhou Muqiao's portrait of a fashionably dressed Chinese woman in BAT's calendar poster for 1914. Wu Hao, Zhuo Botang, Huang Ying, and Lu Wanwen, *Duhui modeng: yuefenpai 1910s-1930s* (Calendar Posters of the Modern Chinese Woman, 1910s-1930s)(Hong Kong, 1994), 2.

calendar poster for 1914 (see illustration 2.2), he showed a lady next to a rock, which was an old-style juxtaposition in Chinese art,[18] but he clothed his subject in a new-style Chinese costume, the *qipao*, a high-collared jacket with slits up the sides and buttons running from the neck across the chest and down the right side. Zhou's choice of costume was strikingly fashionable because Han Chinese women had only recently begun wearing the *qipao*; prior to the revolution of 1911, it had been worn only by Manchu women, and ironically, it achieved its first popularity with Chinese women after the revolution overthrew China's Manchu rulers.[19]

Zhou made the woman in his calendar poster of 1914 appear still more fashionable by placing on her unbound feet a pair of Western-style stiff leather shoes with medium high heels, bows, and laces rather than giving her Chinese-style flat, soft slippers. In the context of the time, this choice of footwear had far-reaching implications because Zhou's calendar poster appeared during an anti-footbinding campaign in China.[20]

Even as Zhou was attentive to changes in fashions, so too was he attentive to changes in politics. In this same 1914 calendar poster, he continued to use traditional painting techniques and he retained some motifs from New Year's pictures: ribbons and flowers along the upper border, the Chinese characters for "auspicious" and "[year of the] goat" at the top right-hand corner, and the traditional lunar calendar down the right-hand side. But these bits are small and marginal in relation to the painting as a whole. The characters for "auspicious" and "goat" are dwarfed by the large gold ones which emblazon the name of the company (a subsidiary of BAT) across the top and chant "Long Live the Republic of China" in the two upper corners. The lunar calendar on the right is offset by the Gregorian calendar on the left and is given a title that makes it seem anachronistic, "The Third Year of the Republic according to the Old

---

18. See Ellen Johnston Laing, "Commodification of Art through Exhibition and Advertisement," a paper prepared for the annual meeting of the Association for Asian Studies, Chicago, March 13-16, 1997.

19. Wu Shenyuan, *Shanghai zui zao de zhongzhong* (The first things to appear in Shanghai) (Shanghai, 1989), 158-160. As used here, the term *qipao* refers to the Chinese descendant of the Manchu garment in the 1910s. As Antonia Finnane has recently pointed out, scholars differ in their interpretations of whether the later *qipao* of the 1920s and 1930s was derived from the Manchu garment or from a Chinese sleeveless dress, the *majia*. See Finnane, "What Should Chinese Women Wear? A National Problem," *Modern China* 22.2 (April 1996): 127, note 1.

20. On the campaign against footbinding and its effects on the popular conception of feminine beauty in China during the first decade of the twentieth century, see Pao Chia-lin Tao, "The Anti-footbinding Movement in Late Ch'ing China: Indigenous Development and Western Influence," *Jindai Zhongguo funu shi yanjiu* (Research on women in modern Chinese history) (June 1994): 170-171.

Calendar's Cycles," compared with the title of the left-hand calendar, "The Western Calendar for 1914," which China's newly founded Republican government had adopted as its official calendar in 1912.[21]

Zhou's calendar posters marked a significant turning point in the history of Chinese commercial art. In retrospect, it is relatively easy to see his ties to the past—his use of traditional painting techniques and his portrayal of women with faces and bodies like those of classic Chinese beauties—and it is undeniable that his work became passé as early as 1915 when younger Chinese commercial artists introduced new painting techniques and began depicting Chinese women with shapely figures and seductive smiles.[22] But it would be a mistake to overlook Zhou's departures from past practices. In painting calendar posters for BAT, he showed a new fashion-consciousness and an interest in revising popular conceptions of feminine beauty which set precedents and subsequently became the hallmarks of successful artists in Chinese commercial culture.

The popularity of the calendar poster. Following Zhou's lead, other Chinese commercial artists working for BAT and other businesses all adopted the calendar-poster advertising painting as a standard form of advertising in China because of its immense popularity. Before publishing a calendar poster, BAT first estimated its potential popularity by circulating a preliminary sketch among BAT's far-flung Chinese sales agents who evaluated it, checked to see that the writing in it carried no potentially damaging puns or double meanings in local dialects, and cast votes for or against it. Once a calendar poster was selected for publication, BAT put to work the company's Western-made

---

21. Derk Bodde, *Festivals in Classical China* (Princeton, 1975), 220.

22. Among Chinese painters on BAT's staff, probably the most creative was Hu Boxiang who became famous for using Western-style watercolors to make Chinese-style landscape paintings. See Ding Hao, "Wencai fengliu jin xiang cun—qian tan jindai wo guo guanggao huazhong yu guanggao huajia" (Evidence of a style still in existence today—a casual conversation about modern China's pictorial advertisements and advertising designers) *Zhongguo guanggao* (China's advertising) 4.2 (1982): 33-34; Ren Yunhui, "Haiku hechu you Wusong—fang Hu Boxiang huashi" (When the seas dry up where is Wusong—introducing the artist Hu Boxiang), *Zhongguo guanggao* (China's advertising) 4.2 (1982): 34-35; Chen Ziqian and Ping Jinya, "Ying Mei yancao gongsi shihua" (Stories about the British-American Tobacco Company), *Wenshi ziliao xuanji diqi ji* (Collection of cultural and historical materials, no. 7)(Shanghai, 1961), 5; Zhang Yanfeng, I, 93; Wu Hao, 162. BAT also commissioned paintings by Chinese free lance artists. On two of the most influential commercial artists, Zheng Mantuo and Hang Zhiying, see Sherman Cochran, "Marketing Medicine and Advertising Dreams in China, 1900-1950," a paper prepared for the conference "Becoming Chinese: Passages to Modernity and Beyond, 1900-1950," Oakland, California, June 2-4, 1995.

technology, lithographing it in more than ten colors. Then in final form the calendar poster was distributed in time for Chinese New Year.

BAT's aim was to turn out a calendar poster that would be accorded a prominent place in as many shops and homes as possible, and according to both the company's employees and other observers, it was remarkably successful at achieving this aim. One American on BAT's staff who later returned from China to become a successful copywriter with the New York advertising firm of J. Walter Thompson and Company, for example, recalled that BAT's calendar became its "big advertising smash every year" and was distributed "in every nook and corner of the nation."[23] Others not employed by BAT, including American government officials, anthropologists, and journalists, all noted the prominence of BAT's calendars as decorations in the homes of both rich and poor Chinese during the early twentieth century.[24]

Why did BAT's calendar posters achieve such enormous popularity in China? As shown here, part of the explanation lies in the production process, especially the company's reliance on Western technology and Chinese artists. But BAT popularized calendar posters by investing in more than a system for producing advertising in China. The company also invested in a system for distributing it there.

Popularizing Chinese Commercial Culture

Even as BAT used a combination of Western technology and Chinese artists to produce advertising, so, too, did it use a combination of Western and Chinese staff members to distribute advertising. Its teams of Westerners and Chinese blanketed China to an extraordinary extent, distributing the company's advertising first in Shanghai, then in other cities, and ultimately in small towns and villages.

Advertising in Shanghai. In Shanghai, BAT encountered China's most sophisticated commercial center, a city complete with major institutions of commercial culture that are described elsewhere in this book. In dealing with these institutions, Westerners on BAT's staff formed contacts and made deals by relying on Chinese intermediaries. In particular, BAT's American manager James Thomas counted on his chief comprador Wu Tingsheng to make contacts with Chinese members of Shanghai's commercial elite, especially the ones from Wu's native place of Ningbo, and Thomas also delegated authority

---

23. James Lafayette Hutchison, *China Hand* (Boston, 1936), 266-267.

24. J.W. Sanger, *Advertising Methods in Japan, China, and the Philippines*, U.S. Department of Commerce, Special Agents Series no. 209 (Washington, D.C., 1921), 81-82; Daniel H. Kulp, *Country Life in South China: The Sociology of Familism* (New York, 1925), 265; Harry A. Franck, *Roving through Southern China* (New York, 1925), 164.

to BAT's leading commission agent, Zheng Bozhao, a well connected Cantonese who had migrated to Shanghai from another native place that had spawned many Shanghai compradors, Xiangshan county in Guangdong province near Hong Kong.[25]

Working together, this combination of Westerners and Chinese succeeded in linking BAT with institutions of commercial culture in Shanghai in much the same way that businesses did in New York. As William Taylor has noted in *Inventing Times Square*, American institutions of commercial culture forged this kind of linkage in New York by employing "new marketing strategies of 'tie-ins'" in the early twentieth century,[26] and BAT employed a similar marketing strategy of "tie-ins" in Shanghai during the same period. With newspapers, BAT tied in by buying the most advertising space that was used by any business in China.[27] As a public proclamation of its strong connection with newspapers, BAT installed a neon sign on top of the building that housed *Shenbao*, China's oldest newspaper.[28] With transport companies, BAT tied in by posting billboards at key intersections, docks, and railroad stations, by painting advertisements on ship's sails, and by making vests for rickshaw pullers and mats for their rickshaws.[29] With amusement parks, BAT tied in by signing contracts in which the parks granted it the exclusive right to advertise and sell cigarettes on their premises. It paid annual fees in accordance with each park's attendance—$7,000 to Great World (Da shijie), $5,000 to Little World (Xiao shijie), $3,750 to New World (Xin shijie) in the 1920s—and devoted special attention to parks with gambling because, as reported by one of BAT's salesman, "the gambling tables use cigarettes exclusively as a

---

25. Sherman Cochran, *Encountering Chinese Networks: Western, Japanese, and Chinese Corporations in China, 1880-1937*(Berkeley, in press), ch. 3.

26. William R. Taylor, "Introduction," in Taylor, ed., *Inventing Times Square*, xiii-xv.

27. Y.P. Wang, *The Rise of the Native Press in China* (New York, 1924), 45; C.A. Bacon, "Advertising in China," *Chinese Economic Journal*, 5.3 (June 8, 1918): 756-758 and 764-766.

28. Zhongguo gongchan dang (Chinese Communist Party), *Zhandou de wushinian—Shanghai juanyan yi chang gongren douzheng shihua* (Fighting for fifty years—a history of the workers' struggle based on Shanghai Cigarette Factory No. 1) (Shanghai, 1960), 51.

29. Zhongguo kexue yuan Shanghai jingji yanjiu suo Shanghai shehui kexue yuan jingji yanjiu suo (The Shanghai Economic Research Institute of the Chinese Academy of Social Sciences and the Economic Research Institute of the Shanghai Academy of Social Sciences), comps., *Nanyang xiongdi yancao gongsi shiliao*(Historical materials on the Nanyang Brothers Tobacco Company) (Shanghai, 1958), 68; Sanger, 57, 80; Wang Jingyu, comp., *Zhongguo jindai gongye shi ziliao, di'erji, 1895-1914* (Historical materials on modern Chinese industry, second collection, 1895-1914) (Beijing, 1957), 223-224; Chen and Ping, 208.

medium for gambling."[30] With Chinese opera houses, BAT tied in by featuring numerous opera stars on cards inserted in cigarette packages; and with theaters, it tied in by supplying slides and films which had been made in its Shanghai studio—a place characterized by its English cameraman as "one of the most modern and best studios that at the time could be found anywhere in the world outside the United States."[31]

With shops, restaurants, and businesses of various sizes and kinds, BAT tied in by securing space for display windows, painted walls, posters, and billboards. The grand scale on which BAT cultivated Shanghai's merchants was evident in the attendance at its annual New Year's banquet. In 1924, at Shanghai's Fuxingyuan Restaurant, for example, it hosted a total of four thousand guests (eight per table at five hundred tables) and held a celebration that featured several floor shows and lasted three days.[32]

By tying in with these newspapers, amusement parks, opera houses, theaters, restaurants, and shops, BAT created a dense network of visual images for persuading consumers to identify its cigarettes with the other pleasures and sources of excitement along Nanjing Road. As pedestrians strolled along this street, by day they were never out of sight of BAT's posters, painted walls and billboards, and by night they could see BAT's glittering neon signs—including its famous clock which was the single biggest advertising device in China.[33] Every step of the way, they were encouraged to see BAT's cigarettes in relation to other desired objects and exciting experiences. Thus, BAT sought to identify its product with consumers' hopes and aspirations by linking its advertising with the major institutions of commercial culture in the pleasure zone along Nanjing Road.

Proud of this advertising in Shanghai, BAT held it up as a model for its sales staff in other Chinese cities. For example, in 1924, twenty years after establishing the art department at its Shanghai headquarters, BAT sent a team of advertising specialists from Shanghai on a tour of nine other Chinese cities (Tianjin, Beijing, Qinwangdao, Shenyang, Harbin, Jinan, Nanjing, Jiujiang, and Hankou), and, based on its findings, the team urged the company to bring Chinese employees from the other cities to see how advertising was done in

30. Bungey to Fairley, January 1927, Collection of Records of the British-American Tobacco Company, Research Center for Chinese Business History, Economic Research Institute, Shanghai Academy of Social Sciences, Shanghai (hereafter cited as BAT Collection), 13-I-59.

31. Quoted by Jay Leyda, *Dianying: An Account of Films and the Film Audience in China* (Cambridge, Mass., 1972), 44. See also Sherman Cochran, *Big Business in China: Sino-Foreign Rivalry in the Cigarette Industry, 1890-1930* (Cambridge, Mass., 1980), 135.

32. Chen and Ping, 212.

33. Cochran, *Big Business*, 180.

Shanghai. The proposal is worth quoting at length because it not only summarizes BAT's advertising operations in Shanghai but also sets the company's goals for other Chinese cities. The advertising team proposed that

> we inaugurate a temporary advertising class in Shanghai and have each Division, to commence with, send down one first class Chinese. Give him a thorough insight into the Art Department work and what we are trying to attain. Newspaper work—how designs are made up and stereos prepared for the papers—painting in all its aspects—the correct method of using poster boards. A visit around Shanghai will quickly open their eyes to the many sites on which painted signs can be erected. A visit to the Printing Factory [will show them] the great amount of labor and expense involved in getting out good material and the greater need for care when using same. Show them the need for our advertising staff in a general way to keep in close touch with the selling work in the district they are working intelligently to assist sales through the medium of advertising.[34]

As emphasized in this proposal, BAT's advertising was unquestionably more sophisticated in Shanghai than in other Chinese cities, but, as implied here, the company's advertising in China was by no means confined to Shanghai. Long before this trip report was submitted in 1924, BAT had begun using Shanghai as a base from which to supply large quantities of advertising to other parts of the country.

Advertising in other Chinese cities. In Chinese cities outside Shanghai, BAT posted Western salesmen, and they worked with Chinese intermediaries at their level of BAT's marketing organization much as their boss James Thomas worked with high-level Chinese intermediaries in Shanghai.[35] As advertisers, these Western salesmen and their Chinese intermediaries were principally responsible for organizing teams of Chinese "snipers" (to quote the term used by BAT's Western salesmen)— who swept through a city and plastered BAT's advertisements on every available surface.

The Western salesmen's attitudes toward sniping varied even as they led Chinese teams that saturated the urban landscape. Some in BAT were proud of the company's "pioneering" efforts to introduce advertisements where they had never appeared before. One, for example, lauded the "vivid" achievement of a Western BAT representative who "scaled the mighty heights of the Yangtze [Yangzi] Gorges for the purpose of fixing a huge 'Pirate' [BAT

---

34. "Report on Trip," 1924, BAT Collection, 13-I-15.
35. Cochran, *Encountering Chinese Networks*, ch. 3.

brand] sign."[36] Others laughed off their responsibility for BAT's campaigns, joking among themselves about "sticking bills in a Chinese temple."[37] And still others disliked the job but did it anyway. An American who served BAT in China early in the twentieth century later wrote, "It was nasty work—deliberately defacing house walls with a lot of glaring, shouting, colored posters. I loathed it." But neither his attitude toward his work nor floods, famines, warfare and other disruptions seemed to stop him and others from posting BAT's advertising. During the revolution of 1911, the same man noted, "In spite of the daily upheavals in politics, we carried on the dirty work of the company without interruption—selling, sampling, posting, and distributing handbills."[38]

At the highest levels of BAT's management in China, James Thomas and others admitted that BAT's sniping spread to locations where the company did not have permission to post advertising. Nonetheless, they continued to put up posters wherever possible—railway stations, wharves, water tanks, wine shops, tea houses, military headquarters, schools, temples, private residences.[39]

BAT's teams of Western salesmen and Chinese snipers covered cities with advertising at the cores of all nine of China's regional economies: the Northeast, North, Northwest, Southeast, South, Southwest, Lower Yangzi, Middle Yangzi, and Upper Yangzi.[40] In the Northeast, an American journalist remarked that the thousands of placards posted in the city of Yingkou in 1905 reminded him of the sensational billing that the Barnum and Bailey circus arranged in advance of its arrival in American cities.[41] In North China a newspaper correspondent in Kaifeng reported in 1907 that "the whole city has been placarded with thousands of staring [BAT] advertisements."[42] In Northwest China a reporter in Xi'an writing in 1911 described "huge [BAT] posters on the city gates, city walls, on every vacant piece of wall or board in

---

36. *B.A.T. Bulletin*, New Series, 14.37 (May 1923): 835.

37. *B.A.T. Bulletin*, New Series, 3.54 (April 1916): 25.

38. Hutchison, 53, 74.

39. Thomas, 161-162; Zhongguo kexue yuan, 68; Sanger, 80. Even in large Chinese cities, BAT and other advertisers paid only nominal rent for the use of highly valued outdoor sites such as the walls of railway stations and the shoulders of highways, and they handed out an occasional package of cigarettes or nothing at all for the right to post bills elsewhere (Bacon, 756-757; Sanger, 79-80).

40. These nine "macroregions" have been delineated by G. William Skinner. See his "Regional Urbanization in Nineteenth Century China," in Skinner, ed., *The City in Late Imperial China* (Stanford, 1977), 211-249.

41. Wang Jingyu, 216 and 222-228.

42. *North China Herald* (June 14, 1907): 669.

the street, on the brick stands supporting the masts in front of the yamens, in fact anywhere and everywhere."[43]

To the south and west of Shanghai, BAT's sniping in the core cities of China's other regions was equally thorough. In South China an observer commented in 1908 that "the walls of Canton City and the delta towns are literally covered with the brightly coloured [BAT] advertisement posters."[44] West of Canton a Western diplomatic official noted in 1904 that BAT agents had canvassed the area along the West River "in a houseboat gaily decorated with flags and other emblems [from which they distributed] picture placards and samples of their wares, with the result that their cigarettes are now on sale in every town and village along the river."[45] In the Southeast, according to a report from the British consul at Fuzhou in 1909, BAT agents drummed up business by "preaching the cult of the cigarette and distributing millions gratis so as to introduce a taste for tobacco in this particular form into regions where it was as yet unknown . . . The streets of Foochow [Fuzhou] are brilliant with [BAT's] ingenious pictorial posters, which are so designed to readily catch the eye by their gorgeous coloring and attractive lettering, both in English and Chinese."[46] In the Southwest, the British consul general at Kunming observed in 1910 that there was "hardly a bare wall in the town that is not brightened by the [BAT's] flaming posters,"[47] and a journalist making a tour across Sichuan, Yunnan, and Burma in the same year found that he was "rarely out of sight of the flaring posters in Chinese characters advertising the [BAT] cigarette."[48] BAT's campaigns were most intensive of all along the Lower, Middle, and Upper Yangzi, where it inundated every city from Shanghai to Chongqing.[49]

Advertising outside major cities. Outside China's major cities, as within them, BAT assigned the task of advertising to Western salesmen, and they, in turn, worked with Chinese intermediaries who presided over teams of Chinese underlings. As in the big cities, these advertising teams covered a lot of ground, but in smaller cities and market towns they campaigned mainly by

---

43. *North China Herald* (January 27, 1911): 198.

44. Arnold Wright, ed., *Twentieth Century Impressions of Hong Kong, Shanghai, and Other Treaty Ports of China* (London, 1908), 795-796.

45. H.H. Fox, "Report," *Journal of the American Asiatic Association*, 4.11 (December 1904): 345.

46. FO 371/864, no. 24094, Playfair to Jordan, June 8, 1909.

47. FO 371/864, no. 8889, O'Brien-Butler to FO, February 4, 1910.

48. Edwin J. Dingle, *Across China on Foot* (New York, 1911), 100.

49. Du Zhenhua, "Ying Mei yancao gongsi yu Chongqing juanyan shichang" (The British-American Tobacco Company and the Chongqing cigarette market), *Sichuan wenshi ziliao xuanji* (Collection of literary and historical materials on Sichuan), 3 (1964): 111-112, 116; Cochran, *Big Business*, 244, note 46.

setting up portable displays at periodic markets. Like other Chinese itinerant vendors, they traveled from one market place to another according to the regular (but not daily) schedule that buyers and sellers generally followed at the time throughout rural China, and they attracted crowds by building a wooden stand, staging a performance, and giving away prizes and free cigarettes.

In the 1910s and 1920s, members of BAT's advertising teams and other observers documented the company's campaigns at temple fairs (*miao hui*) in towns and villages throughout all of China's economic regions, and BAT's salesmen reported that they encountered different crowds and used different techniques in the countryside than they did in the cities.[50] This difference was noted, for example, in a first-hand account by Frank Canaday, one of BAT's American salesmen, as he led a Chinese advertising team in 1923 across western Shandong province, one of the most impoverished places in China.[51]

According to Canaday, he and his team worked the crowds much more easily in the cities than they did in the countryside. In Jining, the most important city in western Shandong, his team had little difficulty turning one of the city's temple fairs to its advantage. As Canaday reported to the company,

> The local deity "Chung Wang" was due to parade through the city to a temple outside the gate at noon. We heard this was postponed, so in order not to disappoint the crowds gathered in the streets we packed up our tent-top and made a parade of "Chequers" [brand cigarettes] through the streets along the parade route—the music in front, five clowns in red and white chequered suits following, then the big tent top and the Chinese staff and myself bringing up the rear . . . [People in the crowd thought] the religious parade was coming, and they laughed in appreciation of the joke when they saw what it really was. Everyone was

---

50. For descriptions of BAT's advertising teams at work in temple fairs held in Northeast China, North China, the Lower Yangzi, and South China, see accounts originally published during the 1920s in BAT's in-house Chinese-language monthly periodical, *Ying Mei yan gongsi yue bao* (British-American Tobacco Company Monthly), which are currently available in the BAT collection, 13-I-27-29, 46, 49-51, 55-57, 100-104, 108, 116. On advertising in small villages around Xian in Northwest China, see R.H. Gregory and A.C. Moore, "Report," July 3-October 20, 1911, BAT Collection, 13-G-83, 88, 99. On BAT's rural advertising in the Upper Yangzi region, see Du Zhenhua, 111-112, 116. On its rural advertising in Southwest China, see Dingle, 100.

51. On the impoverishment of western Shandong province, see Kenneth Pomeranz, *The Making of a Hinterland: State, Society, and Economy in Inland North China, 1853-1937* (Berkeley, 1993).

laughing and shouting "Chee Pan Pai" ["Chequers Brand"]—and I think they well remember how to say it seriously too . . .

By the time the real "Chung Wang" procession arrived outside the temple our total sales of "Chequers" was close to 1000 packets for the day.[52]

After the festival had ended, Canaday's team continued to enjoy success in the city. On October 14, 1923, he wrote to his American superior in Shanghai, "I . . . succeeded yesterday through the influence of the territory manager here who had a friend 'at court' (Police court), in getting my booth placed right along side the entrance to the Magistrate's Yamen. We made an enclosure against a wall with some tables and bamboo poles and kept a crowd of about one hundred pushing Chinese around us most of the time."[53]

Upon leaving the city, Canaday and his team encountered far less playful and cooperative crowds between the towns of Wenshang and Yuncheng. At the first stop, a market place consisting of "three mud villages," he found a "bare, drab scene of poverty and winter hibernation," according to an entry in his diary, and his team made its pitch to "a skeptical crowd that pinched their coppers very hard." While this crowd seemed overly passive, a crowd that he faced a few days later at a Confucian temple in a nearby market town, Juye, seemed overly aggressive:

> Huge crowds of farmers, soldiers, etc., big hardy fellows, mostly with queues. Their women sitting about on the ground, their bound feet crossed. Crowds fought to buy cigarettes and get prizes. Around us, a picture stand, a story teller, merchants of every ware . . . Played phonograph. Finished by 2. Went back at four to give samples. Was nearly mobbed by the crowd . . . They were like savage beasts trying to get at the free cigarettes . . . Was followed up the street by a crowd of a hundred youngsters . . . not sympathetic and inclined to throw stones . . . such a crowd is dangerous . . . a slight incident can easily change their temper . . . [54]

In Canaday's account, the volatile "temper" of these rural crowds—the "skeptical" penny pinchers in the three mud villages and the "savage beasts"

---

52. Canaday to Huang, August 27, 1923, Frank H. Canaday Papers, Harvard-Yenching Library, Harvard University, Cambridge, Mass.
53. Canaday to Bassett, October 14, 1923, Canaday Papers.
54. Canaday diary, October 18, 1923, Canaday Papers.

in the market town of Juye—contrasted sharply with the "laughing and shouting" cheerleaders at BAT's parade in the city of Jining.

BAT's Chinese agents drew a similarly sharp distinction between city and countryside in their surveys of popular Chinese reactions to the company's advertising. In their evaluations, urban Chinese preferred BAT's advertisements depicting modern scenes, and rural Chinese preferred the ones showing traditional scenes. In North China, according to one of these agents, adults and children all liked a series called "Chinese Society Girl" which showed one Chinese "modern woman" on each of a series of "illustrated cigarette cards" (*xiangyan huapian*) (also known as "stiffeners" because they kept soft packs of cigarettes from bending and breaking). Among urban dwellers in North China, BAT's agent reported, only the elderly avidly collected cigarette cards showing ancient tales which they used for telling their grandchildren traditional stories like "Journey to the West."[55]

BAT's Chinese agents in other regions of the country similarly noted differences between urban and rural reactions to the company's advertising. One writing from Xuzhou in the Lower Yangzi region found that in the countryside the series of cards showing ancient figures was more popular than the one showing modern women. Country people especially enjoyed collecting cards showing the cast of characters from "Romance of the Three Kingdoms," he said, because it "is our old and historic novel in China. Every Chinese knows it."[56] The same point was made by a Chinese agent writing from Yancheng in the Middle Yangzi region. "People are more attracted by stiffeners in the interior counties than in the city," he said. Whenever stiffeners were changed in some of BAT's brands, "plenty country people even doubt the quality of the cigarettes." In distinguishing between BAT's cigarettes and local imitations, his customers assumed that only BAT was capable of making stiffeners and, therefore, that the presence of stiffeners confirmed the authenticity of BAT's product.[57]

These surveys were not done systematically and should not be regarded as the equivalent of marketing research in today's commercial world (with polls and statistically grounded evaluations of popular taste), but they and Canaday's account unquestionably demonstrate BAT's interest in rural Chinese consumers as well as urban ones. To reach these consumers, BAT advertised on an enormous scale, sending teams into poor rural areas along the peripheries of China's economic regions as well as into rich urban metropolises at the cores of these regions. To place the scale of this advertising in perspective, it

---

55. Y.S. Hsu to BAT, April 30, 1933, BAT Collection.
56. Chen Hsiang Yen to BAT, April 30, 1933, BAT Collection.
57. Lincoln S.P. Lu to BAT, April 4, 1933, BAT Collection.

is worth comparing BAT's record with the record of other propagandists in China at the time.

Measuring the reach of BAT's advertising. A bizarre episode that occurred during World War I suggests the extent of BAT's penetrating power compared to that of other organizations at the time. The episode originated in May 1916 when members of the British Secret Service hatched a plot to compete with Germany for China's support during World War I by launching a propaganda campaign to appeal directly to the Chinese people. This proposal was absurd, for, as Sir John Jordan, the British minister in Beijing, pointed out to his superiors in London, the "great mass of Chinese are completely indifferent to causes and progress of the war."[58] Nonetheless, the British officials' discussion of how to carry out this assignment is very revealing.

Without exception, the members of the British Secret Service all agreed that whatever propaganda was to be made and distributed in China could be handled more effectively by BAT than by any other organization. As two put it, BAT would be the perfect distributor because it "gets into the closest touch with the people."[59] The British Secret Service was especially keen on inserting British anti-German propaganda as stiffeners in packs of BAT's cigarettes because "commercial and political propaganda should go hand in hand, if we really wish to achieve success."[60] Eager to enlist BAT's help, the British Secret Service contacted BAT's management in China, received enthusiastic support for the project from James Thomas, and arranged for BAT to translate, produce, and distribute highly pictorial propaganda in the form of newspaper articles, maps, and posters.[61]

These tasks were performed by BAT to the full satisfaction of the members of the British Secret Service. BAT was "admirable" and "most public-spirited," one of them remarked. "I can think of no more effective means of getting our propaganda work before the Chinese public."[62] The only snag was that Western missionaries in China complained that the British Secret Service should have given this assignment to themselves rather than to BAT. The missionaries were "jealous" of BAT, one British official observed, but he preferred to give BAT a "complete monopoly" on distributing the propaganda because "for credit,

58. FO 395/125058, Jordan to FO, June 28, 1916.

59. FO 395/16/1623/113151, Nicholson and Long to Gowers, June 7, 1916.

60. FO 371/2827/1623/F1623, Lampson to Macleay, May 4, 1916.

61. FO 395/16/1623/113151, Nicholson to Gaselee, June 26, 1916; FO 395/16/1623/ 131742, Nicholson to Lampson, July 6, 1916.

62. FO 395/16/1623/131742, Lampson to Nicholson, July 18, 1916.

activity, pervasiveness & popularity, the BAT considerably exceeds the missionary bodies."[63]

As a compromise, the missionaries and BAT divided responsibilities and handled the propaganda jointly, but the British officials continued to comment on BAT's greater effectiveness. BAT had "absolutely unrivalled facilities for distribution in China," one noted in March 1917 after the propaganda campaign had been going on for almost a year, and he added, "I think there can be no doubt that they have facilities greater and better organized for this purpose" than the missionaries had.[64] Another agreed that BAT's "organization has a mobility and a wider range, in the interior of China, than that of the Mission Stations."[65] This view that BAT was superior to missionaries as a propagandist in China prevailed among British Secret Service officers until they ended their propaganda campaign later in 1917 when China entered World War I on the side of the Western allies.

The British Secret Service's evaluation suggests that BAT had a greater capacity than any other foreign organization—religious, diplomatic, military, or otherwise—to disseminate propaganda in China on a nationwide scale. But perhaps even this seemingly high assessment does not go far enough, for it is possible that BAT reached more Chinese people than any other propagandist—Chinese as well as foreign. Those skeptical of such an assertion might doubt that BAT's advertising system could possibly have rivalled the communication system of China's central government under the Qing or the Republic, for these governments distributed official proclamations throughout the country at the provincial and county levels. To reach semi-literate and illiterate people, Qing emperors ordered local magistrates in every county to give periodic lectures, but few Chinese in rural areas had ever heard these lectures, and by the nineteenth century the district magistrates had lost interest in giving them.[66]

By contrast with official proclamations, BAT's pictorial advertising was deliberately designed to communicate with unlettered people, and it reached a large number of them. The result, according to one Chinese journalist who watched Chiang Kai-shek's government compete directly with foreign businesses for attention in the late 1920s and 1930s, was that BAT proved to

---

63. FO 395/16/1623/190656, unsigned comment on Jordan to Fraser, August 9, 1916.

64. FO 395/93/2399/46109, Gowers to Montgomery, March 1, 1917.

65. FO 395/93/2399/79146, M. deB. to Alston, April 23, 1917.

66. Hsiao Kung-chuan, *Rural China: Imperial Control in the Nineteenth Century* (Seattle, 1960), 184-205; Ch'u Tung-tsu, *Local Government in China under the Ch'ing* (Cambridge, Mass., 1962), 162-163; John R. Watt, *The District Magistrate in Late Imperial China* (New York, 1972), 196.

be more effective than the government as a propagandist. Writing in 1934, after seven years of the Nationalist government's indoctrination according to Sun Yat-sen's Three Principles of the People (*san min zhuyi*), he remarked that "many rural Chinese villages still don't know who in the world Sun Yat-sen is, but very few places have not known Ruby Queen (*Da Ying*) [brand of BAT] cigarettes."[67]

Thus, compared to foreign missionaries, Chinese governments, or any other propagandist, BAT disseminated its message widely in early twentieth century China. It was by no means the only foreign firm to do so; various American, British, German, Russian, and Japanese firms used similar techniques, and by 1915 these firms marketed at least 11 percent of China's imported goods, including kerosene, alkalis, soaps, dyes, medicines, and textiles.[68] Nor was BAT the first to make Chinese art available; members of the Chinese elite had long circulated paintings, book illustrations, and other works among themselves, and people from a cross section of Chinese society had seen paintings and sculpture displayed in Chinese temples and had hung New Year's pictures and woodblock prints as decorations in their homes. But it is probably no exaggeration to say that, compared to BAT, no other organization (including governments, temples, missionaries, newspapers) produced such a variety of Chinese illustrations and distributed them on such a massive scale in the early twentieth century—not even in the 1920s and 1930s when the first art museums were opened in China.[69]

Conclusion

Does the case of BAT in China provide evidence that the origins of Chinese commercial culture are traceable to foreign sources and specifically to New York City's Times Square? As shown here, some origins of BAT's advertising in China may be traced almost literally to Times Square. BAT's founder, James Duke, set up its headquarters near Times Square and reached out from New York to China by appointing his fellow North Carolinian James Thomas as manager of the company's headquarters for China at Shanghai. Moreover, Thomas consciously tried to follow the example that Duke had set as an

---

67. Xichao, "Ying Mei yan gongsi duiyu Zhongguo guomin jingji de qinshi" (The British-American Tobacco Company's penetration into China's national economy), *Zhongguo jingji lunwen ji* (Essays on China's economy) (Shanghai, 1936), I, 93. See also Hutchison, 307, 328.

68. G.G. Allen and Audrey G. Donnithorne, *Western Enterprise in Far Eastern Economic Development* (London, 1954), 45-46; Cochran, "Marketing Medicine."

69. On China's first art museums, see Margaret Mayching Kao, "China's Response to the West in Art, 1898-1937" (Ph.D. dissertation, Stanford University, 1972), 145-146.

advertiser in the American market. Even as Duke had produced advertising on newly available American-made continuous-process printing presses and had distributed it through a bureaucratic organization of American salesmen in the United States, so Thomas set out to do the same in China. To this extent, there is undeniably a connection between Times Square and the myriad regional and local markets throughout China touched by BAT's advertising in the early twentieth century.

And yet, the description of BAT's of advertising given here suggests that the transmission of culture was not simply a matter of an American business unilaterally exporting to China advertising that had been invented in America. Not until BAT's Western owners and managers began to team up with local Chinese did the company become effective at producing and distributing advertising in China. Despite its sophisticated American printing technology, BAT failed to produce advertising of interest to Chinese consumers until it began to enlist the services of Chinese artists. For all of BAT's vaunted resources and financial backing, its American managers "tied in" with China's commercial institutions only through the good offices of Chinese intermediaries. However much its American salesmen pioneered as distributors of advertising, they remained dependent on Chinese to form their advertising teams, guide them through local communities, and give them evaluations of popular taste.

In the early twentieth century, the key to BAT's approach was its transnational shift from American- to Chinese-oriented advertising. After its advertising's initial failures, BAT abandoned the strategy of merely importing American-made advertising and switched to the strategy of delegating authority to Chinese artists as producers of advertising and to Chinese commercial agents as distributors of it. These Chinese became the pivotal figures in BAT's advertising system in China. Insofar as Chinese artists retained control over production, BAT's advertising images for China were invented not on Times Square but on Nanjing Road, and insofar as Chinese commercial agents retained control over marketing, BAT's advertising was distributed in China not from New York but from Shanghai at the crossroads of the Chinese world.

Part II
Inventing Shanghai-style
Commercial Culture

Invention, Industry, Art: the Commercialization of Culture in Republican Art Magazines

Carrie Waara

Nanjing Road as a metaphor for Shanghai's commercial culture points to the origins of that culture in the retail businesses of Shanghai. The Shanghai lifestyle has long been described in terms of its restaurants, clothes stores, and entertainments. The invention of this style clearly owes most to the driving force of Shanghai's commercial market, but the fashioning of that consumer culture also owes a fair amount to an extraordinary alliance of artists, publicists, businessmen, and technical experts. In the Republican period, mass market publications, department stores, and radio broadcasts promoted the consumption of luxury commodities through advertisements that glorified the "Shanghai style" (*Haipai*) as refined, dashing, cosmopolitan, and, above all, "modern."[1] The urge to be modern was at the core of Shanghai's identity as a treaty port receiving the latest imports from the industrialized West. Nonetheless, this urge to be modern was compounded by the impulse to shape a modern Chinese identity to face the challenges of the twentieth century. Chinese national interests were more and more threatened through the first decades of the Republic, and nowhere more conspicuously than in Shanghai, where the world powers dominated entire areas of the city. The modernism of

---

1. In fact, the term *Haipai* originated in the late Qing phrase *haishang huapai* to disparage Shanghai painters and craftsmen for catering to the market, and the term continued in the Republican period to express the negative connotations of the marketplace, equated with frivolity, vulgarity, emptiness and deception. It was partially to counter that condescending view of business that the artists and editors in this study promoted commercial and industrial art. For a discussion of the history and meaning of the term *Haipai*, see Zhang Zhongli, ed., *Jindai Shanghai chengshi yanjiu* (Modern Shanghai Studies) (Shanghai: Shanghai renmin chubanshe, 1991), 1130-1159.

the new Republican-era Shanghai style was not a Western import, but was consciously invented to capitalize on and transform modern Western cultural elements for Chinese purposes. This modernism-as-nationalism was a new element in Shanghai's commercial culture.

The publishing industry in particular pictured itself at the center of the Chinese struggle for a higher position in the hierarchy of nations. Rather than challenge the technological criteria that Western (and Japanese) societies held as standards for international status, some Chinese publishers promoted technical or industrial arts as the primary measure of national progress. A significant group of artists and entrepreneurs engaged in periodical publishing in order to help generate and shape a Chinese-style modernism based on a cult of technology and entrepreneurial commercial nationalism. This modernism came to be conflated in the periodicals with a middle-class consumer culture. It emphasized the spread ("democratization") of a domestic lifestyle replete with all the latest news and fashions, amounting to a kind of nation-building based on comfortable, healthy homes managed by informed and educated women. The consequence for Nanjing Road was a highly gendered consumer culture. Advocating an ideal integration of art with daily life, essays supported all kinds of practical and applied arts like furniture, clothing, housewares, interior and architectural design, and commercial art like advertising, display design, and even wrapping paper and package design, as fields for artists and manufacturers to pursue—fields most visible in the shop windows and department stores on Nanjing Road frequented by the female shoppers described by Carlton Benson. Light manufacturing of such goods was also well suited to the Nanjing Road area, which, as Hanchao Lu points out, housed a variety of commercial/residential mixes in shikumen compounds in the alleyways off the main streets. And Fuzhou Road, one of the main commercial thoroughfares that belonged to the Nanjing Road sphere, was Shanghai's noted booksellers' street, where readers purchased current periodicals, including the art magazines at the center of this study.

Three popular magazines in particular, each edited by prominent artists and backed by powerful political or business interests, exemplify the goals and strategies of Shanghai's new commercial culture: *Zhenxiang huabao* (The true record) was established in the dramatic first year of the Republic by two of the founders of the Lingnan (Cantonese) School of Painting. The brothers Gao Jianfu and Gao Qifeng were among the first Chinese artists to be identified with the nationalist movement. Allegedly funded by Sun Yat-sen,[2] their

---

2. Wang Bomin, ed., *Zhongguo meishu tongshi* (A General History of Chinese Art) in Vol. 10 of *Jinxiandai meishu* (Modern and Contemporary Art) (Jinan: Shandong jiaoyu chubanshe, 1988), 113.

bookstore-publishing house in Shanghai produced in *Zhenxiang huabao* a new form of publication in China, the photographic art pictorial, which set the pattern for the art magazines that followed it. In particular, it hailed its own use of advanced printing technology and claimed a guiding role for itself as a promoter of industry and technology in China. *Liang you tuhua zazhi* (The young companion pictorial magazine), published from 1926 to 1941 by Wu Liande, a nationalistic entrepreneur with broad overseas connections, was one of Shanghai's most popular and successful pictorial magazines of the 1920s and 1930s. It frequently joined its coverage of the native goods movement with enthusiastic promotion of small-scale industrial and commercial arts. Moreover, its signature portraits of glamorous "covergirls" call to mind the statement by Cao Juren: "*Haipai* is like a modern girl."[3] *Meishu shenghuo* (Arts and life) was published in 1934-1937 by a leading Shanghai print industry entrepreneur and edited by a virtual Who's Who in Chinese art for this period.[4] This prestigious periodical clearly targets women consumers in its "art and life" messages promoting commercial art and consumer industries, but each of these Shanghai art magazines couches its consumer agenda in nationalistic terms and addresses potential producers as well as consumers.

The joint participation in these publications of the cultural elite of the art world and the modern Shanghai business bourgeoisie was a conscious effort to promote the new culture of the city as a model for all of China. They attempted to reconstruct Chinese national identity through an urban focus on the industrialization (*gongyihua*) of art to meet the needs of society, the practical needs of consumers as well as the commercial needs of industry. They promoted new ways for retailers and manufacturers to join forces with artists for economic growth and national development. As a result, the Shanghai search for a new national culture became inextricably linked to the commodities of domestic life.

Gongyi Meishu: Industrial Arts and Artistic Industry

The magazine editors recognized that the modern movement penetrates most widely in the forms of everyday life, and the decorative, applied, or industrial arts comprise the field of art that most embodies the modernist movement. The *Meishu shenghuo* editors stressed consistently that the *gongyi meishu*

---

3. Quoted in Zhang Zhongli, *Jindai Shanghai chengshi yanjiu*, 1137.
4. Founder and publisher Jin Youcheng has an entry in Qi Zaiyu, ed., *Shanghai shiren zhi* (Biographies of Notable Shanghai Men) (Shanghai: Zhanwang chubanshe, 1947).

movement[5] represents a significant link between fine art and socioeconomic life. The decorative industrial arts were seen as the artists' bridge between the "masses" and "beauty."[6] This movement in China had a double impetus: not only was it a logical extension of the "art for life" movement to promote the practical and applied arts for national glory, it also promoted national economic rejuvenation through consumer culture. Many artists encouraged the development of items for sale and for export.[7] *Meishu shenghuo* especially emphasized the productive possibilities of art for life's sake.[8] Such

---

5. In Chinese, *gongyi* can refer both to technical arts like printing or textile manufacture and to decorative art and design, as well as to craftsmanship and technique. The *Zhongwen da cidian* (Encyclopedic Dictionary of the Chinese Language) translates *gongyi meishu* as "industrial art," and describes it as the production of objects of everyday use that are subject to aesthetic criteria. In other words, *gongyi meishu* refers to various kinds of goods meeting the needs of practical life and on which artistic skill or ornamentation is applied. Examples are lacquerware, woodwork, pottery, textiles, and metalwork. *Zhuangshi meishu* is another term used for "decorative arts," but *gongyi meishu* also came to indicate machine production of consumer goods, as well as to refer to industrial design and tool and machine use (common Western associations with the term industrial art). In this work, *gongyi* and *gongyi meishu* will usually refer to the "applied arts" or "decorative arts," except where handicrafts are specifically indicated, as in *Meishu shenghuo*'s promotion of hand-crafted commodities. To distinguish clearly, however, it is important to note that the *gongyi meishu* movement in Republican China had several sources, a major one being the contemporaneous European modern design movement dating approximately from 1890 through the 1930s. Its sources, in turn, lay with the English arts and crafts movement, the nineteenth-century revival of handicraft art championed by the socialist William Morris and emphasizing "art for use" in society, and with the European Romantic tradition in the arts, including interests in folk arts, "Oriental" trends, and nationalistic revivals. Chinese artists also relied on Japanese sources on modern European industrial and handicraft arts.

6. Zhe An, "Zhuangshi meishu zhi xin gujia" (A new appraisal of the decorative arts) serialized installment begun in *Meishu shenghuo* 4 (July 1934). Here Zhe An develops a theory of the relationship between the decorative arts and "national" (*minzu*) spirit: Great spirit is expressed in decorative art, evident in such examples as the arts of Greece, Rome, and Paris. Each people wants to express its greatness and glory by building great cities and incomparably beautiful government buildings. Public gardens and handcrafted architecture lead to city and national pride, just as the Champs Élysees nourishes French patriotism. When art and beauty are valued and widely available, a people's spirit will be strong and refined.

7. For example, Gao Jianfu, the esteemed cofounder of *Zhenxiang huabao*, promoted decorated porcelain as a potential export industry and as an art form. See Ralph Croizier, *Art and Revolution in Modern China: The Lingnan (Cantonese) School of Painting, 1906-1951* (Berkeley: University of California Press, 1988), 68.

8. See Liu Lin, "Tichang gongyi meishu yu tichang guohuo" (Promote industrial art and promote national goods) in *Meishu shenghuo* 4 (July 1934); Liu Suijiu, "Wei gongyi meishu yan" (Speaking for the applied arts), *Meishu shenghuo* 3 (June 1934); Lang Shu, "Shangye meishu" (Commercial art), *Meishu shenghuo* 3 (June 1934); Zhang Derong, "Gongyi meishu yu rensheng zhi guanxi" (The relationship between the applied arts and human life), *Meishu*

encouragement worked to overcome the anti-business bias inherent in the so-called "amateur ideal" that selling one's artwork devalued it. "A New Appraisal of Decorative Art" set forth the *Meishu shenghuo* argument against the amateur ideal:

> From the previous art scene emerged a superiority theme that declared that in order to preserve the respectability of art, artists must be forbidden from engaging in the applied arts. . . . It also claimed . . . artists are just not in the same category [as artisans and that] artwork is not sold for money; whatever is sold is not art. [It also claimed] artwork is not useful; whatever is useful is not art. . . . Yet, in fact, people who condemn the selling of art, . . . who despise applied arts for having no artistic value, . . . will buy pretty patterned fabric and fashionable furniture, and say, . . . "How beautiful this is to look at!" This self-contradictory talk is something we often hear.[9]

Moreover, failure to acknowledge the caliber and the role of artisans and painter-craftsmen in creating great monuments to art like churches and palaces reveals not only a lack of expertise on the part of so-called artists, but an inflated sense of their own worth that is embedded in pre-Republican notions of class and social prestige.

> While most people cannot recognize the value of decorative art and the greatness of the "artisan," they fall head over heels for the empty name of "artist." In fact, most . . . artists . . . do not reach the artisans' level of skill. . . . Thus Roger Marx, in his *Le Rapide* magazine article "Salons and the Decorative Arts," says, "We would rather have fewer ordinary painters and a few more useful painter-craftsmen."

> There is another group of people who, in order to prop up their stinking airs of being "artists," determine never to do decorative art for fear their status will fall to that of "painter-craftsmen." This is all abnormal thinking that comes out of a people whose . . . art ideology is unhealthy. We must know that the work of the painter-craftsman is of the same artistic value as the artist's. We absolutely cannot ignore them or slight them on account of social status.[10]

---

shenghuo 1 (April 1934); and Tang Jun, "Tashang shiyong yishu di daoshang" (Step onto the road of practical arts), *Yi feng* 2:3 (March 1933): 22-23.

9. Zhe An, "Zhuangshi meishu zhi xin gujia."

10. Zhe An, "Zhuangshi meishu zhi xin gujia."

Meishu shenghuo emphasized the appeal of modern, up-to-date applied arts technology, which supported national development and growth. With more and more advanced techniques available to artists in China, it would be unprogressive to reject such work as unartistic. "If we now want to enter the 'city' of modern civilization, we must purge the empty talk on art and energetically apply ourselves to the decorative arts," one writer urged.[11]

Industrial art was promoted in *Zhenxiang huabao* and *Liang you* as a way to compete with foreign manufactures in China. In an essay titled "The Relationship between Industrial Arts and Human Life," Zhang Derong remarks that the makers of Chinese decorative arts failed to adapt to the changing requirements of human life. Chinese goods could not compete economically with machine-made foreign products, resulting in the contemporary situation of Chinese economic decline. Zhang bemoans the comparatively backward, even regressive nature of Chinese handicraft arts, and urges art's modernization (*xiandaihua*) and enlivening (*shenghuohua*) through the "industrialization" (*gongyihua*) of art. Zhang saves specific blame for the Chinese art world's negligence in this area. Art academies' failure to institute specialized courses in the applied arts deprive their students of the skills to "meet the needs of society"—including the practical needs of both middle- and working-class consumers as well as the commercial needs of industrial society.[12]

On the pages of *Liang you*, *Meishu shenghuo* and *Zhenxiang huabao*, these promoters of the industrial arts constantly sought new ways for education and commerce to join forces for economic growth and national development. Some were inspired by the ways that commercial artists succeeded in joining their talents to modern industry and business. Perhaps with an eye to encouraging employment on Nanjing Road for art school graduates, both *Meishu shenghuo* and *Liang you* were especially drawn to reproduce the works exhibited by students in the graphic design department at the Shanghai Academy of Art, one of the few modern commercial art programs in the country. *Liang you* featured a vivid selection of the students' designs in a special section on the applied arts titled in English "Decorative and Ad Drawings." The designs included advertisements for Ford cars, a newspaper, and for the state lottery (the last illustrated by an airplane and a new car). The short text that

---

11. Liu Suijiu, "Wei gongyi meishu yan."

12. Zhang Derong, "Gongyi meishu yu rensheng zhi guanxi" (The relationship between the applied arts and human life) *Meishu shenghuo* 1 (April 1934). From the opposite position, Sanyi Printing Company pledged as its mission the "aestheticization of the industrial arts" (*gongyi meishuhua*). Both agenda ultimately lead to the same goal, the union of art and industry.

accompanied the display stated, "The development of commerce depends on art. Various aspects, like design composition and color, are able to catch the viewer's attention . . . and prove effective in soliciting customers. It is a pity our Chinese art world has paid so little attention to this."[13] As Sherman Cochran notes earlier in this volume, Chinese entrepreneurs and artists alike had initially ignored the American advertising techniques of the British-American Tobacco Company in Shanghai. But when the BAT brought advanced printing technology to Shanghai and began to win over Chinese customers, advertising started to develop there.

By the 1930s, commercial art was vigorously promoted by some in the Shanghai art world. One *Meishu shenghuo* author noted that advertising had become more and more important in the recent era of commercial competition. As more businessmen invested in advertising, advertising itself had become more competitive, he asserted, noting that typeface had become a major way to attract consumers' attention. A second article on commercial art declared that although the term was fairly new, the phenomenon of commercial art had existed for a long time, and was now influenced by the most advanced art techniques and forms. The development of the field worldwide was attributed to the stimulus of capitalist competition. The author's use of examples from advertising campaigns in Paris underscored the global competitiveness of Shanghai's commercial art scene.[14]

Showcasing the two Chinese arts academies that had already instituted design curricula, one issue of *Meishu shenghuo* reproduced examples of graphic art from the West Lake National Art Academy in Hangzhou and from the Shanghai Academy of Art. All of the pieces exhibited decidedly Art Deco influences, in the sans-serif-like typography on a set of advertisement designs, and in the curvilinear yet flattened female forms dominating the three other designs. Presumably these student works represented the cutting edge of the movement to combine avant-garde and decorative arts in China.[15] According to Scott Minick and Jiao Ping, imported American and European Art Deco designs of the nineteen-twenties attracted Chinese middle-class consumers,

---

13. "Shiyong meishu zhanlan" (Exhibition of applied arts) *Liang you* (February 1937).

14. Zhang (or Zhou?) Yifan, untitled article on advertising and typeface; Yifan, "Chuchuang chenlie" (Window displays); and Liu Guantong, "Meishu ziti" (Artistic typeface) in *Meishu shenghuo* 3 (June 1934).

15. Two of the works, from a West Lake Academy exhibition, are anonymous. The Shanghai Academy of Art works are attributed to Lin Yu and Xu Minying, relatively unknown artists.

who saw them as representations of modern life.[16] The so-called Shanghai Style of graphic art not only incorporated Western elements of Art Deco (such as its crisp lines, geometric forms, and flattening of pictorial space, borrowing from Cubism—which has roots in both African and Asian art) but also incorporated patterns and motifs found in traditional Chinese decorative arts. The accompanying illustrations show how the Shanghai Style often combined Chinese and Western Art Deco forms.

Invention and Technology

It is clear by now that the Shanghai art magazines of the Republican era participated in a much wider cause. *Gongyi meishu* (industrial or decorative arts) was art and more. Alongside the magazines' endorsement of consumer culture and economic development was a fascination with the power of machine technology and advanced processes. Some editors may have appreciated that the prosperous economy of pre-1800 China had depended on a highly developed handicraft industry. The capacity of Chinese industry to "catch up" to Western levels depended to a certain extent on its handicraft economy. For instance, ingenuity and enterprise, identified so closely with the rise of American industrial democracy, were qualities long known to Chinese society—but now were perceived as lying moribund and in need of rejuvenation.[17] The American public's infatuation with machines and inventors also spread world-wide at this time. The growing mass market press, particularly magazine publishing, was integral to the diffusion of this interest in Shanghai.

Therefore, many Chinese publications seriously took on the responsibility to disseminate news of science and technology. This news also became a source of entertainment for readers, enhancing the marketability of Chinese magazines. With the combined zeal of the missionary and the publicist, periodicals set about informing the Chinese public of new inventions and discoveries and their marketable applications. For example, in *Zhenxiang huabao,* a lengthy, serialized translation appeared of a Japanese work titled

---

16. Scott Minick and Jiao Ping, *Chinese Graphic Design in the Twentieth Century* (New York: Van Nostrand Reinhold, 1990), 44. See also the variety of designs for advertisements, packaging, tablecloths, and screens exhibited by students of the Shanghai Academy of Arts in *Meishu shenghuo* 36 (March 1937).

17. John Schrecker has implied that these qualities had long been stock resources among the secular, mercantile Chinese, but the nineteenth-century decline of the *junxian* system in China, concurrently with the rise of the Western Industrial Revolution, led to a certain cultural amnesia. John E. Schrecker, *The Chinese Revolution in Historical Perspective* (New York: Praeger, 1991), 77-80.

"On recent world discoveries." Its self-promoting preface proclaims that the current scientific and material age was dominated by Europe and America precisely because of the widespread popularization of scientific knowledge in the West via publishing. To foster such popularization in China, the article intends to introduce the general reader to the recent history of contemporary Western science and invention.[18] By making new scientific knowledge accessible to general readers, and by offering models of applied science, many Republican periodicals sought to rouse the imagination and innovation that would lead to material and social progress in China.

Feature articles ranged from entertainingly wacky to potentially transformative topics. One amusing piece in *Zhenxiang huabao* spotlighted the "waterbike," an impractical, muscle-powered cycle that moved on the surface of water. Intending "to encourage new invention" the article emphasizes that the Hong Kong inventor was ethnically Chinese. Articles and photographs on the new science and industry of aviation appeared frequently throughout the Republican period in Chinese periodicals of all kinds. They promoted readers' understanding of advanced technology in a developing field where the Chinese could establish themselves at the beginning, ostensibly rendering international competition more equitable.

Frequent reminders of the arms race in popular Republican era magazines admonished that the development of industry and technology in China was a life-and-death enterprise. The international context of Western and Japanese military domination is explicitly represented in the periodical press. In *Zhenxiang huabao* and *Meishu shenghuo*, whole pages of photos and charts detail British, French, German, and American naval ships and commanders stationed in China; photomontages proclaim the latest advances in weaponry; illustrated news articles compare the armies and navies of the world; great warships and their commanders are portrayed in in-depth stories about modern military training and strategy; and cartoons caricature the brutality of modern arms technology and mass warfare.[19] The early Republican press, including these three popular art magazines, frequently used the example of Japan's

---

18. Bu Guosheng, trans., "Jinshi famingtan" (On recent world discoveries), *Zhenxiang huabao* 1 through 8, non-consecutively.

19. See for example the accompanying illustration, as well as "Lun lieqiang zhu Hua jiandui zhi shili" (On the strength of the Powers' fleets stationed in China) in *Zhenxiang huabao* 8 and the first and second issues of *Meishu shenghuo* (April and May 1934), which feature photos of a new style of American tank and its inventor, an article on international developments in chemical warfare, and photographs of Japanese and Soviet arms, German, British, and Japanese military airplanes and airplane carriers, and British warships and gas masks.

military-industrial complex to demonstrate how modernization could lead to national strength and international status.[20]

"Guide to the Industrial Arts" represents *Zhenxiang huabao*'s definitive statement on the subject. This detailed analysis takes a world historical perspective to craft a critique of China's comparative lack of progress in the industrial arts and to provide a firm rationale for their promotion. The article opens with this preface:

> Since the mid-seventeenth century, the various countries of Europe and the West have competed in promoting the industrial arts, which have steadily advanced. Until now, the world's powers . . . have seen their industrial arts excel and their authority expand. Similarly, [we have] the recent [example of] Japan, whose . . . imitation, research, and advance [in industrial arts] have stunned Europe and America. Now, today's world is an industrial arts world. . . . [and] those who do not think about how to advance, promote, and manage their industrial arts . . . will not be able to [compete] in the world.[21]

The rapidity of change becomes pressing when research in the ascendant nations can advance "one thousand *li* in one day" while "countries with thousands of years of civilization can only watch their backs."[22] So, the article accuses, "to be content and not to seek progress, to taste the world and not to plan reforms, to hoard wealth and be unwilling to invest it" could have tragic consequences for China. The article warns that China's independence is at stake in this competition. "Twentieth century commercial battles intensify into the drama of military battles. For this reason, every country in the world competes (economically) to eliminate (its rivals.)"[23]

The article contends that the few workshops and schools built in recent years in China "do not amount to a drop in the ocean," especially given the size and resources of the country. Moreover, it maintains, the government's hardpressed financial administration exacerbates the situation by devoting all its funds to the military. "The economy would not be this bad if the government paid more attention to the industrial arts."[24] Instead of developing

---

20. After Japan took Manchuria, however, it served less often as a popular media model for Chinese modernization.

21. Haifeng, "Gongyi zhinan" (Guide to the industrial arts), *Zhenxiang huabao* 17, 5.

22. Haifeng, "Gongyi zhinan," 5.

23. Haifeng, "Gongyi zhinan," 7.

24. Haifeng, "Gongyi zhinan," 5.

new manufactured goods, as other countries were doing, China continued to experience only the decline of her ancient arts. The essay continued:

> Various countries . . . seek unethical profit from us, and we, paradoxically, have no [will] to resist and boycott. Won't we be sorry! In the shops, foreign goods are everywhere. . . . Even for small daily necessities we are willing to let foreigners profit from us and we do not seek out or promote [native] copies [of foreign goods]. That is the reason we have no industrial arts consciousness. And without industrial arts consciousness, then there is no industrial arts reality. And without it, it is hard to speak of competing [with the West].[25]

Promoting "industrial arts consciousness" thus was meant to solve the problem of the increasing consumption of foreign goods at the expense of a decreasing consumption of Chinese goods. This version of economic nationalism is an adjunct to the patriotic boycott and native goods movements, especially after Tokyo pressured the Nanjing government to suppress anti-Japanese boycotts after the Tanggu truce. It is the tactic seized by many of the professional, commercial, and industrial elite, whose interests, not surprisingly, are most served by such a strategy. The new element in this form of economic nationalism is the urgent focus on technological awareness and development. As the article enthuses, public education and enterprise in the industrial arts could no longer be delayed, and multi-class and multi-generational solidarity over this issue held the promise of success:

> The poor give their labor, the rich give their capital, the young study its principles, the strong plan its achievement. . . . Unity of purpose is a formidable force. Our industrial arts will have its day of flourishing. . . . We must plan for roads, mines, forestry, shipbuilding, management, architecture, medicine, textiles [and so on].[26]

The article presents a painstaking analysis of the relationship of the industrial arts to society and to the nation, addressing the need for advances in agriculture, manufacturing, and academia, and the role of the military, government treasury, and rights and privileges under the Republic. Its mention of household commodities and clothing, "the small daily necessities" that competed with foreign manufactures and were a focus of the native goods movement, raises a topic that later became prevalent in both *Liang you* and

---

25. Haifeng, "Gongyi zhinan," 5.
26. Haifeng, "Gongyi zhinan," 5-6.

Meishu shenghuo. Those magazines often presented the decorative or graphic design potential in such light manufactures. *Liang you* urged the promotion of small-scale industrial arts by reporting on native goods exhibitions and by publishing regular "how-to" features on specific products like glassware and laquerware.[27] *Meishu shenghuo* also regularly published features and photographic spreads on various industrial and decorative arts that lent themselves well to the production of consumer commodities.

Liang you kicked off one series with an article titled "Should small industrial arts be promoted?" The article acknowledges that obstacles like limited capital, technology, and other resources made large-scale manufacturing dependent on foreign assistance. But it reprimands the Chinese people for their willingness to buy small foreign manufactures and "to let silver coins one by one fly away to foreign countries." It focuses its attack, however, on Chinese capitalists and entrepreneurs, who

> think they always have to spend money building houses to rent. . . and that running a factory is dangerous. . . . and that things with tiny profit margins like toys, cosmetics, and writing utensils are naturally to be looked down on. Young students think that if they study law and politics, when they graduate they can become officials or lawyers . . . [or] military officers. [They feel that] doing small-scale industrial arts is time consuming and troublesome, so the only people who engage in it are those from poor families with no means to study [their fields]. With low goals [in mind], they attain success. . . . But I see a lot of unemployed people seeking work who don't even think of learning an industrial art and standing on their own feet.[28]

Meishu shenghuo encouraged Chinese entrepreneurs to invest in consumer goods manufacturing in very concrete and educational ways. *Meishu shenghuo* saw itself as an active participant in China's modern industrial sector, and often printed diagrams and instructions for light industrial products, especially textiles. For example, one three-page article offers three different weave patterns, with loom instructions and photographs, to help China's textile factories "adapt to current world trends in consumer desires for beauty." It is

---

27. See, for example, Lin Er, "Xiao gongyi (kehua boli di yanjiu)" (Small industrial art (Research on glass engraving)), *Liang you* 6 (July 15, 1926): 14 and Lin Er, "Xiao gongyi: Meishu qiqi di zuofa" (Small industrial art: How to make artistic lacquerware), *Liang you* 4 (May 15, 1926): 24.

28. Lin Er, "Xiao gongyi yinggai tichang di ma?" (Should small industrial arts be promoted?), *Liang You* 2, 5.

followed by another illustrated article explaining fabric samples.[29] *Meishu shenghuo* published numerous articles and photo spreads on Chinese factories, providing shots of machines, processes, and workers' conditions. One two-page article describes in detail the writer's visit to a fabric dying mill in Changzhou, complete with scenic photos of old bridges, fields, and trees around the exteriors of the women workers' dormitory and the main plant, lending a certain amount of country charm. Shots of the interior of the factory show it to be ultra-modern, with huge rows of machines.[30]

Frequently *Meishu shenghuo* published photo essays on manufacturing processes for goods that modern citizens might take for granted on Nanjing Road, like light bulbs, tin, and salt. These kinds of essays often focused on China's natural resources (tungsten for lightbulb filaments, for example) and on the types of labor needed (such as for young workers with fine eyesight and dexterity to make lightbulbs).[31] They also emphasized advanced technical processes and equipment, such as in an early piece on a native cotton textile factory, which showed rows and rows of immaculate, complicated machinery. *Meishu shenghuo* even published a photo essay on a "scientific" chicken factory.[32] In fact, these examples work well to illustrate *Meishu shenghuo*'s breadth of coverage of native industries, from advanced machine-processed goods to labor-intensive enterprises. Such articles show a continuing concern by Chinese modernizers to educate the public on new technologies and approaches, just as *Zhenxiang huabao* had published articles on inventions and industrial models of applied science.

By the seventh issue, these types of articles are enshrined in their own regular "industrial" applied arts section in *Meishu shenghuo*, complete with a heading in which the word *gongyi* in stylized, Art Deco-influenced calligraphy is incorporated into an impressive photograph of factory towers,

---

29. Ling Donglin, "Fangzhi: Zhiwu zhi sanyuan zuzhi" (Weaving: Three patterns of cloth) and Ling Donglin, "Zhiwu yangben jieshuo" (Explanation of fabric samples), *Meishu shenghuo* 7 (October 1934).

30. Zhang Sanli, "Canguan Changzhou dacheng fangzhiranchang jilue" (A record of a visit to Changzhou's fabric dying plant), *Meishu shenghuo* 9 (December 1934). This discussion has tones of the New Village movement for workers' housing that the Chinese YMCA promoted in the 1920s. See also the article by Hua Lin, "Xincun yu xuequ" on creating industries in the countryside in *Meishu shenghuo* 4 (July 1934).

31. Luo Gusun, "Diandengpao zhizao" (Making lightbulbs), *Meishu shenghuo* 7 (October 1934); see also "Guangxi xikuang zhi cailian gongchang jishi" (Factual recording of the tin refining process in Guangxi), *Meishu shenghuo* 41 (August 1937).

32. "Guohuo baozhi zhizaochang zhi yi" (A native products cotton textile factory) and "Guohuo tangzi zhizaochang zhi yi" (A native products enamel ware factory), *Meishu shenghuo* 4 (July 1934). See also "Kexuehua di yangji" (Scientific poultry raising), *Meishu shenghuo* 3 (June 1934).

smokestacks and rail lines. In the next issue, the photo is replaced by a print of a Western painting of multiple belching smokestacks in a changing natural landscape, capturing the sense of dynamism and growth that *Meishu shenghuo* hoped to inspire. While this scene is a far cry from Nanjing Road's commercial scenery, it is the imagined source of growing numbers of goods to be sold there.

In an editorial postscript, the motivation behind the *gongyi* section is explained in this way: "The spirit of this section consists in its equal emphasis on theory and practice. . . because we understand clearly: National salvation lies first in relieving our rural communities and promoting industrial enterprise."[33] Elsewhere, an editorial states that the relationship of *gongyi* to the native goods movement was critical, and "We feel that this is truly 'real life,' worth our special advocacy.[34] *Gongyi* as the arts of everyday life, with their basic connection to everyday livelihoods, gave concrete materiality to the magazine's calls for national rejuvenation. Aimed at a bourgeois audience with the means for developing China's technological capacity, the message ultimately championed middle-class consumerism and utopian populism as the way to address the social, political, cultural, and economic issues of modernization. As Carlton Benson notes elsewhere in this volume, Shanghai culture found a way to undermine the New Life Movement's anti-consumerist messages even as it incorporated the ideal of national rejuvenation. Interestingly, the rhetoric almost anticipates some of Deng Xiaoping's economic reforms of the 1980s, and particularly his promotion of consumer goods industries after 1989.

Inventing the Shanghai Style Home and the Gendering of Shanghai's Consumer Culture

A great deal of the discussion about commercial and applied art in these Republican era magazines is aimed at businessmen to try to get them to think in terms of the needs for artistic talent in their field as well as at artists to try to get them to think of applying their skills to economically productive enterprises. Middle-class women are also central to the magazines' promotion

---

33. "Bianhou" (Postscript), *Meishu shenghuo* 8 (November 1934). This view echoes Dong Ruzhou's position in the liberal debate over China's modernization priorities. See Susan Mann's analysis of the "reconstructionist paradigm" of Chinese urbanization in her "Urbanization and Historical Change in China," *Modern China* 10:1 (January 1984): 100-107.

34. "Bianhou" (Postscript), *Meishu shenghuo* 3 (June 1934). Photos of native goods rallies and exhibitions that were held as part of the government's New Life movement also appeared in *Meishu shenghuo*.

of economic modernization and Chinese consumerism, particularly through the championing of decorative arts for the home. For *Meishu shenghuo* especially, female subscribers were the foundation of its readership. Many sought and found in these art magazines the opportunity to polish their cultural proficiency through exposure to reproductions of Chinese and Western art and to gain information about news and trends while preparing to raise families under the radically new circumstances of urban Shanghai. As Wen-hsin Yeh has noted,

> Already in Republican cities a new breed of cultured women was being brought forth through . . . [new-style] schools. Compared with old-fashioned ladies, these women saw the importance of speaking softly and conducting themselves with style. Those who had attended missionary schools had even acquired a love for Western visual arts and music for the elevation of the spiritual state of everyone in their future families.[35]

Women consumers, responsible for outfitting and maintaining stylish Shanghai homes, could be counted on to pay close and enthusiastic attention to the decorative arts works on display in the magazines and to seek them in the stores on Nanjing Road.

Images of the modern Shanghai woman, confidant, stylish and beautiful, abound in advertising and pictorials of the Republican period. By the mid-1920s, popular magazines often included large-scale, colorful photos and paintings of beautiful young women. In fact, the covers of *Liang you* magazine were almost exclusively pictures of beautiful women. Usually they were glamour portraits taken at commercial photographic studios. Color was applied to the black-and-white photos by artists. Each of the "covergirls" was identified by name, and sometimes also by school or vocation. Most were movie stars or students, who wore their hair fashionably bobbed, dressed in the latest Shanghai styles, and represented *Liang you*'s standard of modern Chinese womanhood: poised and confident, exquisitely coiffed and attired, the model of contemporary, urban propriety. Thomas Lawton has noted that the convention in Chinese figure painting was for women to illustrate moral stories, where well-bred, virtuous women represented paragons of filial

---

35. Wen-hsin Yeh, "Progressive Journalism and Shanghai's Petty Urbanites: Zou Taofen and the Shenghuo Enterprise, 1926-1945" in Frederic Wakeman and Wen-hsin Yeh, eds., *Shanghai Sojourners* (Berkeley: Institute of East Asian Studies, 1992), 210.

piety.[36] There is something of that tone in these covergirls' portraits, even those of movie stars. Their seductive beauty was clothed in a certain wholesome, covergirl respectability. They represented both *Liang you*'s physical and social ideal of the modern woman: the beautiful and virtuous prospective wife.

In Western art history, John Berger's well-known essay on the female nude broke new analytical ground in suggesting the correspondence between Western representations of women in oil painting and in contemporary mass media, and some of his ideas about the social presence of women seem relevant here. The importance of a woman's looks, her appearance to others, has been critical to her success in life—a success conventionally predicated on marriage—both in the West and in China. The prevalence of foot-binding is the telling evidence that this was so in China, and not just among the middle and upper classes. The artistic representation of women thus has been the abstraction of socially-constructed standards of ideal beauty intended for the male gaze.[37] While each of the *Liang you* covergirls had her own distinctive "look," nevertheless, just like the court ladies in traditional paintings, "their faces were sweet and expressionless, conforming to ancient standards that emphasized elegantly arched eyebrows, hooked nose, and pursed lips."[38]

Furthermore, most of the covergirls look directly at the camera, returning its gaze, fully aware of being seen, of being on display. Alice Hyland remarks of a Qing dynasty female portrait, "Her direct gaze implies erotic overtones."[39] This was also the case with the fetching portraits on the covers of *Liang you*, intimating fulfillment of the fantasies of the male audience/spectator of the magazine. Female *Liang you* readers would also have been attracted by the covers, in a "way of seeing" by which John Berger explains glamour as a function of social envy.[40] Given the lack of role models for the dawning

---

36. Thomas Lawton, *Chinese Figure Painting* (Washington, D.C.: Freer Gallery of Art, 1973), 9-12.

37. Berger has also noted that painting has traditionally been a celebration of material property and status in the West, and this may also be evident both in traditional Chinese court figure painting and in modern magazine covers. John Berger, *Ways of Seeing* (London: BBC and Penguin, 1977), 45-64, 108-110, and 139.

38. Alice R.M. Hyland, *Deities, Emperors, Ladies and Literati: Figure Painting of the Ming and Qing Dynasties* (Birmingham: Birmingham Museum of Art, 1987), 70-71.

39. Hyland, *Deities, Emperors, Ladies and Literati*, 72.

40. Berger, *Ways of Seeing*, 146-149, and Naomi Wolf, *The Beauty Myth: How Images of Beauty are used against Women* (New York: William Morrow, 1991), 58 and passim. Ellen Laing has admirably demonstrated that mildly erotic themes could also be suggested in the shinü genre through poetic imagery or references.See her "Chinese Palace-style Poetry and A Palace Beauty," *The Art Bulletin* 72:2 (June 1990), 284-295; "Erotic Themes and Romantic Heroines Depicted by Ch'iu Ying," *Archives of Asian Art* 59 (1996), 68-91; and

modern world, readers sought them "on the screen and glossy page."[41] Shanghai was the Hollywood of China and many of the covergirls were movie stars—celebrity glamour incarnate. One of the most famous international stars to grace the cover of *Liang you* was Anna Mae Wong (Huang Liushuang), the Chinese American actress, who signed her publicity portraits "Orientally yours."[42] Wong capitalized on exoticism in American society and at the same time afforded modern Chinese the image of an Asian woman successfully competing in a business dominated, like Western culture in general, by notions of white supremacy. The posh theatres on Nanjing Road showed mainly Western-made films starring caucasian actors and actresses, but *Liang you* had a Chinese face.

Female readers wanted to look like the covergirls, but at least two of *Liang you*'s readers objected to the glamorous imagery, demanding "reforms" to place "real people" (*zhen ren*) on the magazine covers. The editor promised "reforms," publishing a photo of a decidedly plain-looking young student reading the next issue, which sported a cover showing a less colorful, more austerely elegant woman's portrait.[43] However, subsequent covers were richly glamorous, as before. The fantasy of being beautiful supported the new-style daydream of modern love and romance preceding marriage.

The hierarchies of gender are similarly reinforced by all three magazines. They presented images of women as fashion plates and as objects of the male gaze, even though the women pictured also represented the new "modern woman" who was challenging traditional female social roles worldwide. They contributed to the *modern* social construction of the docile female body, self-regulated through fashion, through advertising, and through her beauty role. In a sense, the magazines fostered the democratization of beauty and of the New Woman through mass production of these images. In another sense these images are symbols for prescribed female behavior and for the reordering of

---

"Notes on Ladies Wearing Flowers in their Hair," *Orientations* 21:2 (February 1990), 32-39.

41. Wolf, *The Beauty Myth*, 58.

42. Editor Liang Desuo notes that the *Liang you* cover of Ms. Wong sported her "new style of writing her signature." These were publicity portraits Ms. Wong presented to the founder of *Liang you*, Wu Liande, while he was visiting Hollywood. She also introduced Wu to her co-star Douglas Fairbanks. In the next issue of *Liang you*, a photo of Wu and Fairbanks appeared, and Wu wrote about seeing the Japanese house in which Fairbanks and Mary Pickford lived in Hollywood. See "Xie zai bianzhe zhi ye," *Liang you* 16 (June 30, 1927): 35.

43. "Bianzhe yu duzhe," *Liang you* 28 (July 1928): 38.

the social hierarchy itself.[44] The idealization of female beauty and domesticity, with an almost exclusive focus on appearance, contains a consumer imperative essential to the development of industrial society.[45]

By the 1930s, Chinese women of means were told that they could play an important role in reconstructing the nation as homemakers, mothers, and consumers of art and household goods. *Meishu shenghuo* culminated this tendency to fuse popular interests in fashion, style, art and technology with modern industrial society's cult of domesticity. There are obvious parallels with the Victorian cult of domesticity, which, like *Meishu shenghuo*, emphasized the cultivation of taste and style among the middle class.[46] Both *Meishu shenghuo* and the Victorian cult of domesticity fostered bourgeois attempts to distinguish oneself through lifestyle. Given the difficult conditions that the Chinese majority lived in, the middle class no doubt did seek a superior lifestyle, particularly in material terms. Many articles in *Meishu shenghuo* are geared toward presenting new living options for modern families, such as one devoted to "the practice of artful living," which describes a Chinese version of the garden city movement. The piece is illustrated with photos of upper-class children, some artfully posed and others at play and study, a Western-type (Sears bungalow-style) model home, and bird's-eye view of "Rose Garden New Village." The article outlines the benefits and responsibilities of suburban versus city living. It even includes ideas about how women's businesses like silkworm and honeybee raising, embroidery, weaving, and sewing enterprises could be established to give women "opportunities for service." This describes a new, nationally contributive role

---

44. The *xiao jiating* (nuclear family) movement in Republican China is treated briefly in Wen-hsin Yeh, "Progressive Journalism," 205-214, and is a central theme in Susan Glosser's work.

45. Naomi Wolf, *The Beauty Myth*, 18. See also Janet Wolff, "Reinstating Corporeality: Feminism and Body Politics," in her *Feminine Sentences: Essays on Women and Culture* (Berkeley: University of California Press, 1990), esp. 124-125.

46. Among the many works on this subject, one with direct relevance to *Meishu shenghuo*'s focus on home-making is the excellent book by Clifford E. Clark, Jr., *The American Family Home 1800-1960* (Chapel Hill: University of North Carolina Press, 1986).

for women, as well as new kinds of urban-rural relations.[47] In Issue 4 (July 1934) Hua Lin writes in "Xincun yu xuequ" about a plan to create new suburbs and "academic districts" that would support a new, cultured and productive lifestyle.

Clifford Clark has noted the transformative effect of magazine reading on Victorian American women through the creation of "an imaginative world of new opportunities and experiences . . . (which) implied the possibility of a new individualism founded upon commodity consumption."[48] *Meishu shenghuo* published many "how-to" kinds of articles directed toward homemakers, such as one on fashion that includes directions for making a stylish child's coat, one on autumn snacks that includes recipes for mooncakes and dumplings, several on knitting, complete with patterns, and even a serialized feature on family medicine and hygiene.[49] *Meishu shenghuo*'s sixth issue was devoted to children, and the seventh issue was devoted to family life, making it very clear that the "modern girl" to whom it addressed itself was going to be married and have a family and still be concerned with China's future.

Meishu shenghuo's fourth issue is devoted to the theme *Funü guohuo*, "Women [for] national goods," 1934 having been designated the Women's Year of Domestic Products in support of China's native goods movement. The cover of the magazine shows a high-heeled woman doing embroidery at an Art Deco dressing table and seated in a modern, chrome-legged easy chair (see illustration 3.1). She is surrounded by tastefully decorated items of household

---

47. "Ertong yu xincun: Meishu shenghuo zhi shijian—Xincun shenghuo di jiazhi yu renwu" (Children and New Village: The practice of artful living—The value and responsibilities of New Village life), *Meishu shenghuo* 7 (October 1934). The Chinese name of the "ideal community" described in the article is Qiangweiyuan Xincun, but I have been unable to find more information about it beyond this article. One ideological assumption shaping this Republican discourse is the antinomious stereotype of corrupt city vs. pure countryside. See Susan Mann's valuable analysis of Republican Chinese paradigms of urbanization, "Urbanization and Historical Change in China," *Modern China* 10:1 (January 1984), esp. 87-113.

48. Clark, *American Family Home*, 140.

49. See "Shizhuang" (Fashion), "Qiutian di jiyang dianxin" (Several kinds of autumn snacks), and an untitled photo-article on women's fall fashions, featuring glamorous evening wear in *Meishu shenghuo* 7 (October 1934); Yu Zaixue, "Jiating yiyao weisheng jiangzuo" (Lectureship on family medicine and hygiene), "Chi xie di yishu" (The art of eating crab), and "Maoxian bianwu zhi jiben jishu ji qi yingyongfa" (Basic techniques and applications of hand knitting) (including diagrams and step-by-step instructions) in Issue 8 (November 1934); and a serialized article for pregnant women, "Renfu xuzhi" (What women with child should know), *Meishu shenghuo* 11-12 (February-March 1935).

3.1. The magazine cover for the fourth issue of *Meishu shenghuo* on "Women's National Goods" (*funü guohuo*) is shown here. Middle-class women were central to *Meishu shenghuo*'s promotion of consumerism and light industry. *Meishu shenghuo* 4 (July 1934).

use, such as a vase, carpet, lamp, and spittoon. An editorial explaining the illustration declares, "We take 'Promote Native Goods' as a way to advance toward the goal of 'mass production' and 'practical life.'"[50] *Meishu shenghuo* urged its audience in rhetoric echoing New Life Movement themes: "Citizens' most urgent tasks are to promote a national culture, build productivity, and reform social life."[51] Yet, as with the *tanci* described by Carlton Benson, the actual implied task was to heighten female consumer demand on Nanjing Road.

Readers of the art magazines were especially encouraged to pay attention to the more private realm of home interior design and decorative arts. The tradition of interior design in China had been refined to exquisite extremes by the literati elite from the eleventh century on. Furniture, desk accessories, tea ware, and paintings together were taken as an embodiment of the taste and character of the owner.[52] In Republican times, domestic material culture was likewise an important aspect of the Shanghai style. It is possible that the opening of the Forbidden City in the mid-1920s to sight-seers and photographers, whose photos were reproduced nationally in the pictorial magazines, contributed to a new popular focus on the aesthetics of private home life, but this attention was evident even in the first year of the Republic in *Zhenxiang huabao* .

In an ironic contrast to the New Life Movement's later encouragement of austerity, the magazine attacked traditional Chinese domestic austerity, initiating the pattern of subsequent periodical press coverage of home interior design by merging national social, political, cultural, and economic considerations with a concern for individual family attainment of middle-class domestic comfort. An intriguing article titled "Republican lens: American family and society" compares Asian and Western domestic practice, suggesting significant conclusions about the need for greater Chinese consumerism.

---

50. The magazine regarded this cover as very special, and provides background information about it in an editorial postscript. "Although we say our editing is all done by committee and the responsibility for ideas is collective, this time we especially applied Liu Puqing's main theme, ideas, and design." Liu Puqing was one of the editors who was intensely involved in promoting the decorative and industrial arts. The editorial thanks several "native goods" companies for supplying items for the cover, and it thanks Ms. Chen Yanyan, "who fervently promotes native goods, and who is the main subject of the photograph." "Bianhou" (Postscript), *Meishu shenghuo* 4 (July 1934).

51. "Fakanci" *Meishu shenghuo* 1 (April 1934): n.p.

52. See for example the catalog of the 1991 exhibit titled *Chinese Scholar's Studio: A Literati's Paradise* held at the Seattle Art Museum.

Asian people's lifestyles are cheap and mean. Westerners' are the opposite. Chinese use the pretext of being thrifty and frugal not to be particular about food, drink, and clothing. We treat ourselves meagerly. The places we live are damp, narrow, and cramped. Even the wealth of the middle class and above is hidden behind poor, small doors of bamboo. . . . How can we blame the people? Simplicity has become common practice, and this restraint still has not opened up.[53]

Objecting to "miserly" Asian lifestyles, the author's critique of Chinese austerity has as much to do with reconstructing national identity as it does with material culture. This condemnation of Chinese austerity is very much a part of the Republican attempt to create a new Chinese culture to contravene and replace that of the Qing dynasty.[54] It is interesting to note that the material culture of the home suggests a site for the creation of personal and national identity. What a person makes of his or her immediate private or family environment is an expression of identity.[55] The material culture of the home is thus a means of self and group expression. This focus on the home shifts the reader's gaze from public to private spheres and establishes the importance of the latter to the former. The article advocates loosening customary Chinese restraint in home design and furnishing, for instance maintaining that Chinese conventionally allocate half of the space in their homes to the traditional altar and receiving room,

and rooms where they live are dark, narrow, unhealthy, and don't count [for anything in the house plans]. In the West, no matter whether parlor, dining room, or bedroom, all are deliberately arranged so that there is no difference among them in quality.[56]

This implication of egalitarianism in Western home design ostensibly represents "democratic" (in effect a code for Western middle-class) well-being and comfort to the Chinese audience. In criticizing traditional Chinese house

---

53. Youke, "Gongheguo zhi jing: Meiguo jiating ji shehui" (Republican lens: American family and society), *Zhenxiang huabao* 3, 17.

54. The historical inversion of this process may be found not only in the New Life Movement, but much earlier in the promotion of a relatively austere aesthetic by Confucians reacting to the highly ornamented styles of the Han aristocracy, which is a main theme in Martin Powers's *Art and Political Expression in Early China* (New Haven: Yale University Press, 1991).

55. Mencius' strong sense of the influence of environment on the person would be a familiar notion to early Republican artists advocating such changes.

56. Youke, "Gongheguo zhi jing," 17.

design the article blames domestic environmental factors for personal ill health. Thus, drawing on the accepted duty to promote a strong and vital nation, the article obligates modern Chinese families to seek and create healthy home environments.

A Question of Class

Inevitably, one must recognize that the Shanghai consumer culture was a bourgeois-centered restructuring of Republican society that benefitted its own class based on its access to expertise and income. For example, in the first issue of *Meishu shenghuo,* contributing editors of the magazine provided examples of industrial arts that they had designed. Notable are the clean, functional lines of Zhang Derong's furniture designs for Bauhaus-type modular storage units and a desk belong to the emerging International Style of modernist art. Zhang's submission was titled "Economical Wood Furniture."[57] The accompanying text echoes the same concerns voiced by Deutscher Werkbund designers: economy, simplicity, and beauty. "An item must be multi-functional, its form beautiful, assembly simple, and price cheap in order to be enjoyed in human life."[58] German design themes likewise stressed the utilitarian, versatile, and standardized in order to bring costs down to middle-class affordability.[59] In fact, although modern German design repeatedly gave cheap industrial production as its raison d'être, many designs were barely industrial and not cheap. This paradox seems to have been replicated in China, where simplicity and economy were also empty slogans of the New Life Movement.

Much of the work *Meishu shenghuo* introduced as industrial arts, particularly that relating to home and interior design, could hardly have been accessible to middle-class families, even when they were portrayed as "economical." For example, three house plans, complete with artists' renderings of the landscaped homes and variations on the plans, were titled "Economical Homes" (*Jingji zhuzhai*).[60] The designs could have been taken

---

57. Zhang Derong, "Jingji muqi," *Meishu shenghuo* 1 (April 1934).

58. Untitled essay accompanying furniture designs by Zhang Derong and laquer painting by Lei Kueiyuan, *Meishu shenghuo* 1 (April 1934).

59. Tim Benton, Charlotte Benton and Aaron Scharf, *Design 1920s: German Design and the Bauhaus 1920-1932; Modernism in the Decorative Arts: Paris 1910-30* (Milton Keynes, U.K.: The Open University Press, 1975). See also Tim and Charlotte Benton, eds., *Form and Function: A Sourcebook for the History of Architecture and Design, 1890-1939* (London: Crosby Lockwood Staples, 1975).

60. Peng Baigang, "Jingji zhuzhai yifu" and Liu Jiasheng, "Jingji zhuzhai erfu," *Meishu shenghuo* 1 (April 1934). Pattern books for building family homes were popular in the United States beginning with the early nineteenth-century Victorian housing reform

straight out of American or English magazines, although they are attributed to members of the Shanghai Architecture Association. The first was a colonial-style frame house with bay and dormer windows, wooden shutters, columned porch, shingle roof and brick chimney. The second is described as a simple variation on the colonial theme, a cosy English-style cottage with stone path and inset fireplace illustration. The third is a small version of a half-timbered Tudor manor house, complete with peaked gables.[61] These designs are a far cry from the shikumen houses that housed the majority of Shanghai residents.

The cost of construction could not have been within the budgets of most of Shanghai's residents, although grand versions of these kinds of homes, such as the Sassoon Tudor mansion, were built—mostly by wealthy foreigners—in the Western "suburban" area off Bubbling Well Road in the International Settlement. Apparently a number of smaller, Western-style homes were also built around the western portion of Avenue Joffre in the French Concession where well-off Chinese lived.[62] These house plans had a potential consumer audience both among the upper economic "crème" of *Meishu shenghuo* readers and among the imaginations of its other readers. As with many designs, *Meishu shenghuo* furnished models of upper class standards to a rising middle class. If we compare these designs in *Meishu shenghuo* with home designs in contemporary American magazines, doubtless very few American readers could afford such designs either. But "window shopping" continues to be a most popular entertainment both in Manhattan and on Nanjing Road. The elements of fantasy and glamour in wealthy lifestyles help to explain the wide popular appeal of *Meishu shenghuo* and the peculiar consumer culture of Republican Shanghai epitomized by Nanjing Road.[63]

---

movement and may have provided the source for these designs. I am grateful to Trudi Abel for directing my attention to this subject.

61. A later issue ties such house designs to the New Village Chinese suburban ideal mentioned earlier in this chapter. The house sample illustrating that article resembles a standard American prefab family home available in the 1920s through the Sears mail-order catalog. See "Ertong yu Xincun" (Children and New Village) in *Meishu shenghuo* 7 (October 1934).

62. Sun Yat-sen's home there is a famous example.

63. Although the need for affordable middle class and working class housing was a driving force in the modern architecture movement in Europe and the United States in this period, the innovative designs rarely met the criteria for affordable housing. Nevertheless, the designs ended up having a profound impact on later art and architecture. It is interesting to see Shanghai design participating in this international movement—and intriguing to conjecture about its ultimate impact on Chinese design. In the early 1980s, I saw appliances and household goods in tourist hotels and in department, stores on Nanjing Road that had decidedly 1930s Art Deco influences.

Meishu shenghuo's examples of furniture and interior design also seem unlikely to have been affordable for most readers. An elegant, modernist design for the lounge of the West Lake National Art Academy utilizes clean, straight lines of chrome tubular chairs and a simple, streamlined aesthetic to convey functionalism and economy. The European theorists of this style expounded on the value of new materials and claimed that these forms were best suited to machine mass production.[64] Contrary to their views, the machines in Europe and the United States were not able to mass produce these avant-garde designs with given materials, and they promoted an aesthetic that was ultimately elitist or even utopian.[65]

Nonetheless, furniture design and manufacture coverage in *Meishu shenghuo* is extraordinarily wide-ranging. Photographs of the latest French room designs and avant-garde designs by Chinese artists were published alongside photos of working students and their furniture products from the Shanghai School for Blind Boys. Or, for example, photographs of the "Moroccan Room" ("Salle Marocain"), a French interior designer's exoticized, highly ornamented entry in a design competition, precede a page of sketches of "1935-style small wooden furniture," which included mostly simple (and affordable) shelf units, dressing tables, planters, and desks.[66]

Another "useful art" that *Meishu shenghuo* promoted was porcelain and glassware design and manufacture. Perhaps as part of the attempt to persuade potential investors and artists that China had a long-standing engagement in this area of useful decorative art, in one issue priceless Qing and Song dynasty porcelains were displayed right before a page of modern European crystal and glassware.[67] In another issue, a full page of "Europeanized" Chinese porcelain designs were displayed and followed by a full-color, full-page print showing a very practical thermos, cup and saucer and two tumblers from the Shanghai Bakelite Products factory, and decorative mirrors and cosmetics cases

---

64. Alastair Duncan, *Art Deco* (London: Thames and Hudson, 1988), 34.

65. Tim Benton et al., *Design 1920s*, esp. 37 and 61.

66. "Morogeshi di shineibu zhi tu (yi), (er)" (Two interior designs of a "Moroccan Room" ["Salle Marocain"]) and "Yijiusanwu-shi xiaomuqi" (1935-style smallscale wood furniture), *Meishu shenghuo* 12 (March 1935).

67. The Chinese porcelains were Kangxi Qinghua vases and Sung "tortoise-shell" glazed bowls; the European crystal and glassware were designs from Marianne Rath of Vienna's J. & L. Lobmeyer factory, O. Haerdtl of the Vienna firm of E. Bakalowits, G. Stromberg of the Swedish Eda glass manufacturers, Keith Murray of Stevens & William, Stonbridge, and Barnaby Powell of the London firm of James Powell and Sons (Whitefriars) Ltd., *Meishu shenghuo* 3 (June 1934). That *Meishu shenghuo* printed the manufacturers' names is completely in keeping with its interest in developing manufacturing in China, even though manifestly it endorses foreign manufactures.

produced at the Zhongxing Celluloid factory.[68] In another instance, Wedgewood china, stylish table lamps, and examples of interior decoration with plants received a two-page photo spread.[69] Clearly *Meishu shenghuo* was a consumer culture booster.

All kinds of "practical arts" engaged the editors of *Meishu shenghuo*. Public architecture is featured in Issue 3 in a particularly striking juxtaposition of an elaborately ornamented Chinese Buddhist temple on the same page as a Belgian architect's rendering of a new Art Deco Shanghai apartment building.[70] The implicit message seems to be that past greatness in Chinese architecture and art more than matches the magnificence of modern skyscrapers, and makes such avant-garde work seem attainable for China.

In fact, *Meishu shenghuo* editors seem to have been quite struck by the modernism of their own city's architecture, and printed photo collages that highlight the dynamism and richness of Shanghai's modern buildings. One two-page spread, titled "Uphold Shanghai's Thriving Big Businesses," portrays hotels, theaters, banks, apartment buildings, and shops, many of them on Nanjing Road, with the added message that capitalism and art make impressive partners.[71]

Conclusion

The ongoing professionalization of the Chinese art field combined with the needs and strengths of the business elite favored the conception of industrial arts as good for everyone: artists, businessmen, manufacturers, consumers and the greater Chinese economy and nation. In Republican art periodicals, *gongyi* often appears to be a euphemism for the design and manufacture of consumer goods. These magazines' remarkable attention to the industrial arts thus constituted a strong endorsement of consumerism. Republican Chinese

---

68. Zhang Yifan, designer, "Ouhua zhi Zhongguo taoqi" (Europeanized Chinese porcelain); "Shanghai jiaomu wupin zhizaochang chupin" (Items from the Shanghai Bakelite Products factory) and "Zhongxing sailuoluchang chupin" (Zhongxing celluloid factory products) all in *Meishu shenghuo* 4 (July 1934).

69. "Xinshi xiyang ciqi" (New-style Western porcelain), "Xiandai zhaoming zhi zhuangshi yishu" (Decorative art in contemporary lighting), "Shinei xiaochenshe" (Small-scale interior decoration), *Meishu shenghuo* 14 (May 1935).

70. "Wanshoushan foxiangta houfang fotang (Hebeisheng Beiping jiaowai)" (Buddhist hall behind the Wanshou Mountain Buddhist pagoda in the suburbs of Beiping in Hebei Province) and "Shanghai zuixinshi zhi gonggongzhuzhai (zai Fazujie Shafeilu)" (Newest style of Shanghai apartment building [on Avenue Joffre in the French Concession]), *Meishu Shenghuo* 3 (June 1934).

71. "Zhichi Shanghai fanrong di daqiye" (Uphold Shanghai's thriving big businesses; English title "Vanity Fair of Shanghai"), *Meishu shenghuo* 3 (June 1934).

promotion of the industrial arts incorporated many aspects of global economic and technological competitiveness. It championed the connection between the industrial arts and a prosperous economy, strong nation, and comfortable society. The promotion of light industry was seen as a contribution to economic growth and national strength through full employment. And import substitution, a key initial element in the later, mid-twentieth-century rise of several East Asian economies,[72] was explicitly favored by many early Republican Chinese. Patriotic Chinese were obligated to consume what Chinese industry produced, including the images and ideas put forth in Shanghai's art periodical press. Often designed and edited by avant-garde artists with new and foreign ideas, the magazines also used and advocated advanced technology to broaden access to culture.

Judging from these leading Shanghai art periodicals, the relationship between art and the developing consumer culture engaged many Chinese concerned about the aims and conditions of modern aesthetic practice and Republican nationhood. The commercialization of Chinese art and the Shanghai art press is thus a central thread in the story of the invention of Nanjing Road.

Artists and publishers were self-conscious inventors of Shanghai's new-style consumer culture. Literate, especially foreign-educated Chinese, and especially those living in the foreign administered sections of the treaty port, had investments—social, educational, and economic—in certain directions of cultural development. Ironically, it was their international orientation combined with their strong economic and cultural nationalism that gave the Shanghai style its own unique and local flavor.

Moreover, the bourgeoisie was the class most identified with Shanghai the city and, not surprisingly, the Shanghai style. As the promoters of the industrial arts, through their own strategic and pragmatic interests, acted to establish the idea of *gongyi* as an internalized element of Chinese culture, they also guaranteed their own role and position in that culture and society. As Ernest Young explains with regard to late Qing-early Republican reformers, "What had come to seem so admirable about the new, Westernizing policies to a socially privileged Chinese nationalist was the conjunction of a vigorous reform movement with his class interests."[73] Their subjective intention was to

---

72. East-West Center, "Developing Economies of the Asia Pacific Region," in Mark Borthwick, ed., *Pacific Century: The Emergence of Modern Pacific Asia* (Boulder: Westview, 1992), 281.

73. Ernest P. Young, *The Presidency of Yuan Shih-k'ai: Liberalism and Dictatorship in Early Republican China*, Michigan Studies on China (Ann Arbor: The University of Michigan Press, 1977), 82.

help determine Chinese attitudes toward modern urban life, to synthesize a new necessary ethos that coincided with their own.

Magazine contents show how these reformers shifted focus away from the public political sphere toward the private sphere of personal and family culture, all the while affirming the importance of the latter to the former, just as the arts were seen also as integral to changes in the society and culture-at-large. Permeable boundaries between public and private are evident in Confucian thought as well, which encouraged the "gentleman" to identify his private interests and values directly with the interests and values of the community and state. Art periodicals promoted the modern movement in Chinese art as a means, editors claimed, to invigorate the culture with fresh ideas and styles, proclaiming that art's place was in Everyman's home. The popular press, in other words, was used to promote and disseminate images of a new private culture while it simultaneously engendered a new public culture among its reading audience.[74]

Zhenxiang huabao was Shanghai's prototypical Republican art magazine. Its key themes, of art and cultural reconstruction, truth and national rejuvenation, and industrial arts and global competition, articulated and shaped the concerns of middle- and upper-class urban Chinese in its and later reading audiences. The leadership role of the printing industry in building a strong Chinese Republic assumed by all three magazines was intimately connected with their own technological basis and capacity to appropriate and match the technologies of the West. Their editors' education and social class provided a basis of familiarity with cultural works and with the categories of perception of the dominant culture. Consequently, within the democratizing society of the new Chinese Republic and the expansion of the urban Chinese middle class under industrialization, existing cultural hierarchies were ultimately reinforced by means of these magazines.[75]

As described above, Republican period artists and entrepreneurs were often among the liberal elite who advocated a Chinese-style modernism as the solution to China's search for material and political power. The three

---

74. Letters to magazine editors are evidence of how individual reading means consciously to join a group of other readers—in a sense taking part in public life. See Alain Corbin, "The Secret of the Individual," in *From the Fires of Revolution to the Great War*, ed. Michelle Perrot, trans. Arthur Goldhmmer, *A History of Private Life*, Vol. 4 (Cambridge: Belknap Press, 1990), 536.

75. See Pierre Bourdieu, "Artistic Taste and Cultural Capital," in *Culture and Society: Contemporary Debates* ed. by Jeffrey C. Alexander and Steven Seidman (Cambridge University Press, 1990), 206-208 and 212-213; and Tom Gretton, "New Lamps for Old," in *The New Art History* ed. by A.L. Rees and Frances Borzello (Atlantic Highlands, New Jersey: Humanities Press International, 1988), 67.

periodicals highlighted in this study serve as key examples of the relationship between the cultural elite, the modern business bourgeoisie, and advanced technology. Their roles in the "modernization project" were an expression of the goal to promote the new urban consumer culture as a model for all of China. Those involved in the project hoped to bolster Chinese national identity by focusing on the industrialization of art to meet the needs of society, including the practical needs of consumers as well as the commercial needs of industrial society. By advocating an integration of art with daily life through the publishing of articles on practical and applied arts, these periodicals commodified and promoted an urban, middle-class lifestyle for Republican Chinese society that carried messages for women and men about their roles both as shoppers on Nanjing Road and as inventors and managers of a new culture for China. While new social and cultural hierarchies appear to be under construction in contemporary China, we would be well advised to look closely at this earlier era.

Shanghai commercial culture as an expression of modernism has become an increasingly relevant topic for study since the priority granted to modernization over revolution in the 1980s began prompting the reappearance in China of elements of the emergent Republican Shanghai culture, together with the century-long critique of traditional culture that it had sought to replace. Chinese commercialism in the 1990s, while in many ways unprecedented, also resounds clearly with the nationalistic tones of Republican Shanghai culture. If these elements are significant constituents of the contemporary transformation of Chinese culture, then their history can provide a vehicle for understanding past and future cultural developments in China.

Consumers Are Also Soldiers: Subversive Songs from Nanjing Road During the New Life Movement

Carlton Benson

In traditional China, consumption was a vice. The state was encouraged to practice austerity, according to Confucian orthodoxy. And its subjects, the least exalted of whom were merchants, were urged to practice frugality.[1] These notions remained in circulation during the Republican period (1911-1949), when Shanghai witnessed the emergence of an exuberant bourgeoisie and a thriving system of capitalism. For the Guomindang (GMD), which opposed these developments,[2] the traditional emphasis placed on restraint acquired new relevance. A rising tide of consumerism accompanied the rise of capitalism in Shanghai, diverting its wealth and human talent from other pursuits that directly empowered the state. To stem this tide and impose austerity on a free-wheeling city, it consequently unleashed the New Life Movement on Shanghai in April 1934.

How was this initiative greeted by local entrepreneurs? They were certainly unable to ignore the Movement; the Guomindang's ability to subdue, and even terrorize, the city's most powerful capitalists is well-documented.[3] But 1930s Shanghai was also known by contemporaries for the inexorable

---

1. A few thinkers who dissented from the Confucian orthodoxy are discussed in Lien-sheng Yang, "Economic Justification for Spending—An Uncommon Idea in Traditional China," *Harvard Journal of Asiatic Studies* 20 (1957): 36-52.

2. According to Marie-Claire Bergere, "the leftist anti-capitalism of the Guomindang was replaced by a rightist anti-capitalism overlaid with Confucian precepts and fascist slogans" in the 1930s. See *The Golden Age of the Chinese Bourgeoisie, 1911-1937* (Cambridge, England: Cambridge university Press, 1986), 286.

3. See, for example, Parks M. Coble, Jr., *The Shanghai Capitalists and the Nationalist Government, 1927-1937* (Cambridge, Mass.: Harvard University Press, 1986).

local culture that was designated *Haipai*, or "Shanghai style." This designation was first employed by late Qing literati to disparage local painting and opera, which to them was suffused with the city's commercial ethos. Merchants were identified as the arbiters of local culture, which resisted, or absorbed, non-commercial forces from beyond the city limits.[4] If this was indeed the case in 1930s Shanghai, the Guomindang might have encountered some unexpected obstacles when the New Life Movement was imposed there.

These obstacles are indeed highlighted in *tanci*, a traditional storytelling genre that became an important instrument of cultural mobilization in the 1930s. During that decade, entrepreneurs were eagerly developing new methods to penetrate urban society and advertise their products. For example, they sponsored storytelling programs on the radio to create a broad audience of potential consumers and saturate it with advertising. In the process, they transformed *tanci* into a representative form of local culture that was not only highly commercialized, but also simplified to attract uninitiated listeners. The *kaipian*, a brief song that traditionally opened a storytelling performance, in fact became an increasingly prominent feature of radio *tanci*. A wider audience favored the *kaipian*, especially when it was accompanied by text, and advertisers found it a useful package in which to wrap their commercial messages.

The Guomindang was anxious to capitalize on Shanghai's new publicity techniques and also broadcast *kaipian* live from its radio station in Nanjing during the New Life Movement. These songs reveal the party's effort to counter local trends and incorporate Shanghai into a national culture of austerity by promoting its own vision of modernity. This invoked traditional values, to be certain, but also invoked a militant strain of nationalism that was self-consciously borrowed from European fascism by the Guomindang. It envisioned a spartan society composed of well-disciplined and self-sacrificing patriots, one in which women, as quintessential consumers, renounced consumption and withdrew from the public realm to save the nation. The storyteller hired by the GMD to publicize its vision was unwilling to alienate his audience entirely, however, and softened the Guomindang's message when he performed at Central Station.

The Guomindang's message was also mediated by local entrepreneurs, including silk merchants and advertising agents. In the early 1930s, these individuals employed the *kaipian* not only to sell domestic and imported

---

4. The meaning of *Haipai* and the evolution of the term's use are explored in Zhang Zhongli, ed., *Jindai Shanghai chengshi yanjiu* (Research on modern Shanghai) (Shanghai: Shanghai renmin chubanshe, 1990), 1130-1159. Also see Jeffrey C. Kinkley, *The Odyssey of Shen Congwen* (Stanford: Stanford University Press), 194-202.

goods. They also promoted a modern consumer society in which women adopted new styles of consumption and played a prominent public role as unrestrained and self-indulgent shoppers. After the New Life Movement was inaugurated, silk merchants assumed a patriotic cloak by condemning the purchase of foreign goods, and also manipulated the regime's idiom of militant nationalism to justify their own vision of modernity. Suddenly a mass-merchandising strategy that entailed lowering profit margins to raise demand for luxuries was presented as a panacea for the nation's economic decline. And suddenly consumers were recast as soldiers who served the nation by shopping. Meanwhile, advertising agents proffered songs for the Guomindang as well as local merchants, and simultaneously peddled competing visions of modern life for their clients. The New Life Movement, apparently, did not simply fade into irrelevance; its message was distorted by local mediators who shrewdly absorbed it into their local agenda.

Songs From Central Station

In the early 1930s, Chiang Kai-shek's fledgling regime was threatened on two fronts. The Japanese were engulfing Manchuria and the Communists were organizing a revolution in south China. Chiang responded by turning his back on the Japanese and mounting a major military offensive against the Communists. To complement his military efforts, he also unleashed the New Life Movement, a social campaign that was designed to transform society by inculcating Chinese citizens with a new ideology.

According to Lloyd Eastman, the ideology of the New Life Movement contained elements of Sun Yat-sen thought, Confucianism, and Christianity, but its primary inspiration lay in fascism.[5] He attributes the New Life Movement to the Blue Shirts, an elite vanguard within the Guomindang that

---

5. Eastman gives short shrift to the non-fascist elements of New Life Movement ideology. See Lloyd E. Eastman, *The Abortive Revolution: China Under Nationalist Rule, 1927-1937* (Cambridge, Mass.: Harvard University Press, 1974), 66-70. James Sheridan's interpretation of the New Life Movement concurs with Eastman's. According to him, "Confucian views provided much of the facade . . . Christianity played a part . . . but Chiang's ideas about the effect of military discipline on individual and group characteristics . . . and Fascist ideas . . . formed the heart of the movement." See James E. Sheridan, *China in Disintegration: The Republican Era in Chinese History, 1912-1949* (New York: The Free Press, 1975), 218. Arif Dirlik also concurs with Eastman, arguing that "the movement bore a strong resemblance to European movements described by the generic term fascist." But Dirlik also argues that its ideology was "lacking in the tone of hostility or myth-making that permeates Fascist and National Socialist writings." See Arif Dirlik, "The Ideological Foundations of the New Life Movement: A Study in Counterrevolution," *Journal of Asian Studies* 34, no. 4 (August 1975): 979.

was largely composed of ex-cadets from the Whampoa Military Academy. These individuals were committed to revitalizing the Party in order to strengthen China, and identified fascism as a powerful instrument of national salvation. Although Eastman argues that the New Life Movement's original inspiration may not have been provided by the Blue Shirts, it was ultimately orchestrated by them "to implant . . . [the] spirit of fascism" in the Chinese people.[6]

Nowhere was the spirit of fascism more evident than in the Movement's rejection of Western liberalism, which granted the individual excess license, in favor of self-sacrifice. The Blue Shirts reacted with horror to the new styles of consumption practiced in cities like Shanghai, styles they associated with self-indulgence and weakness, and to eliminate these, they provided detailed lists of rules to govern conduct. While these rules, which dictated everything from table manners to hemlines, might appear trivial, they were designed to transform society. First, they would accustom individuals to strict military discipline; and second, they would promote ascetic norms of behavior like those practiced by the Blue Shirts, whose namesake, after all, was a coarse blue cotton garment.[7]

As Jonathan Spence has indicated, women became a whipping post during the New Life Movement. To eradicate the evil customs that women had begun to practice in modern cities like Shanghai, the Blue Shirts placed especially rigid guidelines on female clothing and public behavior.[8] By obeying these guidelines, women would gradually acquire self-discipline, learn to practice spartan lifestyles, and sacrifice their selfish interests for the state and its paramount leader. The Generalissimo himself captured the Movement's essence in a brief rhetorical statement:

> What is the New Life Movement that I now propose? Stated simply, it is to thoroughly militarize the lives of the citizens . . . so that they will cultivate . . . the endurance of suffering and tolerance for hard work, and especially the habit and ability of unified action, so that they will at any time sacrifice for the nation.[9]

One way to instill these ideals in the public was with radio. In 1928, the Guomindang had established the Central Broadcasting Radio Station

---

6. Eastman, 67.

7. See Jonathan D. Spence, *The Search for Modern China* (New York: W.W. Norton & Company, 1990), 416.

8. Ibid., 415-416.

9. Cited in Eastman, 68.

(*Zhongyang guangbo wuxian diantai*) in Nanjing. Originally located at Party headquarters, Central Station was equipped with a small, 500-watt transmitting device.[10] Its broadcasting range was disappointingly narrow, but the GMD expanded its capacity in the early 1930s. It relocated Central Station outside the city, equipped it with a 75-kilowatt transmitter purchased in Germany, and established affiliated stations in cities across China. Central Station thus became the nation's largest radio station in the 1930s, and disseminated party propaganda as far as San Francisco, not to mention Shanghai.[11]

The GMD appealed to listeners by packaging its propaganda in popular forms of radio entertainment like the *kaipian*. After the New Life Movement was inaugurated in 1934, Central Station began to publish *Broadcasting Weekly* (*Guangbo zhoubao*), a new journal that was distributed in a network of cities from Shanghai to Kunming. It clearly addressed a far-flung audience, and consequently its programming was quite diverse, but Central Station did broadcast the local storytelling genre for a national audience. It played recordings by popular performers and hired storytellers to sing *kaipian* in its Nanjing studio. It also announced the songs and printed their lyrics in *Broadcasting Weekly* so listeners who did not speak the storyteller's dialect could read along while they listened.

When the first issue of *Broadcasting Weekly* appeared in September 1934, Wang Gengxiang was performing at Central Station. This was an attractive assignment for contemporary storytellers because the station paid well, provided a dormitory and cafeteria, and placed few demands on the storyteller's time.[12] Like most performers with some degree of celebrity, Wang was a member of the Guangyu Storytelling Guild. He distinguished himself from his peers, however, by composing his own songs and expressing a cheerful willingness to participate in state-sponsored campaigns. If the GMD instructed the guild to provide its members with a propagandistic *kaipian*, for example, Wang would agree to compose it.[13] He therefore proved a likely candidate for an easy assignment at Central Station, and in late 1934 he

---

10. See Zhongguo guangbo gongsi, ed., *Zhongguo guangbo gongsi dashiji* (Chronicle of the China Broadcasting Company) (Taibei: Kongzhong zazhi she, 1978), 1-2. The station sent technicians to assemble and operate receiving sets in municipal and provincial party headquarters throughout China, and to provide local newspapers with transcriptions of its broadcasts. See pp. 2-3.

11. See Shenbao nianjian she, ed., *Shenbao nianjian* (Shanghai: Shenbao guan, 1933), 0-60; also see Shenbao nianjian she, ed., *Shenbao nianjian* (Shanghai: Shenbao guan, 1935), 119. Throughout Jiangsu province the station's broadcasts could now be received both night and day with a crystal receiving set. See *Zhongguo guangbo gongsi dashiji*, 16.

12. Yao Yinmei, interview by author, tape recording, Shanghai, 9 July 1993.

13. Ibid., 9 July 1993.

performed *kaipian* in its studio on Tuesday and Friday evenings from 7:00 to 7:40.

Wang cultivated a relationship with his audience that was based on unconventional principles. To begin with, he addressed its invisible members as fellow countrymen, or *tongbao*, explicitly linking himself and them by nationality rather than shared presence in a neighborhood teahouse or theater. He also played the role of an official messenger and attempted to mobilize proper conduct by disseminating overt, and sometimes threatening, propaganda. But Wang, in effect, acknowledged that many listeners were alienated by his message. To soften its blow and preserve a warm rapport, he ended his songs by posing as an understanding companion who endorsed their customs even when they rejected New Life ideals.

On Friday, 21 September, for example, Wang performed "An Exhortation to Quit Smoking Opium." This *kaipian*, addressed to "my dear fellow countrymen," first condemned in strident language the reckless self-indulgence of hateful young men who neglected their studies and frequented opium parlors. He then detailed the effects of opium in a way that was designed to frighten an audience concerned with appearing well-fed, well-dressed, and well-connected. Addiction, he sang, resulted in a skinny body, sloppy clothing, and loss of respect from friends and family. If this scenario failed to discourage drug use, Wang reminded listeners that the GMD was prepared to take violent action.

> The government is determined to ban opium
> (And calls on all you)
> Opium-smoking friends to register soon.
> You have until the end of September;
> Do it by then or be shot.

To avoid execution, Wang prescribed a rehabilitation program that included two parts. The first reflected the Blue Shirts' demand for total submission of the individual to the state. The addict would register his vice with the GMD, and then—if he was unable to break the addiction independently by purchasing his own medication—he would check into a free, state-run hospital for drug users. The second part, which also reflected Blue Shirt ideals, entailed a personal struggle to strengthen one's will.

> Exercise your body daily.
> Exercise until you're blazing with vigor
> And you can help society accomplish its task.

By adhering to a strict physical regimen, the hateful addict would cultivate willpower, self-discipline, and strength, three qualities that prepared him to endure hardship and serve the nation selflessly.

Wang realized his portrait of a self-sacrificing dynamo who obeyed the dictates of a New Life regimen was less than appealing to many listeners. He therefore encouraged his wealthier fans to recuperate in the comfort of their own bedrooms, attended by excellent doctors and bevies of doting women. He also extended them a special invitation to lie back and listen to their bedside radios every Tuesday and Friday evening, when "I reverently sing for you a simple *kaipian*."[14] Juxtaposed to the official image of a fiery citizen who submitted to the state and struggled to practice self-discipline and sacrifice was Wang's image of a wealthy man who sensibly lived in the lap of luxury.

Almost two weeks later, on Tuesday, 2 October, the storyteller performed "An Exhortation to Use National Goods," which opened on the decadent city of Shanghai:

> The ten-*li* foreign strip is most extravagant,
> With beautiful clothing, food, housing, and
> transportation.
> Families live in high-rise apartments
> And drive in motorcars when they step out.
> (Most comfortable)
> Is the rich young mistress of the house—
> And a couple of modern girls
> Who consider shark's fin [soup] and sea cucumber
> ordinary dishes.
> All day long they won't do a thing
> But deck themselves out in the latest fashions.

Here Wang first identified Shanghai as a foreign enclave whose inhabitants enjoyed luxurious Western housing and transportation. He then identified the quintessential residents of this alien paradise as self-indulgent women whose diet consisted of expensive delicacies, and whose clothing was always stylish. Thus he equated Shanghai with a nonproductive female whose raison d'etre was the satisfaction of her pampered palate and overblown vanity.

He next described in great detail her appearance and voiced his disapproval in non-strident but clear language. Her hair was set in a permanent wave. Her face was powdered snow-white. Her lips were painted bright red.

---

14. See "Quan jie yan" (An exhortation to quit smoking opium), *Guangbo zhoubao* 1 (17 September 1934): 44.

Her legs were bare. And she wore black high-heel shoes. "Yet this is considered," he sang with surprise, "the ultimate school of modernity!" It was clearly not the GMD's vision of modernity and Wang proceeded to reprimand the misled women of Shanghai.

> All that concerns you is
> Spending your lives in the limelight.
> Why not stop to consider
> How quickly time flies?
> It's only a matter of decades
> Before each one of you is an old lady.
> (So I advise you all when you're young)
> To spend money frugally.
> The money you save can rescue the poor.

In accordance with New Life ideals, Wang expressed displeasure with the modern forms of consumption that were practiced by women in Shanghai. These were guided by vanity, and were grotesque not only in terms of degree, but especially in terms of their immodest and alien character. He therefore encouraged women to halt their public displays, practice frugality, and help the disadvantaged. He also promoted nationalism.

> If you must buy fabric,
> Let everyone unite in purchasing national goods.
> You mustn't . . .
> Serve as a living advertisement for imported
> merchandise.

Here he condemned the purchase of imported goods, as dictated by the ninth tenet of the New Life Public Pledge, and condoned shopping when it reflected patriotic sentiments.[15]

---

15. The eleven tenets of the "New Life Public Pledge" were as follows: 1) clothing must be simple and plain, neat and clean; 2) buttons must be buttoned; 3) shoes and socks must be worn; 4) hats must be worn properly; 5) hats must be removed when saluting; 6) hats must be removed during rallies; 7) hats must be removed indoors; 8) torn clothing must be mended; 9) for clothing we must use national goods; 10) clothing must not be hung in the street; 11) a handkerchief must always be carried. See Xin shenghuo yundong tuixing tuan, ed., *Xin shenghuo yundong* (Shanghai: Xin shenghuo yundong tuixing tuan, 1936), 139-140. Both Eastman (pp. 68-69) and Sheridan (p. 218) argue that such tenets were designed to foster strict military discipline in Shanghai.

Having no desire to appear dogmatic and alienate his audience, Wang ended the song with a comic appeal for sympathy that was calculated to reveal his own, more tolerant stance.

> Female compatriots!
> Hear my *kaipian*—
> But don't get upset and scold me;
> Let everyone clap their hands and laugh out loud.
> And now, little ladies, gather in countless numbers
> And descend on silk stores to buy national goods.
> Beleaguer the clerks till they're busy as bees.[16]

Wang clearly believed his message would be greeted with displeasure by female listeners, and implicitly asked them to understand his predicament as a performer employed by the state. He was forced to tow the official line, but still expected forgiveness for spouting propaganda that contained sensible elements. Wang encouraged women to boycott foreign goods even as he provided his listeners with a final image of female consumers descending on luxury retailers in anxious hordes.

This image contrasted sharply with the New Life ideal of a citizen who submitted to strict military discipline and subscribed to principles of austerity rather than self-indulgence. It also reflected a declaration of solidarity with an audience whom Wang considered less than committed to New Life ideals. Even if these ideals were not internalized by the storyteller and his audience, however, his songs reinforced the public awareness of righteous conduct as it was defined by the state. And awareness of state expectations, which determined the content of Wang's lyrics, could also inform the public behavior of listeners who did not wish to appear completely out of step with present trends.

Songs From Nanjing Road—and then Beyond

Silk retailers in Shanghai were also constrained by the Blue Shirts, whose *Disciplinary Code* listed "traitorous merchants" as "heartless creatures . . . who produce no emotions of loving the nation," and whose violent methods inspired terror in contemporary Shanghai.[17] Yet these entrepreneurs, while unwilling to

---

16. See "Quan yong guo huo" [An exhortation to use national goods], *Guangbo zhoubao* 3 (29 September 1934): 36.

17. Cited in Eastman, 47. Marie-Claire Bergere points out that after 1932, "veritable terrorist attacks were mounted against the delinquent merchants [who failed to comply with boycotts] by clandestine groups whose names speak for themselves . . . 'The brigades of iron

challenge the Guomindang directly, were surprisingly bold under the circumstances. They paid lip service to the New Life Movement after it was inaugurated in Shanghai, but also continued pursuing their private agenda. To illustrate, this section considers three silk stores that manipulated *tanci* to conform with the rhetoric of the New Life Movement and increase consumption of luxury fabrics at the same time. First, I focus on the pioneering manager of Lao Jiu He, a silk store on Nanjing Road that paved the way in developing techniques to raise demand for silk. His techniques presented a challenge to competing silk stores that were not located on Nanjing Road, and I subsequently examine two competitors who followed in his footsteps.

Lao Jiu He. When the Lao Jiu He Silk and Foreign Goods Emporium opened on Jiujiang Road in the early 1870s, it catered to an elite clientele who "only valued quality . . . and rarely deigned to inquire after prices."[18] In 1928 it relocated to Nanjing Road, however, and Wang Zhongnian, its manager, introduced a variety of innovations to awaken demand for silk in a broad-based clientele of price-conscious shoppers whom he designated "consumers" (*xiaofeizhe*).[19] He adopted, for example, a new mass-merchandising strategy that entailed "lowering the profit margin to expand sales" (*boli duomai*).[20] He also initiated new methods of displaying fabric in the store, inaugurated a purchase-by-phone sales strategy, and provided his customers with an easily-remembered telephone number that rhymed with the name of his store.[21]

To publicize its operations, moreover, Wang developed an effective advertising strategy that employed modern and traditional media. On the one

---

and blood,' and so on." The concessions, moreover, provided merchants with little shelter from the GMD. See Bergere, 279.

18. According to one source, the store opened in 1875. See "Shangye dengji shengqingshu," n.p., 1947. Shanghai shi dang'anguan, Shanghai shi shehuiju shangye dengji shengqingshu, 1947, juan hao 418. According to another source, it opened forty years before the establishment of the Republic, presumably in 1871. See, "Lao Jiu He chouduan yanghuo ju qianyi zhounian jinian zixu," in *Wei wei ji* 1 (30 September 1933):6. The quotation is cited in *Wei wei ji*, 6.

19. The store first reopened at the intersection of Nanjing Road and Stone Road. Then in 1932 it relocated a second time to the Mainland Shopping Arcade at the intersection of Nanjing Road and Wangping Street. Ibid., 6-9.

20. Ibid., 9. This retailing practice excited bitter controversy among competing stores that were not eager to follow Wang's example and attempted to prevent silk-producing factories from supplying Wang with fabric. See "Lao Jiu He boli zao duji" (Lao Jiu He's narrow profit margin incites jealous attacks) *Jin'gangzuan*, 15 September 1934, p. 1.

21. See Wu Yunmeng, "Zuo you feng yuan de Lao Jiu He" (The fortunate Lao Jiu He), in *Shanghai bai nian ming chang lao dian* (Famous factories and venerable stores in Shanghai over the past one hundred years), ed. Gan Gu (Shanghai: Shanghai wenhua chubanshe, 1987), 118-19.

hand he turned to the mass medium of radio to broadcast commercials into every neighborhood with receiving sets, while on the other hand he sponsored *tanci* to attract potential consumers. This strategy was first employed by the store in 1932, when Yang Binkui was hired to perform *The Dream of the Red Chamber* at a local radio station. When Yang succeeded in attracting customers, Wang quickly purchased air time from several radio stations and hired several storytellers to perform during peak listening hours throughout the day.[22] Henceforth *tanci* was not only used to entertain a live audience for the simple price of admission to a teahouse or theater; it was also used to generate demand for an increasing variety of goods and services, and to promote a new constellation of values and customs.

One year later, Wang's advertising division magnified the impact of its strategy by complementing its use of radio with an effective use of print. In September 1933, it began to publish *Moving Tunes*, a periodical collection of *kaipian* that was designed as a guide for radio listening and distributed free to consumers. Its editor invited them to browse through each edition and select their favorite songs for storytellers to perform during store-sponsored broadcasts. Consumer response was overwhelmingly positive; the first issue of 10,000 copies was in fact gone within two weeks and the store printed 10,000 additional copies for immediate distribution.[23]

Connoisseurs were unsatisfied with the magazine's artistic merits, however. "I have read several criticisms of *Moving Tunes* in the newspapers," one man claimed in his letter to the editor. "Most indicate that your *kaipian* ignore traditional rhyming patterns." The editor responded by expressing his appreciation for the man's concern, but explained that it was impossible to alter the songs for three reasons. First, he and his staff were too busy to edit the lyrics carefully. Second, he would never wish to offend the composers who donated *kaipian* to store-sponsored performers. And third, many of the songs were actually performed before they were published, and, if the lyrics were altered, performers and fans would feel cheated.[24] They clearly expected the songs to conform with a script, but not with the formal requirements of literary excellence. In *Moving Tunes*, the *kaipian* was a popularized vehicle for the enjoyment of consumers, not connoisseurs.

---

22. See "Xian sheng duo ren" (Off to a good start), *Wei wei ji* 1 (30 September 1933): 4.

23. See "Zai ban zhui yan" (Superfluous note before second printing), *Wei wei ji* 1 (30 September 1933): 1.

24. See Bian zhe, "Da Hu Hanyun xiansheng" (Reply to Mr. Hu Hanyun), *Wei wei ji* 3 (Chinese New Year Day, 1934): 45-46.

When the first issue of *Moving Tunes* appeared in September 1933, the Year of National Goods, Wang was overtly marketing foreign merchandise.[25] In an illustration on the magazine's cover, Lao Jiu He's proud facade towered over a crowd of tiny shoppers. The magazine's name was printed vertically on the left margin, while a subtitle was printed on the right: A Special Issue to Commemorate the First Anniversary of the Relocation of "The Lao Jiu He Silk and Foreign Goods Emporium (*Lao Jiu He Chouduan Yang Huo Ju*)." This full designation also appeared on the store's facade in no less than six places, as well as in the preface. "The Emporium is deeply aware that promotion of national goods is fundamental to nation building," its editor here proclaimed. "But among foreign products are items that China does not produce, and to satisfy the demands of everyone . . . we supplement our silk with foreign merchandise."[26]

Five famous storytellers were also prepared to sing *kaipian* that celebrated the flamboyant styles of modern consumption which so disgusted proponents of the New Life Movement. On a moonlit evening highlighted in the "Second Song for Lao Jiu He," a young woman is suddenly overcome with joy at the prospect of getting married. Immediately she succumbs to an impulse, makes an appointment with her girlfriends, and they speed to Nanjing Road in an automobile. After noticing that "richly attired women" gather at Lao Jiu He, they slowly enter the store and discover friendly service and "modern" fabric at inexpensive prices.[27] Thus the song encouraged women to venture out with their friends and emulate the shopping habits of other well-dressed consumers.

Xu Yunzhi, a storyteller whose voice was often cited for its special appeal to female listeners, also promoted unconventional fashions in a song entitled "Modern Women." Such women "completely abandon traditional getup" in favor of short hair, which liberates them from "needless worry" (*fannao*),

---

25. Wu Yunmeng notes that Wang also profited greatly by disregarding accepted trade practices and retailing high-quality imported fabrics. See Wu Yunmeng, 119. The National Goods Movement was inaugurated in March of 1915 when the Chinese leaders of twenty major guilds met in Shanghai to organize an anti-Japanese boycott in response to the Twenty-one Demands. See Sherman Cochran, *Big Business in China: Sino-Foreign Rivalry in the Cigarette Industry, 1890-1930* (Cambridge, Mass.: Harvard university Press, 1980), 68. After 1927, however, the GMD assumed control of the boycott movement, and used boycotts as an effective weapon to weaken the bourgeoisie. See Bergere, 277-79. Also see Christian Henriot, *Shanghai, 1927-1937: Municipal Power, Locality, and Modernization*, trans. Noel Castelino (Berkeley: University of California Press, 1993), 70-71.

26. See "Lao Jiu He Chouduan Yanghuo Ju qianyi zhounian jinian zixu" (Preface noting the anniversary of Lao Jiu He Silk and Foreign Goods Emporium's relocation), *Wei wei ji* (30 September 1933): 10.

27. See Zhang Lirong, "Lao Jiu He *kaipian* zhi er" (Lao Jiu He *kaipian* number two), *Wei wei ji* 1 (30 September 1933): 8.

heavy cosmetics, revealing clothes, and precious gems. They also "take a daily stroll on Nanjing Road," naturally stopping at Lao Jiu He to buy fabric, without eliciting any condemnation from the performer. He in fact drew an analogy between female consumers and soldiers in the song's conclusion. "From ancient times we strengthened the nation first by strengthening men." Let them "display their martial vigor," and "among women there will also be heroes, with equal fame and glory."[28] Thus, just as men fulfilled their patriotic duty on the battlefield, the modern woman fulfilled her own destiny by shopping on Nanjing Road. She was portrayed by Xu as a model for female listeners, and celebrated for leaving the past behind her. She followed her impulses. She abandoned the isolation of her bedroom—where she presumably listened to Lao Jiu He's commercials on the radio. And she gathered with friends in public places to shop for modern clothing that revealed not only her arms and legs, but also a glorious lack of self-restraint.

By December 1933, the store's message was somewhat less brassy. Its facade still towered over a bustling crowd of tiny shoppers on the cover of *Moving Tunes*. But its lengthy designation as "The Lao Jiu He Silk and Foreign Goods Emporium" graced the facade in four places rather than six and was not highlighted in a subtitle. Clearly it was circumspect to deemphasize the trade in foreign goods that winter, but management continued to profile pent-up women succumbing to wild desires. "Whenever [Zhu Yaoxiang and Zhao Jiaqiu] perform, every listener falls in love with our store," the editor of *Moving Tunes* proclaimed.[29] Consequently he enlisted both men to excite unbridled desire in consumers by singing "The Little Nun Goes Down the Mountain." The errant nun who longed to marry was a familiar stereotype in Chinese literature, and *kaipian* that exposed her deep frustration were still popular in Republican Shanghai. But Zhu and Zhao portrayed the nun as one possessed by unconventional lust. She watches "modern girls" who pray for husbands in revealing silk dresses and finally asks, "where did you buy such stylish fabric?" When she learns it was purchased at Lao Jiu He, her longing becomes unbearable.

> (When can I)
> Wear powder and rouge—indulging my desires?
> (When can I)
> Adorn myself in silk and satin clothing?
> (I lose control)
> The more I think—the more my heart grows bitter.

---

28. See "Modeng nuzi" (Modern women), *Wei wei ji* 1 (30 September 1933): 51.
29. See the preface to Part Two, which listed songs that Zhu and Zhao were prepared to sing for consumers, in *Wei wei ji* 1 (30 September 1933): 13.

Finally she flees the convent and descends the mountain to search for silk and a handsome husband.[30] At the end of 1933, as the Year of National Goods approached its unsuccessful conclusion, here was another example of the pent-up woman who cast away her ancient shackles to embark on a self-indulgent search for personal happiness.

Then in 1934, which was designated the Woman's Year of Domestic Goods, Chiang Kai-shek formally unleashed the New Life Movement in Shanghai. Designed to foster strict military discipline, spartan norms of conduct, and patriotic self-sacrifice, its goals were in sharp contrast with the advertising campaign that was currently underway at Lao Jiu He. Wang Zhongnian responded swiftly, however, and avoided a confrontation by altering his message in superficial ways. First, he adopted an increasingly patriotic front. And second, he justified the behavior of consumers by eliminating the most offensive aspects of modern consumption and underlining its contribution to national wealth and power. With language designed to echo the rhetoric of the New Life Movement, he meanwhile distorted its fascist vision.

Published on Chinese New Year in 1934, the third issue of *Moving Tunes* marked a turning point for Wang's Emporium. On the magazine's cover, the store was reborn as Lao Jiu He (see illustration 4.1), and elsewhere in the collection as the Lao Jiu He Silk and Woolen Goods Emporium (*Lao Jiu He Chouduan Nirong Ju*). Any explicit reference to foreign goods was erased. Meanwhile, however, one of the tiny shoppers pictured on earlier covers was magnified. With a permanent wave, she poses in white gloves, high-heel shoes, an overcoat that hugs her figure, and an opulent fur collar. Clearly the magazine's editor continued to promote the silk merchant's vision of the modern woman, a self-indulgent consumer who lavishly spent money on the cultivation of an immodest, anti-traditional style—and flaunted it publicly.

In the current issue of *Moving Tunes*, Wang Zhongnian printed a New Year's Greeting to torytelling fans that justified such indulgence by claiming it was an expression of patriotism, and by advocating consumerism.[31] He first lamented China's economic crisis, and then lamented a failure to improve the economy with patriotic commercial practices in 1933. "Wasn't last year acknowledged by everyone to be the Year of National Goods?" he asked with rhetorical flourish.

---

30. See Gu Zhongying, "Xiao nigu xia shan" (The little nun goes down the mountain), *Wei wei ji* 2 (December 1933): 18.

31. Consumerism, as defined in the Oxford English Dictionary, is "a doctrine advocating a continual increase in the consumption of goods as a basis for a sound economy."

4.1. This cover of the third issue of *Moving Tunes* (Wei wei ji) introduced the new name of Wang Zhongnian's shop, Lao Jiu He (shown at the top), which eliminated any reference to foreign goods, but it also continued to promote his vision of the modern Chinese woman as a consumer. *Wei wei ji* 3 (1934).

In this year, although it was impossible to completely eliminate foreign goods from our national markets, we should have at least reduced the trade deficit to a limited degree. But upon inspection, [one] not only sees no reduction; on the contrary, [our deficit] grew. This really must be viewed as a tremendous disgrace in the Year of National Goods![32]

To explain the campaign's failure, Wang blamed the Guomindang for negligence. "Before it began, officials never clearly identified our target during the Year of National Goods." Consequently consumers only boycotted products from enemy nations and continued to buy goods from other countries with a clear conscience. Then Wang softened his criticism of the GMD and claimed that consumers were ultimately responsible. He admitted that it was improper for merchants to sell imported merchandise, but claimed it was necessary. Certain products were not manufactured domestically, and "merchants who themselves do not lack patriotic sentiments must in reality sell foreign goods to satisfy their customers."[33] In Wang's view, it was consumers who lacked patriotism in 1933.

Wang, meanwhile, had behaved impeccably. "During the Year of National Goods we completely exhausted our energy by promoting Chinese products," he stated. And in 1934, the Woman's Year of National Goods, he proclaimed himself "the vanguard in promoting female consumption of domestic products" after selling a large consignment of Chinese fabric at a low profit margin. "When we broadcast the news" of our sale, Wang proudly announced, women "flocked to the store by the thousands daily."[34] He then argued that mass-marketing techniques, which excited these episodes of rampant consumption, not only promoted the patriotic commercial agenda of 1934 and benefited consumers. They also benefited manufacturers by accelerating the cycle of production and consumption.

When the Emporium places a low price on new and beautiful goods, market demand is tremendous. If market demand is tremendous, we can replenish our stock without too many fears—unlike stores that sell low-quality merchandise at a high price and therefore have limited sales. Consumers and producers will benefit one another by mutually interacting in a cause and effect relationship! Because the national

32. See Wang Huicheng, "Xin nian xian ci" (New year dedication), *Wei wei ji* 3 (Chinese New Year, 1934): 26.

33. Ibid., 27.

34. Ibid., 27-28.

economy remains extremely weak, the Emporium will from now on focus its efforts on passing profits on to customers and facilitating the rapid flow [of goods] for manufacturers and merchants.[35]

Wang, in effect, argued that mass consumption was the key to economic recovery and national salvation. He therefore promised to continue promoting demand for silk with an already proven mass-merchandising strategy.

As the modern woman who was magnified on the magazine's cover would suggest, Wang also continued to portray women as an important linchpin in the modern consumer society. But during the 1934 campaigns, the rhetoric of nationalism was again on the rise and as it reshaped popular discourse it also affected Wang's presentation. His magazine now portrayed women as consumers of national goods alone, and thus presented an increasingly patriotic front for the store's operations. With regard to modern styles of behavior and appearance, however, *Moving Tunes* sent mixed signals to its clientele. In a *kaipian* entitled "The Woman's Year of National Goods," which the editor reprinted from the pages of *Xinwen bao*, the modern woman symbolized overconsumption. Her gross expenditure on clothing, food, housing, and transportation was not only conspicuous; it was also unpatriotic.

> You all know Shanghai's an extravagant city,
> Unique for indulgence and luxury.
> Modern women can capture the limelight
> By vying for beauty without regard for the cost.

They perm their hair, paint their eyebrows, and wear lipstick, powder, perfume, high-heel shoes, and silk stockings. Then, when the styles change, they discard their outdated fashions. For transportation, they ride in automobiles. For entertainment, they frequent dance halls. For nourishment, they dine in fancy restaurants, drink fine wine, and smoke cigarettes. And finally for housing, they live in Western-style homes with all of the modern conveniences. In sum:

> To be modern, they reject Chinese goods.
> (They view)
> National goods as worthless,
> (And even their)
> Sanitary napkins are a Western import.

---

35. Ibid., 28.

Finally the song exhorted all women to "fervently love your country first" and "never forget the Woman's Year of National Goods!"[36] Like Wang Gengxiang at Central Station, the management of Lao Jiu He now paid lip service to the GMD and risked alienating its female audience with insulting rhetoric.

But the current issue of *Moving Tunes* also celebrated the assertive style of modern women. In "The Sixth Song for Lao Jiu He," the female consumer was portrayed as a positive model. Here the season is changing and:

> Everyone wants new clothes.
> (So the young mistress and maiden)
> First order the chauffeur to prepare,
> And then invite their girlfriends to go on an outing.
> In a flash they arrive at Nanjing Road.

With Lao Jiu He towering above them, the women emerge from their automobiles and enter the store holding hands. Thus they respond like clockwork to seasonal fashion, indulge in extravagant forms of transportation, and join their companions in public places to shop for silk and satin. They do so, moreover, without eliciting condemnation. As far as Wang was concerned, their customs in no way contradicted his patriotic agenda. "We promote national goods," his song reminded the listener, "and render the nation strong!"[37]

Female consumers in fact contributed to the battle against imperialism by shopping. "Onshore at Shanghai," which the Chen brothers were prepared to sing in early 1934, glorified Nanjing Road and the modern women who represented it.

> For real prosperity look at Nanjing Road.
> On both sides it is lined with great stores,
> And beautiful women come and go in modern fashions.

They dress in Western clothing, their white teeth and red lips are lovely, and their perfume fills the air with a wonderful fragrance. Even the sound of their high-heel shoes on the pavement excites no bitter remark. On the contrary, modern women who capture the limelight in their nontraditional fashions are noted for their patriotic consciousness.

---

36. See "Funu guohuo nian" (The woman's year of national goods), *Wei wei ji* 3 (Chinese New Year, 1934): 6.

37. See Wang Xixian, "Lao Jiu He *kaipian* zhi liu" (The sixth song for Lao Jiu He), *Wei wei ji* 3 (Chinese New Year, 1934): 4.

Graceful as willows they enter the store.
As one calls out to an older woman,
Another calls out to a girl.
You and I should buy some [fabric] for new clothing.
My girl! Just look at those Chinese silks . . .
Suitable in spring, summer, winter, and fall.
No harm in making more clothes for your wedding day!

Designed to stimulate female consumers, the song promoted new customs of consumption: displaying oneself in public, socializing in stores, and shopping continuously for national goods. Finally the Chen brothers directly equated consumer behavior with patriotic resistance.

When shopping, always demand Chinese goods.
Resolutely save the nation—and carry on the resistance
By cutting the outflow of currency to Japan![38]

In 1934, Wang Zhongnian urged women to fulfill their patriotic duty by practicing customs that were in many ways inimical to New Life ideals.

Lao Jie Fu. The management of Lao Jie Fu, a competing silk store that also opened on Jiujiang Road in the late Qing dynasty,[39] duplicated Wang's innovative advertising strategies. In the early 1930s, the store purchased air time for storytellers who served as its spokesmen, and in March 1934, six months after Lao Jiu He initiated publication of *Moving Tunes*, Lao Jie Fu introduced *Lucky Star*. This periodical collection of *kaipian* was also distributed free to consumers, whom its editor encouraged to select songs for performance during store-sponsored broadcasts. Hoping that *Lucky Star* would appeal to the masses (*da zhong*), he also "welcomed submissions, especially from anonymous authors."[40] Like Wang, he extended his hand to a broad-based clientele and employed an advertising strategy that combined the forces of radio, print, and *tanci*.

---

38. See Zhang Sujuan, "Shanghai tan" (Onshore at Shanghai), *Wei wei ji* 3 (Chinese New Year, 1934): 34.

39. The store opened in 1860. See *Shanghai cidian*, 312. Like Wang Zhongnian, its manager, Cheng Yongliu, hailed from Anhui province. The store's second in command, Lu Hesheng, hailed from Suzhou. See "Shanghai shi chouduan ye tongye gonghui huiyuan mingce," n.p., 1939. Shanghai shi dang'anguan, 230.1.73. The store was almost twice as large as Lao Jiu He, employing eighty individuals in 1939 as compared with forty-five at Lao Jiu He. See "Shanghai shi chouduan shangye tongye gonghui benhui huiyuan mingce," n.p., 1939. Shanghai shi dang'anguan, 230.1.73.

40. See a notice to the readers of *Lucky Star* in *Fu xing* 1.3 (May 1934): 30.

Lao Jie Fu responded to the political campaigns of 1934 with less haste than Wang Zhongnian. When the first issue of *Lucky Star* was published in March, an illustration of the store's facade appeared on its reverse cover, along with the store's full designation as the Lao Jie Fu Silk and Foreign Goods Emporium (*Lao Jie Fu Chouduan Yanghuo Ju*). Its management also continued to promote modern styles of consumption with respect to entertainment and clothing. In "The Modern Girl," a beautiful young woman who excels in athletics is presented as an exemplar. Unwilling to stay at home and "sit quietly in her room," she wanders the city freely, visiting parks, movie theaters, and dance halls in nontraditional clothing.

> Her high-heel shoes sound a distinctive note,
> And her brand new clothes are the latest fashion.

Even when she falls in love and chooses her own husband, the song suggests that her marriage will be successful.[41] Printed beside the lyrics, moreover, are specific instructions for women who wished to emulate her lifestyle. "A Modern Guide" announced that "Modern women wear modern clothes, and Lao Jie Fu's silk is completely modern . . . If you don't wear Lao Jie Fu's modern fabric, you can't be considered a modern girl."[42] The editor clearly intended the members of his female audience to idealize women like the one portrayed in his song, and invited them to realize their ideal by purchasing silk.

The store meanwhile articulated with more clarity than Lao Jiu He the female consumer's contribution to a new society characterized by a patriotic spirit of hard work and sacrifice on the one hand, and the spirit of mass consumption on the other. Even as Lao Jie Fu proclaimed its foreign goods in March 1934, the store's management established its patriotic credentials by urging women to focus their shopping energies on Chinese products. "This is the Woman's Year of National Goods," it announced in "A Report to Female Compatriots."[43] "Our women must fulfill their obligation with utmost seriousness and defend the [campaign's] goals." The report then underlined the importance of clothing in popular mentality, and prescribed increased consumption of Chinese silk as a practical means to promote the campaign. "If our women purchase more domestically-produced silk . . . this year, our obligation to promote [national goods] will be met." The store was in fact

---

41. See Xiao Yuan, "Modeng nulang" (The modern girl), *Fu xing* 1 (March 1934): 35.
42. See Huang Yi, "Modeng zhinan" (A modern guide), *Fu xing* 1 (March 1934): 35.
43. For all citations, see Ling Yu, "Gao nutongbao" (A report to female compatriots), *Fu xing* 1 (March, 1934): 18-19.

eager to facilitate the woman's patriotic fulfillment of her duty by following Wang Zhongnian's example and cutting its profit margin:

> Firmly embracing the spirit of self-sacrifice, Lao Jie Fu slashes prices on a huge volume of Chinese silk to increase sales . . . and help women continue their work (*gong zuo*) of promoting national goods. With this kind of assistance, our women should labor with special zeal (*gewai nuli*) to accomplish our noble agenda.

Like Wang, Lao Jie Fu's management justified a new mass-merchandising strategy that did not promote spartan behavior. On the contrary, it was designed to excite feverish shopping activity in a broad-based clientele. But Lao Jie Fu surpassed Wang in the manipulation of an idiom that would appeal to proponents of the New Life Movement. In *Lucky Star*, the marketing of luxury fabrics was construed as self-sacrifice, and its consumption was equated with a noble form of hard work conducted in the national interest.

As 1934 passed, the Emporium fine-tuned both its patriotic image and its vision of female labor. In April, when the second issue of *Lucky Star* was published, its editor eliminated explicit reference to foreign goods. He printed an identical illustration on the reverse cover, but rechristened his store The Lao Jie Fu Silk and Woolen Goods Emporium (*Lao Jie Fu Chouduan Nirong Ju*). He also invited customers to select *kaipian* that portrayed indulgence in a positive light by conflating it with patriotism.

"The Second Song For Lao Jie Fu" opened on a spring day with singing birds, blooming flowers, and gentle breezes. Meanwhile:

> Richly-attired men and women inhabit the scene.
> Immensely satisfied and happy as immortals,
> They call for their late-model cars
> (And proceed to Lao Jie Fu)
> For silk and satin fabrics.

Lao Jie Fu met its "constant stream of customers—racing for first place" with a broad selection of Chinese fabric. "We promote the sale of national goods as a principle," the song proclaimed.

> (Therefore)
> The masses are united with a firm conviction.
> Who is not responsible for restoring [national] power?

Women, of course, were most accountable during the Woman's Year of National Goods, and the song encouraged them to rescue the nation by shopping:

> Female compatriots, combine your labor (*nuli*)
> By taking national goods to heart.
> Everyone can help to solve the crisis.[44]

If female consumers failed to understand this point, on the next page they found a clear bulletin entitled "Practical Labor" (*Shiji gongzuo*).

> Female compatriots who wish to perform the practical labor of promoting national goods should proceed to Lao Jie Fu and buy more low-priced but beautiful Chinese silk . . . Truly you'll set an example with your action and kill two birds with one stone.[45]

Suggesting that women could contribute to national wealth and power while they satisfied their desire for new clothing, Lao Jie Fu assigned to them the patriotic task of shopping for silk.

In May 1934, the store's tone was on the one hand increasingly strident. When the editor of *Lucky Star* published his third collection of songs, he printed an essay entitled "The New Life [Movement] and Clothing."[46] Here the store presented for its clientele the regime's vision of a spartan new order that employed two idioms: one recalling a golden age of traditional Chinese ethics, and another invoking strict military discipline. Both idioms were used to condemn contemporary customs and apparently posed a direct threat to luxury retailers.

> The major goal of the New Life [Movement] is to revive the abandoned virtues of propriety, justice, honesty, and self-respect, and to rectify the customs of luxury and indulgence that currently prevail. Therefore a public pledge has been taken, stipulating that clothing, food, housing, and transportation shall be regulated with extreme rigor so that life will be rendered simple and plain. This is the so-

---

44. See Jin Shude, "Lao Jie Fu—di er bian" (The second song for Lao Jie Fu), *Fu xing* 2 (April 1934): 3.

45. See "Shiji gongzuo" (Practical labor), *Fu xing* 2 (April 1934): 4.

46. For all citations, see "Xin shenghuo yu yi" (The New Life Movement and clothing), *Fu xing* 3 (May 1934): 20.

called discipline-ization (*jilu hua*) and soldier-ization (*junren hua*) [of life].

But Lao Jie Fu's management, which currently led a campaign to stimulate consumption, neutralized the threat by placing a favorable spin on New Life pronouncements. First, it enthusiastically joined the regime's campaign by declaring that "we should realize each tenet of the public pledge that pertains to clothing. The ninth tenet, 'For clothing we must use national goods,' should be promoted above all." Thus the store seized on one of eleven tenets and ignored the implications of the other ten, which had as their agenda the transformation of Shanghai into a boot camp. The store even employed the ninth tenet to justify its attempt to bring luxury items within the grasp of an increasingly broad clientele.

> The Lao Jie Fu Silk Emporium has always cherished the goal of increasing market demand for domestic goods by reducing its profit margin. It appears we harmonize perfectly with the ninth tenet of the "New Life Public Pledge," and . . . provide an extremely helpful boost to the New Life Campaign.

Finally the essay reminded storytelling fans that "shopping for more domestically-produced fabric at Lao Jie Fu constitutes the important work (*gongzuo*) of promoting the New Life Movement," and encouraged them to "carry on with the hard work to accelerate its success." By presenting the purchase of silk as both a patriotic form of hard labor and a gesture of compliance with the regime's campaign, Lao Jie Fu recast the activity in an idiom that echoed official propaganda. It also represented its own goal—the retailing of luxury items on a mass scale—as consistent with the regime's agenda. Thus it interpreted the New Life Movement in a self-serving fashion and blunted its fascist thrust.

In contrast to the strident tone of his essay, the editor of *Lucky Star* continued to provide amusing songs for his customers. "The Fourth Song For Lao Jie Fu," which he urged them to select for broadcast, actually delineated the store's mass clientele in a playful manner.[47] After noting Lao Jie Fu's venerable status, ethical business practices, and friendly service, the song

---

47. See Ling Yu, "Lao Jie Fu—di si bian" (The fourth song for Lao Jie Fu), *Fu xing* 3 (May 1934): 2-3. The fourteen categories of customer included wealthy young women, young men, middle-aged men and women, infants and children, GMD party members, government officials, famous figures and politicians, peasants, laborers, merchants, students, soldiers, judges and lawyers, and journalists.

underlined the store's patriotism in sharp terms. Lao Jie Fu "loves its country with an especially ardent heart," declared the composer. "Foreign goods cannot get through the door." Then he listed fourteen types of customer and highlighted the good fortune of each type when it purchased silk at Lao Jie Fu. Wealthy young women naturally topped his list, but he also claimed some unexpected customers. These customers were rarely pictured in silk by contemporary storytelling fans, and by upsetting their expectations he provided them with amusement. The list, for example, included political cadres, who were commonly pictured in Party uniforms.[48]

> When comrades in the GMD
> Buy our silk for clothing,
> The revolution succeeds and the world is respectful.

It also included soldiers, who were fortunate to obtain uniforms, much less silk garments.

> When comrades in arms
> Buy our silk for clothing,
> Lost territory is recovered and bandits are eradicated.

And even less likely to appear in silk was Shanghai's working class, which barely scraped by.

> When workers and manual laborers
> Buy our silk for clothing,
> Labor is in harmony with capital and production rises.

In this way the composer captured a variety of conventional figures in an unlikely gesture and transformed them all into figures of fun. From the store's perspective, a world in which everyone purchased silk was naturally appealing, and the song ended with a light-hearted wish.

> If millions of fellow countrymen
> All dressed in domestic silk,
> (Then certainly)
> The nation would be rich and powerful, and all its
> affairs would flourish.

---

48. Party uniforms were commonly associated with military vigor and discipline. See Wen-hsin Yeh, *The Alienated Academy: Culture and Politics in Republican China, 1919-1937* (Cambridge, Mass.: Harvard University Press, 1990), 222-226.

> If fellow countrymen fail to believe me,
> Please just ask around.

The composer realized that his audience was unlikely to accept a claim that national wealth and power depended on the mass consumption of silk. But he suspected it would find the prospect amusing, and solicited good will by proposing a simple solution to complex problems.

For its next collection of *kaipian*, which the store published in July, Lao Jie Fu drastically altered the magazine's cover. The first three issues of *Lucky Star* had presented comical illustrations of old men and women behaving like children. On the cover of the first issue an old man was kicking a shuttlecock; on the second issue an old woman was flying a kite; and on the third issue an old man was blowing bubbles. The fourth issue suddenly abandoned humorous tableaux that upset the viewer's expectations, and instead presented a sultry woman reclining on a crescent moon without any clothing. A thick bolt of silk flowed over her shoulder, around her waist, and between her bare legs before billowing down from the sky and disappearing beyond an opulent garden of flowers. During the summer of 1934, Lao Jie Fu openly disregarded the ethos of the New Life Movement and represented itself in a visual idiom of sensuality and self-indulgence.

Da Chang. The advertising methods of Wang Zhongnian also spread from Nanjing Road to the Da Chang Silk Emporium, which was located at the Small Eastern Gate of the Chinese city. In mid 1934, Da Chang's advertising division followed the example of its competitors in the International Settlement and began to publish *Happy Tidings*, a magazine devoted to *kaipian*. This journal was also designed to foster a sense of participation in store-sponsored activities, and to that end it announced the Emporium's broadcasting schedule and encouraged its clientele to select a song for broadcast. The editor also invited consumers to voice their sentiments publicly by submitting their own compositions. Soon he was overwhelmed with *kaipian* composed by listeners who hoped to hear their songs performed on the radio, and in the seventh issue of *Happy Tidings* he apologized for being unable to publish every submission. He did note the present collection attracted "several women writers," however, and applauded their loyal support for his store.[49]

Da Chang was perhaps least cautious about representing itself in a consistent, politically correct fashion. Each issue of *Happy Tidings* published between July 1934 and July 1935 advertised the store's trade in foreign goods even as the songs and essays hotly condemned such a traitorous practice. In the

---

49. See Ding An, "Bian yu" (Postscript), *Le wen* 7 (July 1935): 74.

sixth collection of *kaipian*, which the store's advertising division published in April 1935, the store printed an essay decrying the steady inflow of foreign goods and the rapid outflow of currency. The high cost of national goods was partly to blame, as were unpatriotic consumers who proudly purchased foreign items. But the Emporium also took a fierce swipe at the "traitorous merchants" who subverted the Woman's Year of National Goods by selling foreign merchandise in 1934, and who now threatened to subvert the Student's Year of National Goods in 1935.[50] Meanwhile, the editor printed a photograph of Da Chang just two pages before the patriotic essay, and mounted on the store's facade is a sign that announces its trade in foreign items.[51] Clearly he did not expect the clientele to be alienated by Da Chang's business practices, nor by the lip service his store paid to nationalism.

Like its competitors, Da Chang imagined fashion-conscious females with pent-up desire in its audience, and employed psychological insight to encourage their self-indulgence.[52] In the July 1935 issue of *Happy Tidings*, its editor printed a *kaipian* entitled "The Modern Girl."[53] It first introduced a young woman who was filled with anxiety by the rapid pace of changing fashion, and then revealed a solution for all her problems.

> The summer weather is unbearably hot
> And the modern girl is filled with anxiety
> Because last year's clothing is out of style.
> Where can [she] go to acquire new clothes?
> She's lost in thought—without a clue,
> When suddenly she hears the radio announcing
> Da Chang repeatedly.

The modern girl is unable to restrain herself and responds immediately to the store's advertisements.

> She hears and her heart rejoices.

---

50. See Xiang, "XX guohuo nian" (XX year of national goods), *Le wen* 6 (April 1935): 51-52.

51. See photograph in *Le wen* 6 (April 1935): 49.

52. My interpretation is influenced by the insight of Emile Zola, whose hero in *The Ladies' Paradise* is a capitalist who envisioned his ability to attract women into his department store as a form of seduction, and his ability to empty their purses as a successful conquest. Retailers in Shanghai also, apparently, perceived of themselves as shrewd manipulators of women. See Emile Zola, *The Ladies' Paradise* (Berkeley: University of California Press, 1992), 69-70.

53. See Kang Kang, "Modeng xiaojie" (The modern girl), *Le wen* 7 (July 1935): 16.

There's no harm in taking a look!

So she drives to the store and discovers fine fabric at "incredibly low prices" in the "Sacrificed Goods Department" (*xisheng bu*).

Da Chang's management certainly appealed to privileged women like the modern girl, who jumped in the car at a moment's notice and drove across town on an impulse. But its clientele also included other women who emulated her lifestyle. Located many blocks from Nanjing Road in the less affluent Chinese quarter of Shanghai, Da Chang's fortunes depended on attracting women with limited spending power. To attract them, the editor of *Happy Tidings* was forced to highlight a special department with bargain-basement prices, and printed his lyrics beneath a caption claiming that Da Chang's "prices are suited for commoners (*pingmin hua*)." As the New Life Movement ran its course in Shanghai during the mid 1930s, he joined competitors in urging a broad-based female clientele to practice modern consumption.

While it urged women to forego restraint, Da Chang also assigned Gu Jia'an with the task of composing a rabidly anti-modern song. In January 1935, when "A *Kaipian* For National Goods" was published in the fifth issue of *Happy Tidings*, Gu was seventeen years old. "Intelligent by nature" and "fond of literature," Gu excelled in the composition of *kaipian* and was considered by the store's editorial division to be "an extraordinary talent among the magazine's contributors." It even printed for its customers a photograph that portrayed the young scholar in round spectacles, a long gown, and a traditional cap.[54] Gu was by no means a member of the city's educated elite, however. He worked for a company in the Chinese city and earned a living that permitted little indulgence. To avoid paying streetcar fare, which would have consumed one fourth of his income, Gu lived at his workplace and prepared his compositions under an oil lamp in a dilapidated building. Only on Sundays, if he completed his work with time to spare, did he visit his home in the city.[55]

In "A *Kaipian* For National Goods," Gu adopted the strident language of the New Life Movement to condemn the customs of modern consumption and prescribe a spartan lifestyle for female patriots.

> Last year was the Woman's Year of National Goods;
> To save the nation, women brandished the first whip.
> Rejecting luxury and indulgence for frugality and

---

54. See Gu's photograph and the Division's remarks on an unnumbered page in the front of *Le wen* 5 (January 1935).

55. Gu Jia'an describes his circumstances in "Jia ge xie xie ni" (Brother Jia thanks you), *Le wen* 5 (January 1935): 18.

> plainness—
> They were leaders in [the consumption of] simple food
> and clothing.

Then Gu explicitly proscribed eleven decadent customs. He forbade women to perm their hair, paint their lips and powder their cheeks like prostitutes, wear high-heel shoes and panty hose, appear in dance halls, eat Western food in emulation of foreigners, drink brandy, smoke foreign cigarettes, drive in automobiles, and pour money into the construction of Western buildings. While banning customs that smacked of Western decadence, however, Gu justified shopping for silk by presenting it as an act of patriotic self-immolation.

> If you want to buy fabric, go to Da Chang
> For national goods that are already inexpensive.
> (I exhort you all)
> To unite in a common effort to use national goods.
> To promote national goods your hearts must be firm;
> So lie on thorns and taste your gall; study Gou
> Jian's [example].[56]

Here Gu alluded to an ancient king who nursed a desire for vengeance against foreign invaders by subjecting himself to physical torment. In 1935, he suggested, women could subject themselves to similar torment by shopping for silk at Da Chang.

Gu Jia'an also prepared a second advertisement for the Emporium's fifth issue of *Happy Tidings*. Composed as a letter to Da Chang from a satisfied customer, "Brother Jia Thanks You" revealed the young man not as a propagandist for national campaigns, but as Da Chang's spokesman.[57] Here he identified himself as a hard-working man who lived apart from his family and cheerfully endured substandard living conditions to save his meager income. Although his "letter" was ostensibly written for the silk store and placed in its mailbox, Gu was of course addressing its customers, with whom he hoped to establish a new type of friendship. He invited them to compose similar letters of thanks and likewise place them in Da Chang's mailbox. Then, "although you and I don't know each other, our letters will mingle forever and [we can] be friends that have never met."

---

56. See Jia'an zhuren, "Guohuo *kaipian*" (A *kaipian* for national goods), *Le wen* 5 (January 1935): 7.

57. See Jia'an zhuren, "Jia ge xie xie ni," 18-19.

An equally convivial tone was reflected in Gu's account of an episode that produced his feelings of gratitude for Da Chang. One day he returned home to help his younger sister prepare for her wedding. When he stepped through the door, he discovered the young woman in a state of panic because the silk she had purchased for her wedding dress had shrunk and faded terribly. "Didn't I tell you to go to Da Chang!" Gu reminded her. It was too far, she replied, so Gu volunteered to pay for the streetcar and off they traipsed to a distant part of the city. After their shopping trip, because the young woman was so pleased with the fabric she purchased at Da Chang, she paid for her brother's carfare and took him to dinner. Moreover, the next time Gu visited his sister with a gift of cosmetics, he overheard the woman laughing. She had spent the previous afternoon sitting on the couch, he learned, telephoning every silk store in Shanghai to compare prices. Da Chang's prices were lowest, so she wholeheartedly thanked him again. Gu, in turn, was compelled to compose his letter of thanks to Da Chang.

In this brief narrative, Gu's first priority was to expand the clientele for Da Chang's silk. To accomplish this, he invoked a sense of community between himself and his faceless friends by adopting a friendly posture. First he introduced himself as a humble urbanite who was well-acquainted with imperfect living conditions, but still preserved an open heart and fun-loving spirit. Then, drawing the audience further into his confidence, he recounted a personal episode involving his sister's shopping escapades. On the one hand, Gu's community would be linked by their common, but not necessarily concurrent patronage of the Da Chang Silk Emporium. Its members would consist of "friends that have never met," and who lived in scattered neighborhoods throughout Shanghai. Frustrated women would play a leading role in this community, some being drawn to the store in automobiles, while others arrived by streetcar.

But Gu's community would also be linked by good will toward fellow customers, shared experience in a difficult urban environment, and common expectations. For example, women would need to go shopping, and consequently explore the city in search of its greatest bargains. They would also wear cosmetics, eat in restaurants, and sit on sofas all afternoon while they talked on the telephone. Gu did not condemn these customs for reflecting idleness and self-indulgence. Nor did he promote the New Life Movement by prescribing a strict regimen of spartan self-denial. Instead he suggested that men like himself would help their women to cultivate modern customs.

In the same issue of *Happy Tidings*, Gu adopted two personae. In "A *Kaipian* for National Goods," he adopted the fierce rhetoric of the New Life Movement to condemn luxury and indulgence. He also identified himself as the song's composer, suggesting that for Gu and his "friends," each of whom was surrounded by rabid propaganda, it was not only acceptable to echo this propaganda; it was also decent. Gu, like silk merchants and storytellers, could proudly participate in a national campaign and turn it into advertising at the same time. In "Brother Jia Thanks You," meanwhile, Gu accepted his faceless "friends" into his personal confidence and neither espoused the New Life Movement, nor suggested that he would observe its stringent tenets. On the contrary, he suggested that if anything limited his ability to practice the customs of consumption as espoused by the city's retailers, it was his income rather than a commitment to New Life ideals.

Advertising Agents

Advertising agents inhabited the same city and faced similar imperatives. On the one hand silk merchants employed them to raise demand for luxuries, while on the other hand proponents of the New Life Movement enlisted them to promote austerity. As a result, advertising agents like Yuan Fengju and Ni Gaofeng could profit by manipulating the *kaipian* to peddle competing visions of modern life for their clients.

Yuan and Ni adopted contrasting public personae. Yuan presented himself as a concerned yet congenial citizen with powerful connections in political circles and the underworld, while Ni presented himself as a traditional scholar with important contacts in literary circles. But the two men were similar in important respects. Neither man claimed Suzhou, the birthplace of *tanci*, as his native place; their families originated in eastern Zhejiang province.[58] Both men received a middle school education, Yuan's emphasizing business skills and Ni's providing a solid background in Western and Chinese learning.[59] And during the 1930s, when both men were in their twenties, they pioneered in a new career as advertising agents. An advertising agent in Shanghai not only created advertisements; he also placed them in various media. Consequently Yuan and Ni required access to radio and print, and ventured successfully into both industries.

---

58. Yuan's native place was Shangyu. See "Xinwenzhi zazhi dengji shengqing shu," n.p., 1946. Shanghai shi dang'anguan, 6.12.141. Ni's native place was Zhenhai. See "Shanghai shi guanggao tongye gonghui huiyuan mingce," n.p., 1947. Shanghai shi dang'anguan, 315.1.7.

59. Yuan Fengju attended a middle school for commerce (*shangwu zhongxue*). Again see Shanghai shi dang'anguan, 6.12.141. Ni attended the Chengzhong Middle School. See "Shanghai shi guanggao ye tongye gonghui tongye dengji biao," n.p., 1945. Shanghai shi dang'anguan, 315.1.8.

As manager of XHHI in the early 1930s, Yuan gained access to air time and, in his own words, "mixed with storytellers from morning till night."[60] He also recognized the profit-making potential of *kaipian* and decided to publish his own collection. This was his goal when he founded the Singing Phoenix Advertising Agency, which published *Songs of the Phoenix* in 1934.[61] The Agency also designed advertisements and placed them on buses, streetcars, billboards, newspapers, and radio air waves.[62] Yuan, who edited *Songs of the Phoenix*, inserted horizontal advertisements along the top and bottom margins of every page, and also printed full-page ads.

After *Songs of the Phoenix* was published, Yuan worked briefly for a second station[63] before moving his agency onto the fifth floor of Huang Jinrong's Great World Entertainment Palace.[64] XHHL, which broadcast from the Great World, became his agency's mouthpiece. To publicize its programming and provide listeners with photographs and lyrics of current performers, Yuan began publishing the *Singing Phoenix Monthly* in 1936.[65] This journal printed a variety of *kaipian*, sometimes praising modern amusements hosted by the Great World Entertainment Palace, and sometimes attacking modern dens of iniquity such as the dance hall. It also provided space to sell to advertisers and publicized his Agency.

In late 1936, Yuan moved his operations from the Great World, where noise was a major distraction, into three-story offices in Huang Jinrong's mansion on Marco Polo Road in the French Concession. With the studios of XHHL quietly secluded on the top floor and his own office installed on the second, Yuan opened a retail section on the ground floor. There he displayed a dedicatory tablet from Huang Jinrong and sold Chinese-made fire extinguishers as well as imported radios.[66] He also hired repairmen to make house calls and provide free radio-repair estimates. As the scope of his

---

60. Yuan Fengju, ed., author's postscript.

61. See Yu Tingwu, "Xian hua Fengming she," 162.

62. See advertisement, *Fengming yuekan* 1.1 (6 August 1936): 12.

63. Yuan and his colleagues refused to mention the station by name. A scandal erupted when he arrived, and after mediation by the *diantai gonghui*, Yuan departed. See Xiao Li, "Cong Fengming she shuo dao Yuan Fengju xiansheng" (Speaking from the Singing Phoenix Society to Mr. Yuan Fengju), *Fengming yuekan* 1.8 (26 October 1936): 209.

64. Ibid., 209. Zhang Shaokun, manager of the Gong wu tai dance hall, introduced Yuan to Tao Shangbo, manager of XHHL, and the two men became business associates.

65. See Yuan Fengju, "Juan tou yu" (Prefatory remark), *Fengming yuekan* 1.1 (16 April 1936): 1.

66. Yuan Fengju refers to this address as "Huang gongguan." See Yuan Fengju, "Guan yu Fengming she" (Concerning the Singing Phoenix Society), *Fengming boyin yuekan* 1 (undated): 2. For a full description of Yuan's new offices, see Zi Liang, 185.

business expanded, the name of Yuan's agency was shortened to the Singing Phoenix Society.[67]

When XHHL was shut down soon after its relocation, Yuan lost his mouthpiece. He subsequently allowed the *Singing Phoenix Monthly* to cease publication as he scrambled for access to air time. Yuan worked briefly at XHHZ, a station owned by Yu Xiaqing, and in April 1937 he published a final issue of the *Singing Phoenix Monthly*.[68] When the Japanese invaded Shanghai in August, his retail business enjoyed a sudden boom in the sale of fire extinguishers, but radio fell into a temporary slump. Consequently Yuan opened a dance hall, but returned to broadcasting in 1938 when an Italian station hired him to serve as its Chinese manager.[69] After 1949, Yuan withdrew to Taiwan and opened the first commercial radio station in the southern port city of Gaoxiong.[70]

Ni Gaofeng's career followed a similar trajectory. During the early 1930s he worked for three radio stations. As assistant manager at XHHY, his third assignment, Ni controlled access to air time and established connections with many performers. He also edited a collection of *kaipian* for the station in 1934, which contained his own compositions. Meanwhile Ni "hit the pavement for a large Western firm"[71] and acquired access to the printed medium by editing a variety of columns, including "Art and Play (*You yu yi*)" for the newspaper, *Diamond*.

With close contacts in different media, Ni ran his own operation out of a third-floor office in the Siming Bank building on Nanjing Road. His publishing was conducted by one entity, the Lotus Blossom Publishing House, while his advertising was conducted by another, the Great Wind Advertising Agency.[72]

---

67. See Xiao Li, 209.

68. See Yu Tingwu, "Ben kan fu huo xiao yan" (A few words about the revival of this magazine), *Fengming yuekan* 1.9/10 (10 April 1937): 1.

69. See Yuan Fengju, "Guan yu Fengming she," 2.

70. See Ding Yinsun, "'Hua jia fengming' nanbu ren de hao pengyou" ('Sixty year old Singing Phoenix,' good friend of southerners), *Guangbo yuekan* 159 (June 1995): p. 17.

71. Wang Yingzhou did not say which firm, nor how long it employed Ni. See Wang Yingzhou, "Ni Gaofeng xiansheng xiao zhuan" (Brief biography of Ni Gaofeng), *Zhuan kan hui bian*, 30 January 1930, p. 2.

72. The Lotus Blossom Publishing House already existed under that name in 1930, when Ni edited and published *Zhuan kan hui bian*. The Great Wind Advertising Agency already existed in 1939, when it was advertised on the pages of a book published by the Lotus Blossom Publishing House. The two entities shared the same office and the same telephone number. It is impossible to say when the second entity was established under that name and assumed responsibility for advertising and media brokerage.

The first entity published Ni's novels, translations and songs.[73] In 1934, the same year that Yuan published *Songs of the Phoenix*, it produced *The Collected Kaipian of Ni Gaofeng*. The Great Wind Advertising Agency meanwhile hired specialists to decorate windows and store fronts, and prepared "literary" advertisements for radio and print.[74] Ni inserted numerous full-page advertisements in his *Collected Kaipian*, but refrained from placing advertisements along the top and bottom margins of every page. He instead charged two *yuan* for his anthology, while Yuan charged only four *jiao* for *Songs of the Phoenix*. Ni's success in advertising was acknowledged by the Shanghai Union of Advertising Agents, which placed him on its council after the war.[75]

Representing the Retailers. Many of the *kaipian* that Yuan and Ni produced for radio broadcast presented traditional themes.[76] They celebrated heroes of old, fictional characters, Chinese festivals, native place sentiment, and family. Other songs presented novel ideas and images. There were *kaipian* about world leaders, soccer stars, national holidays, cinemas, and divorce. There were also advertisements written and sung in traditional *kaipian* form. These *guanggao kaipian*, a subgenre that Yuan and Ni helped create, introduced consumer goods and stores. Eager fans who browsed through the anthologies to request *kaipian* for performance usually bypassed these. But advertisers paid for air time as well as the storyteller's salary, so they did reach the air waves. The messages they delivered were often reinforced by conventional advertisements and urged listeners to practice the customs of modern consumption.

Advertisers and storytellers established contact in several ways. Sometimes storytellers solicited sponsors, either by hitting the pavement or posting an advertisement. Zhang Mengfei, who performed *kaipian* from 10:00 to 11:00 on XHHF every morning in mid-1933, announced to readers of *Diamond* that he "composed *kaipian* for any large commercial firm," and

---

73. His novels include *Liu shui xing yun*. His translation of *A Tale of Two Cities* was completed in collaboration with his wife.

74. See the advertisement inserted between pp. 56-57 in Ni Gaofeng, *Ni Gaofeng duichang kaipian ji* (Ni Gaofeng's collected *kaipian* duets) (Shanghai: Lianhua chubanguan, 1939).

75. See "Shanghai shi guanggao tongye gonghui huiyuan mingce," n.p., 1947. Shanghai shi dang'anguan, 315.1.7.

76. The songs in both anthologies were clearly intended for radio as well as print. Ni's, for example, was marketed as a guide for radio listening. "All famous storytellers have obtained this collection," one advertisement boasted. "So after you purchase the book, please feel free to select the songs for performance. Every night there are special shows lined up for [the songs] to be broadcast." See Lu Dan'an, *Ti xiao yin yuan tanci*, act 35, p. 13.

printed an address for potential clients.[77] In some cases, the advertiser initiated the search for a popular storyteller by conducting market research. The Shanghai Moving Company hired Xu Yunzhi, for example, after receiving several thousand letters in response to a poll of listeners.[78]

If an advertiser controlled his own radio station, he bypassed media brokers and provided the performer with air time independently.[79] But even merchants who located storytellers without the help of middlemen usually depended on advertising agents to arrange a daily broadcast. Wang Zhongnian, for example, scouted for talent at the Oriental Hotel's storytelling theater and then enlisted Ni Gaofeng, his friend and business associate, to provide air time. When he discovered Chen Ruilin and Chen Yunlin performing in late 1933, he hired both men to perform daily from 11:00 to noon on XHHY, the station managed by Ni.[80]

Ni also disseminated *guanggao kaipian* for Wang Zhongnian. *A Collection of Lingering Tunes* (*Niao niao ji*), which Ni edited for XHHY in 1934, included two *kaipian* entitled "The Lao Jiu He Silk Store." Both songs opened on the prosperous city of Shanghai, and then focused on the imposing facade of Lao Jiu He at the intersection of Nanjing Road and Wangping Street. Inside was a magnificent array of imported as well as domestic silk, and a crowd of indulgent shoppers. The first song identified them as:

> Lovely women—roaming abroad in groups,
> And casually buying fabric for new clothes
> Suitable in spring, summer and fall.[81]

The second song added detail:

> (There are) young married women in powder and rouge—
> Who invite one another to try on new clothes.
> (There are) modern women with fluffy perms—

---

77. See "Zhang Mengfei tanchang shishi kaipian boyin xun" (Notice that Zhang Mengfei performs current kaipian on the radio), *Jin'gangzuan*, 13 July 1933, p. 2. Also see "Tanci mingjia yi lan biao" (A list of famous Suzhou storytellers), *Fengming yuekan* 1.8 (26 October 1936): 210. Three storytellers listed here specialized in "private shows and radio advertisements."

78. See "Maikefeng" (Microphone), *Jin'gangzuan*, 25 November 1933, p. 2.

79. Zhou Bangjun opened a radio station at his Sino-Western Pharmacy and placed Pan Xinyi on the air waves. See Pan Xinyi, "Shutan yu diantai," *Shan hu* 2.7 and 2.8 (1 and 16 April 1933): 1.

80. See Ni Gaofeng, "Chen Ruilin yu di pin ding zi," p. 2.

81. Ni Gaofeng, ed., *Niao niao ji* (Shanghai: Lili guangbo wuxian diantai, 1934), 5-6.

Twittering bird-like, each with a view of her own.[82]

Jiang Zhigang, the manager of Tian Faxiang Fur and Leather Goods, relied on Ni to meet performers, provide air time, and compose *kaipian*. On a cold day in late 1933, Ni Gaofeng met Zhu Yaoxiang, a popular storyteller, in the Lao Jiu He Silk and Foreign Goods Emporium. Zhu had just purchased the silk facing for a new gown, but still needed a fur lining. Consequently Ni led the storyteller to Tian Faxiang and introduced him to Jiang Zhigang. Because Zhu "spread propaganda and expanded sales" for his store, Jiang was delighted and offered his spokesman a discount.[83]

Ni composed at least three *kaipian* for Jiang Zhigang, including "Fur and Leather Goods," which opened on a cozy winter scene. Outside it was bitterly cold, but inside a stove was burning and warmth was flooding the room. If you step outside, "You can't bring the hot stove with you," Ni reminded the audience. One solution was the fur coat, and Ni threw his spotlight on one particular store. "Were you to ask, 'which retailer is best,'" Ni would recommend Tian Faxiang. "In Shanghai it has no match," he promised. Its prices were fair, its stock was excellent, and service was friendly. Ni then reminded the consumer of luxury items that people in Shanghai were freezing.

> How many of our laboring friends
> Have spare cash to buy a fur coat?
> With cold penetrating their bones,
> They cannot find food or clothing—
> Much less scrape together extra cash
> For a sheepskin jacket to stay warm.[84]

Ni displayed a social conscience while tempting consumers to purchase fur. The consumer he portrayed in conventional ads for the furrier. A full-page advertisement for Tian Faxiang on the back of his *Collected Kaipian* presented a stylish woman in mid-stride. She wore a fashionable cap, an overcoat with a fur collar, and high-heel shoes. In her right arm she carried a pocketbook, but her left arm swung freely. She cut off her queue, so to speak, by bobbing her hair, and displayed so much confidence that buildings framing her elegant figure leaned to the side with a start. To inspire his audience, Ni presented a confident woman at home on the streets of Shanghai.

---

82. Ibid., 6-7.
83. See Pan Xinyi, "Shutan yu diantai," *Shan hu* 2.7 (1 April 1933): 6-7.
84. Ni Gaofeng, *Ni Gaofeng kaipian ji*, 264-65.

Yuan Fengju constructed an identical image for He Yizhou, the Cantonese manager of the Minghua Silk Store on Nanjing Road.[85] When fans opened *Songs of the Phoenix*, they discovered an advertisement for the Minghua Silk Store, which boasted that "Every day [we] have new merchandise—[our] variety is modern." Yuan Fengju did not provide a visual illustration of the new woman who desired so much selection. Instead he portrayed her in song.

"A *Kaipian* for the Minghua Silk Store" presented a cheerful spring day. The leaves were out. The flowers and trees were blooming. And the prosperous city of Shanghai was suffused with an atmosphere of freshness. Suddenly a coterie of young women strolled into view wearing cosmetics and modern clothing, and one young woman asked her companion, "Where can I find such fine clothes?" Her companion suggested the Minghua Silk Store, which, being brightly lit, well decorated and spotless, provided a magnificent site for shopping. But even more important was Minghua's variety of fabric. "With a hundred kinds of cloth, its selection is complete . . . On plain white walls are lengths of brilliant fabric, the latest fashions in Shanghai." Another selling point was Minghua's public spirit.

> The *Pearl Pagoda* of Shen and Xue;
> The *tanci* currently broadcast on [XHHX] . . .
> is brought to you as a service from Minghua.

Every evening from 7:00 to 8:00, Shen Jian'an and Xue Xiaoqing performed a traditional love story entitled *The Pearl Pagoda* on XHHX.[86] Listening on the radio, however, was a woman whom retailers urged to practice the customs of modern consumption. She and her companions wore clothing, cosmetics, and hairstyles that were immediately recognized as modern. They also formed intimate coteries and ventured throughout the city on shopping trips that formed a central part of their social lives and daily routines. Rapidly-changing fashion necessitated regular visits to luxury retailers who provided both entertainment in a bid for the affection of consumers, and enough selection for consumers to cultivate their individuality. The ideal woman, as represented by advertising agents for their commercial clients, then displayed her modern identity in public—and in flagrant disregard of traditional virtues such as modesty and frugality.

Representing the Regime. Meanwhile the GMD also depended on middlemen to promote its vision of austerity in storytelling. Pan Gongzhan, the party's Bureau of Education chief, initiated a storytelling contest in November

---

85. See "Shangye dengji chengqing shu," n.p. 1942. Shanghai shi dang'anguan, 14.1.172.
86. See *Jiu Zhongguo*, 120.

1932, for example. His objective was to "improve the character of storytellers," who would "exhort audiences to uphold simplicity and reject luxurious living." Pan needed a middleman with media access and artistic judgement to publicize and judge the contest, so he enlisted Fan Niuweng, a newspaper columnist with expertise in storytelling.[87]

Pan also relied on Yuan Fengju and Ni Gaofeng to inculcate a new ideology in the minds of radio listeners. When Yuan established the Singing Phoenix Advertising Agency in the early 1930s, Pan endorsed his entrepreneurial effort.[88] The Agency in turn hosted a program of radio entertainments dedicated to the promotion of summer hygiene—during which the mayor of Shanghai and at least three bureau chiefs, including Pan Gongzhan, delivered speeches.[89] Likewise, when Pan's Bureau of Education declared 6-12 November 1933, the Anti-Bandit Propaganda Week, Ni Gaofeng announced the news in *Diamond* and reserved air time for the delivery of speeches.[90]

When Jiang Jieshi unleashed the New Life Movement in 1934, both men immediately produced *kaipian* to publicize its message.[91] As a result, they won the endorsement of Wu Tiecheng, Shanghai's mayor when *Songs of the Phoenix* and *The Collected Kaipian of Ni Gaofeng* were published in 1934. Wu placed his stamp of approval on the cover of both anthologies by contributing his calligraphy, signature, and chop. His contribution, in turn, was

87. See Fan Niuweng, "Shanghai shi jiaoyu ju tichang shuo shu jingsai hui ping" (Critical comments on the storytelling contest sponsored by the Shanghai Bureau of Education), *Jin'gangzuan*, 25 November 1932, p. 1.

88. Yuan Ludeng, a powerful merchant and government official, also sent a dedication to Yuan. See Yu Tingwu, "Fengming guanggao she de rongyu" (The Fengming Advertising Agency's honor), *Fengming yuekan* 1.2 (5 May 1936): 15. The two men were possibly acquainted through shared activities as Peking opera buffs. See "Shen shang ming piao" (Well-known amateur performers among Shanghai's merchants), *Fengming yuekan* 1.8 (26 October 1936): 215.

89. See Yu Tingwu, "Fengming guanggao she de rong yu," 15.

90. Ni stated that merchants invited famous people to deliver speeches on every station. Merchants presumably paid for the air time, while station managers like himself reserved it for such an occasion. See Ni Gaofeng, "Maikefeng," p. 2.

91. According to Yao Yinmei, a storyteller who was twenty-seven at the time, performers and fans did not take these songs seriously. Because storytellers and stations were directed to publicize the Movement, however, they quickly performed them on radio and stage to dispense with the task and get on with the entertainment. Yao Yinmei, interview by author, tape recording, Shanghai, 2 July 1993.

a useful ingredient in the sales strategy of Ni, who proclaimed the mayor's endorsement in his advertisements for the *Collected Kaipian of Ni Gaofeng.*[92] Instead of promoting consumption, these songs encouraged good citizenship and spartan conduct. The first *kaipian* in *Songs of the Phoenix,* entitled "The New Life Movement," was composed for Hua Zhenya, a performer who sang *kaipian* nightly on XHHI, the station managed by Yuan Fengju.[93] Its sobering lyrics were composed by Yu Tingwu, a school teacher and Yuan's partner at the Singing Phoenix Advertising Agency, who simultaneously endorsed Tian Faxiang's vision of modernity. This furrier also placed advertisements in *Songs of the Phoenix,* and beside its illustration of a blonde woman with bobbed hair, a string of pearls, and a fur stole, is Yu's proclamation that "Tian Faxiang is King of Fur and Leather." Meanwhile his *kaipian* declared that "old fashioned lifestyles must be reformed," but not on behalf of merchants.

The twentieth-century tide has turned;
Everyone will become a new citizen (*gongmin*).
Just how does one become a new citizen?
The tenets of a New Life are clear.
Desire simple clothing and clean food;
Accept basic housing and transportation.[94]

Yu urged members of the audience to become citizens, but his conception of the role was a narrow one. Because increased consumption would not be the essence of their new lives, the most important thing for new citizens to do was lower their expectations. His lyrics comprised an assault on the vision of retailers, whom he also represented as a partner at the Singing Phoenix Advertising Agency.

Women who accepted Tian Faxiang's prescription for modern living, a prescription that Yuan Fengju delivered in *Songs of the Phoenix,* were a lightning rod for attack in the same collection. "A New *Kaipian* About Modern Women" denounced them for worshipping finery, being seduced by foreign objects, and venturing freely throughout the city. As an alternative, it proposed a spartan New Life:

---

92. See, for example, the advertisement in Lu Dan'an *Ti xiao yin yuan tanci,* "Zhuanzhu *Ti xiao yin yuan tanci* de jingguo" (Experience of writing *Fate in Tears and Laughter,* the *tanci*), 8.

93. See *Jiu Zhongguo,* 119-120.

94. Yuan Fengju, ed., *Fengming ji,* 1.

(The tenets of which are)
None other than propriety, justice, honesty, and self-
respect;
Practice honesty and self-respect in your compartments,
For men administer the world, and women manage the
home . . .
(Only) with thorns for hairpins and cotton skirts can a
wife be virtuous.[95]

The first song in *The Collected Kaipian of Ni Gaofeng* was also entitled "The New Life Movement," and the next four songs elaborated on the meaning of "Propriety," "Justice," "Honesty," and "Self-Respect." In these songs Ni condemned the modern world for rampant materialism and proclaimed traditional values like frugality. He also presented the spartan citizen who renounced luxury and indulgence to serve the nation as a modern exemplar. This citizen contrasted sharply with the modern woman he constructed for his commercial clients, and whom he simultaneously denounced for the GMD.

In a *kaipian* entitled "Vainglory," Ni admitted that men were vain. But:

Women care for appearances most;
They're keen on nothing but clothes.
Blind to hard times, they won't make donations . . .
And wind up damaging youth.

Because the shallow concerns and spending habits of modern women threatened the nation, Ni urged them to exorcise the vanity "lodged in your breast through intensive [self-]criticism."

You must cast vainglory aside,
So youth can awake
And the nation revives.
Wealthy ladies and prominent girls
Should be known for reserve and virtue!
Expel vainglory in favor of motherhood . . .
What good is the love of cosmetics, and
Why let jewels subvert your resolve?[96]

---

95. Ibid., 45.
96. Ni Gaofeng, *Ni Gaofeng kaipian ji*, 320-21.

On behalf of the Guomindang, Ni Gaofeng encouraged women to stop wasting money on selfish trifles, halt their public displays of modern fashion, and commit themselves to grooming the next generation. In other words, they should reject the customs promoted by the propagandists of consumption, including himself, and practice a New Life that entailed self-denial, devoted nationalism, and domesticity. Like Yuan Fengju, Ni paid lip service to the Guomindang in order to avoid trouble and profit from official endorsements. But he was not committed to New Life ideals, and simultaneously undermined an official campaign by promoting an antithetical vision of modern life for the city's merchants.

Conclusion

In the early 1930s, entrepreneurs in Shanghai developed a new advertising technique that combined storytelling with radio and print. Their goal was to tempt a wide audience with concrete pleasures that offered immediate gratification, and thereby unleash a hidden reservoir of desire for a growing number of goods and services. To facilitate consumption, meanwhile, they also adopted a mass-merchandising strategy that entailed lowering profit margins to increase sales. If the essential features of a consumer revolution are a proliferation of consumer goods, an elastic view of demand, and innovative commercial techniques, then such a revolution was well underway in Shanghai during the 1930s.[97]

If we switch our focus from the activities of entrepreneurs to the activities of consumers, however, the revolution is less easily proclaimed. Based on the evidence presented here, any conclusions about the response of ordinary urbanites would be premature. Did consumption indeed become an ideal? Did they respond to fashion, make shopping a daily event, and locate forms of consumer credit? Did the aggregate level of consumption, a fundamental issue, rise by the 1930s?[98] In Shanghai, which began to feel the impact of a world

---

97. These features are cited in Frank Lambert, *Pedlar in Divinity: George Whitefield and the Transatlantic Revivals, 1737-1770* (Princeton: Princeton University Press, 1994), 6. Craig Clunas cites the commodification of art as evidence for a "proto-consumer culture" (p. 38) in late sixteenth-century China, but underlines the opposition to its progress among contemporary elites, who were not to be "midwives present at the birth of consumer society" (p. 173). See Craig Clunas, *Superfluous Things: Material Culture and Social Status in Early Modern China* (Cambridge: Polity Press, 1991).

98. These criteria are cited in Neil McKendrick, John Brewer, and J.H. Plumb, *The Birth of Consumer Society: The Commercialization of Eighteenth-Century England* (London: Europa Publications Limited, 1982); and Eric Lampard, "Introductory Essay," in *Inventing Times Square: Commerce and Culture at the Crossroads of the World*, ed. William R. Taylor (New York: Russell Sage Foundation, 1991), 16-35.

depression at mid decade, the stimulation of new desires undoubtedly resulted in greater frustration as well as increased consumption.

But the evidence also suggests that entrepreneurial activity is highly significant in and of itself. William Leach points out that actual consumption was fairly steady in the United States between 1890 and 1929, but "the character of consumption and its context" were transformed. Critical to their transformation was the broker, an "individual who represses his/her convictions and withholds judgement in the interest of forging profitable relationships between other people." This individual, "essentially indifferent to virtue and hospitable to the ongoing expansion of desire," served in New York a corporate order with great centralizing force.[99] Such an order was less advanced in Shanghai, but the city was indeed home to an expanding group of brokers who were quite willing to foster a "staggering machine of desire" for local merchants. They and their clients altered both the character and context of consumption in Shanghai, and helped to create a local consumer society with Nanjing Road at its epicenter.[100]

This development is important to note because it sheds light on tensions between the state and local culture, and between political and commercial forces, that are recurrent in twentieth-century Chinese history. In 1930s Shanghai, commercial forces promoted a new culture that was based on modern customs of consumption. For example, women would obey the dictates of fashion and regularly join their friends on shopping trips. Together they would explore the city in search of the finest stores with the lowest prices, shop for immodest costumes that reflected Western influence, and proudly display in public their modern identities. Self-restraint was discouraged by merchants, who promised consumers that shopping provided a quick and simple solution to life's frustrations.

These customs were repellent to powerful elements in the Guomindang, which consequently unleashed the New Life Movement to reverse commercial trends and incorporate Shanghai into a new culture based on strict military

99. See William Leach "Brokers and the New Corporate, Industrial Order," in *Inventing Times Square: Commerce and Culture at the Crossroads of the World*, ed. William R. Taylor (New York: Russell Sage Foundation, 1991), 99-117.

100. For pioneering research on early progress of larger companies, including a multi-national corporation, at raising levels of consumption for consumer goods and extending Shanghai's commercial culture into the hinterland, see Sherman Cochran, "Inventing Nanjing Road: Advertising by the British-American Tobacco Company in Early Twentieth-Century China," a paper presented at "The Birth of a Consumer Society? Commerce and Culture in Shanghai, 1895-1937," Cornell University, 1992; and Sherman Cochran, *Big Business in China: Sino-Foreign Rivalry in the Cigarette Industry, 1890-1930* (Cambridge, Mass.: Harvard University Press, 1980).

discipline, self-sacrifice, and nationalism. Women, in particular, would cancel their shopping trips and withdraw from the public arena. This initiative presented a direct threat to local merchants, who were happy to echo the rhetoric of the New Life Movement even as they sabotaged the campaign. Luxury retailers adopted its revolutionary idiom to promote mass consumption, and advertising agents disseminated propaganda to secure profitable endorsements from the regime. Essentially they incorporated the New Life Movement into their advertising strategies along with traditional forms of popular culture and modern mass media. By reexamining the Movement in the context of an emerging consumer society, both its origins and its failure can be interpreted in a new light. In Shanghai during the Nanjing Decade, local merchants were actively promoting a consumer culture that could inspire and swamp an official campaign.

"The Seventy-two Tenants":
Residence and Commerce in Shanghai's *Shikumen* Houses, 1872-1951

Hanchao Lu

Visitors to twentieth-century Shanghai, if they were to pay attention, could easily find a type of row house popularly known as the *shikumen*. Spawned everywhere in the city, shikumen were a part of a broader category of residences known as alleyway houses (*lilong*), which have consistently housed the great majority of Shanghai's people since the late nineteenth century. In the city's busy commercial districts (such as those around Nanjing Road), in its tree-lined elegant residential areas (such as those in the French Concession), and in the Chinese districts (such as Zhabei and Nanshi), shikumen were built as homes for ordinary people. For visitors who were not especially attentive, however, these houses might have been easily overlooked, not only because they were usually located in back alleyways behind commercial enterprises, but also because, paradoxically, their very commonness made them blend into a backdrop against which other urban structures stood out. Visitors were often struck by Shanghai's modern skyline along the Bund and Nanjing Road, or impressed by its European-style villas in the city's western suburbs; more social-minded observers were perhaps stunned by the abject poverty of the city's squatter shacks.[1] But few people paid attention to the shikumen. As for local residents, shikumen were merely the place most people called home and were nothing special. The lack of attention to this common architecture was simply a matter of "paying no attention to a familiar sight" (*shu shi wu du*).

I gratefully thank the University of California Press for permission to use in this article materials from my book, *Beyond the Neon Lights: Everyday Shanghai in the Early Twentieth Century* (California, 1999)

1. See Hanchao Lu, "Creating Urban Outcasts: Shantytowns in Shanghai, 1920-1950," *Journal of Urban History*, 21.5 (July 1995): 563-596.

This neglect of the shikumen at the popular level has also been reflected in the scholarly literature. Given the importance of this type of house in the dev.elopment of Shanghai and its significance in the everyday life of the city's people, it is remarkable how little it has been studied. This neglect, however, has been partly corrected by some recent academic research in China, notably the works of Luo Suwen and Zhang Jishun, which treat the shikumen as a legitimate topic for historical research, and associate the topic with the broader urban culture of Shanghai. None of this recent work, however, rises above generalities, nor does any focus on the structure of everyday life in shikumen neighborhoods.[2] In the English-speaking world, despite a boom in research on the history of twentieth-century Shanghai, which has in recent decades led to a significant number of works covering a wide range of topics, the texture of life in residential neighborhoods remains largely a blank spot.[3]

This article provides some details on the alleyway houses (in particular, the shikumen) and their social implications, which involve primarily the housing market that operated at the rental and subletting levels and its impact on the life of ordinary people. In these neighborhoods, commercial enterprises and residential premises were mixed, and this mixture played an important role in creating modern Shanghai's commercial culture.

The Rise of the Modern Real Estate Market

Shanghai's modern real estate market originated in two wars that occurred near the city's foreign settlements in the mid-nineteenth century: the Small Swords uprising and the Taiping Rebellion. From September 1853 to February 1855, the walled county seat of Shanghai, whose northern gates were located only a block south of the French Concession, was occupied by a rebellious band known as the Small Sword or the Triads. Their fight to seize the county seat brought the first tide of refugees into the foreign settlements which, in spite of the ambiguities of of their legal status, were until then reserved for

---

2. See Luo Suwen, *Shikumen: xunchang renjia* (Shikumen: ordinary homes) (Shanghai: Shanghai renmin chubanshe, 1991); Zhang Jishun, "Lun Shanghai lilong" (On the alleyway houses of Shanghai), in *Shanghai yanjiu luncong* (English title: Papers on Shanghai Studies), no.9, 59-77. (Shanghai: Shanghai Academy of Social Sciences,1993)

3. Jeff Cody has an on-going research project related to this subject. See his "Residential Real Estate in Republican Shanghai," a paper presented at the international conference on Shanghai at the Shanghai Academy of Social Sciences, Shanghai, August 17-19, 1993.

Westerners only. Early in 1854, over 20,000 refugees from the county seat had entered the foreign areas. Later, the number of refugees reached 80,000.[4]

In the face of this crisis, Shanghai's foreign community debated whether to expel the Chinese and maintain segregation, or to build housing for the refugees (to be rented to them for, it was hoped, a profit). Eventually, the idea of continuing segregation was overridden by the undisguised wish to make money by renting land and buildings to the Chinese. But whatever the result of the debate, the dismantling of segregation was soon to prove inevitable: the Taiping Rebellion (1850-1864)—the capital of the Taipings was Nanjing, 200 miles northwest of Shanghai—drove thousands of Chinese in the Jiangnan region to flee to Shanghai seeking safety under European rule. In particular, in 1860-62 when Taiping troops marched toward Shanghai several times, it was reported that refugees in Shanghai's foreign settlements once reached half a million.[5] Given the geographical size of the foreign settlements at that time, this might be an exaggerated estimation. More reliable sources reported that by 1865 the population of the British-American settlements (later known as the International Settlement) had increased to 92,884. Most were Chinese from the vicinity of Shanghai. At the same time, about 50,000 Chinese had moved into the French Concession. By the end of the Taiping Rebellion, well over 110,000 Chinese had moved into Shanghai's foreign settlements.[6]

In spite of the unhappiness of both the British consul and the Chinese daotai over the problem of crime and the threat to public health caused by the refugees, the business of building and renting houses to the Chinese boomed.[7] From September 1853 to July 1854, over eight hundred two-story row houses were built on Guangdong Road and Fuzhou Road in the British Settlement; still more houses were scattered in the northwest part of the Settlement, as well as on the Bund and along the Yangjingbang Creek, which separated the British Settlement from the French Concession. By 1860, there were 8,740 houses in the British Settlement, mostly owned by Britishers and Americans but inhabited by Chinese. Many new clusters of houses continued to be built on

---

4. Kuai Shixun, *Shanghai gonggong zujie shigao* (A draft history of the Shanghai International Settlement) (Shanghai: Shanghai renmin chubanshe, 1980), 347; Guo Yuming. *Shanghai xiaodaohui qiyi shi* (A history of Shanghai's Small Swords rebellion) (Shanghai: Zhongguo dabaike quanshu chubanshe, 1993), 249.

5. H.Lang, *Shanghai, Considered Socially* (Shanghai: Kelly and Walsh, 1875), 27; Kuai Shixun, *Shanghai gonggong zujie shigao*, 359.

6. Zou Yiren, *Jiu Shanghai renkou bianqian de yanji* (Research on population change in old Shanghai) (Shanghai: Shanghai renmin chubanshe, 1980), 3-4, 90-91.

7. De Jesus, C. A. Montalto, *Historical Shanghai* (Shanghai: The Shanghai Mercury, Limited, 1909), 98-99.

Hankou Road, Jiujiang Road, and further north to Nanjing Road and up to the south bank of Suzhou Creek.[8]

These new clusters did not merely change the landscape of Shanghai but, more significantly, they marked the beginning in China of a modern real estate market. In traditional China, residences were usually built as individual, freestanding structures. A row of houses was as a rule formed without plan by a gradual accumulation of structures that were built at different times and in different styles.[9] In that sense, the houses that were built in Shanghai's British Settlement in the 1850s and 1860s were new to the Chinese, for these houses were built in batches of identical units and were, as a modern developer would say, "spec built" (that is, built for the market). The difference in design, arguably, was derived from the difference in purpose: traditional Chinese houses were constructed individually because they were mostly built by or for owners for their personal use, while the row houses in the foreign settlements were constructed solely for commercial purposes. In Shanghai in the mid-nineteenth century, both the design and the purpose of these houses were European innovations. Of course, land and housing had been commodities in China long before the coming of the West. At least from the eleventh century on, house purchasing and leasing were already common in Chinese cities.[10] But these commercial activities were usually conducted on a small scale. House purchasing and leasing were primarily a matter of what might be called self-consumption (e.g., building a home for oneself), of convenience (e.g., renting a house for a sojourn away from home, or selling a house when one relocates), or of a shift of wealth (e.g., selling a house to pay debts, or purchasing a house in order to have *hengchan* or permanent property). To build identical houses on a large scale solely for for the market, as Western merchants started to do in Shanghai in the middle 1850s, was something that the nation had never before seen.[11] In that sense, it could be argued that China's first modern real estate market was born in the gun smoke in Shanghai, or more specifically, on

---

8. Zhu Jiancheng, "Jiu Shanghai fangdichan de xingqi" (The rise of real estate markets in old Shanghai), *Shanghai wenshi ziliao xuanji*, 64(1990):10-13; Wang Shaozhou, *Shanghai jindai chengshi jianzhu* (Urban architecture in modern Shanghai) (N.p.: Jiangsu kexue jishu chubanshe, 1989),75; Kuai Shixun, *Shanghai gonggong zujie shigao*, 347.

9. J.E. Spencer, "The House of the Chinese," in *Geographical Review*, 37(1947): 254-273; Ronald G. Knapp, *The Chinese House: Craft, Symbol, and the Folk Tradition* (Hong Kong: Oxford University Press, 1990), 5-25.

10. Hu Jianhua, "Songdai chengshi fangdichan guanli jianlun"(On the management of urban real estate in the Song dynasty), in *Zhongguo shi yuanjiu* (Research on Chinese history), no.4(1989): 24-31.

11. Zhu Jiancheng, "Jiu Shanghai fangdichan de xingji," (The rise of real estate markets in old Shanghai), *Shanghai wenshi ziliao xuanji*, 64(1990):10-13.

the blocks of Nanjing Road. In the climate of continuing Western encroachment in the late nineteenth century, the modern real estate market was destined to have a profound impact on the life of the Chinese residents of the city.

The end of the Taiping Rebellion brought a temporary decrease in the population of the city in the late 1860s, but the real estate market remained steady. According to a British merchant, by renting land or a house to the Chinese, foreigners in Shanghai could make a profit of at least 30 to 40 percent.[12] A contemporary commented in the early 1870s that renting out houses was the "most profitable business" in Shanghai, a business that until then had remained predominately foreign-run.[13]

By the 1870s the wartime speculation had died away and a more regulated real estate market began to emerge in Shanghai. In September 1869, the Land Regulations, which was regarded as the "constitution" of Shanghai's foreign settlements, was revised and approved by the European envoys in Beijing to create the Shanghai Municipal Council (SMC) to govern the International Settlement, the core of modern Shanghai. One of its first orders of business was to levy a tax on real property. The rate was set at 3 percent of estimated land value in 1874 and gradually increased to 7 percent by 1919. In 1869 taxes levied on houses were set at 8 percent of the rent for Chinese-style houses and 6 percent for Western-style houses. By 1919, taxes for both Chinese and Western houses were levied at a rate of 14 percent. Furthermore, mainly for purposes of taxation, the International Settlement was divided into four districts: the Central, the North, the East, and the West, and periodically all real property was reassessed.[14] A brochure indexing land value and tax was issued by the SMC, by which landlords could easily find the standard taxes for their property. In the period 1869-1933, at least 19 assessments of property value were conduced by the SMC; in other words, there was a reassessment on average every three to four years.[15]

Initiated by Westerners, Shanghai's real estate market was also dominated by them. All real estate magnates in late nineteenth century Shanghai were Westerners. Among them we find the names of such well-known China adventurers as Edwin Smith, Thomas Hanbury (1832-1907), Henry Lester

---

12. Sir Rutherford Alcock, *Capital of the Tycoon: A Narrative of A Three Years' Residence in Japan* (New York: Harper & Brothers Publishers, 1863), 37.

13. Ge Yuanxi, *Huyou zaji* (Miscellanies on Shanghai sojourn) (Shanghai: Shanghai guji chubanshe, 1989), 14.

14. Shen Bojing and Chen Huaipu, *Shanghaishi zhinan* (Guide to Shanghai) (Shanghai: Zhonghua shuju, 1933), 13.

15. Zhang Zhongli and Chen Zengnian, *Shaxun jituan zai jiu Zhongguo* (The Sassoons in old China)(Beijing: Renmin chubanshe, 1985), 34-35.

(1840-1925), the Hogg brothers (William, James, and E. Jenner), the Sassoon family, and Silas Aaron Hardoon (1847-1931). From 1869 to 1933, the top three real estate magnates—whose holdings fluctuated from 36 percent to over 60 percent of the real estate along Nanjing Road—were all foreigners. In the early 1930s, close to half of the real estate along Nanjing Road, which was the most expensive area in the city, was under Hardoon's name.[16]

However, shortly after foreigners launched the real estate market in Shanghai, Chinese merchants started to join the adventure. Among the refugees who came to Shanghai during the Taiping Rebellion were many wealthy landlords and bureaucrats. Some of them soon found that speculation in urban real estate was a much more profitable business than renting out farm land in the countryside. Among the Chinese real estate owners were four families—surnamed Zhang, Liu, Xin, and Peng—known as the "Four Elephants," who owned many shikumen compounds in the Nanjing Road area. These four families shared a few things in common. They all hailed from Nanxun, Zhejiang province, and all owned a great amount of land and controlled the silk and tea markets there. Having come to Shanghai, they continued their silk and tea businesses but shifted the bulk of their capital to real estate.[17]

By the end of the 1940s, Shanghai had over 3,000 Chinese who were qualified to be called great real estate investors (*fangdichan dayezhu*), an epithet commonly applied to anyone who owned more than 1,000 square meters of real property in the city. About 160 of this group owned over 10,000 square meters of real property; 30 owned over 30,000 square meters.[18] Many Chinese real estate investors were compradors.[19]

---

16. Shen Chenxian, "Nanjing lu fangdichan de lishi" (A history of the real estate of Nanjing Road), in *Shanghai wenshi ziliao xuanji*, 64 (1990):18-30.

17. Zhu Jiancheng, "Jiu Shanghai fangdichan de xingqi," 15.

18. Zhu Jiancheng, ibid., 14.

19. The following is a list of some top Chinese real estate magnates in Shanghai, all of whom were compradors for Western companies in Shanghai:

Cheng Jinxuan comprador of Sassoon & Co.
Zhou Liantang comprador of Sassoon & Co.
Bei Runsheng comprador, a "pigment magnate"
Yu Qiaqing comprador of the Dutch Bank
Zhu Dachun comprador of Jardine Matheson & Co. (Yihe)
Chen Binxian comprador of Burkill & Sons (Xiangmo)
Ying Zhiyun comprador of Tonghe
Wei Tingrong comprador of the French Bank
Zhu Ziyao comprador of Banque de L'Indo-chine (Tongfang huili Bank)

See Zhu Jiancheng,"Jiu Shanghai de Huaji fangdichan dayezhu"(The Chinese big real estate Investors of old Shanghai), *Shanghai wenshi ziliao xuanji*, no.64(1990): 14-17.

Both Chinese and foreigners invested not only in commercial property but also residential houses in the Nanjing Road area.[20] From 1910 to 1940, most old houses along Nanjing Road left from last century were remodeled into alleyway (*lilong*) houses.[21] This type of dwelling was derived from the two-story houses built in clusters during the Taiping period but rebuilt with a new and more sophisticated design in the early 1870s (discussed below). First built in the Nanjing Road area, alleyway houses soon spread to other parts of the city and, toward the end of the nineteenth century, they had become the predominant type of housing in Shanghai. By the end of the 1940s, seven decades after the emergence of alleyway houses, over 72 percent of the city's dwellings were alleyway houses, and about three quarters of these were shikumen houses.[22] To the present day, more than a century since the first shikumen was built, alleyway houses remain the predominant type of housing in the city.[23]

Shanghai's real estate market, therefore, was launched with the construction of alleyway houses and much of the market remained connected with the evolution of these houses in the late nineteenth and early twentieth centuries. What was important to the everyday life of the people of Shanghai was of course not the operation of the market at the level of the real estate magnate (whether foreign or Chinese), but its operation at the grassroots level.

Let us now look into how the alleyway houses and the housing market changed to meet the needs of ordinary people, and, in turn, how the daily life of the ordinary people of Shanghai was profoundly shaped by changes in the housing market.

---

20. For the convenience of narration, the "Nanjing Road area" refers to the British Settlement in its early stage. It centered on Nanjing Road, and was bounded by the Bund on the east, Tibet Road on the west, the southern bank of Suzhou Creek on the north, and Yangjingbang Creek (later transformed into Avenue Edward VII) on the south. The boundaries of this, the core area of modern Shanghai, were set by the Shanghai daotai Lin Gui and the British consul Rutherford Alcock in November 1848.

21. Shen Chenxian, "Nanjing lu fangdichan de lishi" and "Shanghai zaoqi de jige waiguo fangdichan shang"(A few foreign real estate merchants in early "treaty port" Shanghai), in *Shanghai wenshi ziliao xuanji*, 64 (1990):129-140.

22. Shanghaishi tongjiju (Shanghai Municipal Bureau of Statistics) (comp.), *Shanghai tongji nianjian,1989* (Shanghai statistics annual, 1989) (Shanghai: Shanghai renmin chubanshe, 1989), 438.

23. Shanghaishi tongjiju, Ibid., 438;Shanghai zhuzhai (1949-1990) bianqibu (Editorial office of the Dwellings of Shanghai (1949-1990), *Shanghai zhuzhai (1949-1990)* (The dwellings of Shanghai, 1949-1990) (Shanghai: Shanghai kexue puji chubanshe, 1993), 147.

The Evolution of Alleyway Houses

The row houses built during the refugee tide of the 1850s and 1860s were constructed in a rush and, since all were made of wood, by the 1870s many of them had become dilapidated. In addition, wooden houses built in rows were particularly unsafe in case of fire. Thus newly built houses in the early 1870s were constructed of brick, wood, and cement. These houses were still built in a row, and a few rows were marked off by surrounding walls to form a residential compound. Paved alleyways between the rows were built within the walled compound, a necessity for access, light, and ventilation. Hence the name for this type of dwelling: *lilong fangzi* or *longtang fangzi*, meaning, alleyway house. Later, alleyway houses evolved into a number of different styles, but the term *lilong* or *longtang* continued to be used to describe all types of alleyway houses in the city.[24]

Naming the Alleyway Houses. The earliest as well as the most common type of alleyway house was known as *shikumen*, a name descriptive of the main entrance of the house. The origin of the term *shikumen* is obscure and needs some explanation. Although virtually everybody in Shanghai knew the word *shikumen*, few could explain its meaning and origin. Literally, it means "a stone warehouse door"; clearly, this interpretation does not help us understand the character of the house itself. The main entrance of shikumen houses was a wooden door of two planks painted in black, with two bronze knockers, one in the middle of each plank. The door was placed within a stone framework (see illustration 5.1); hence the term *shikumen* can mean "a wooden door within a stone frame."[25]

In her recent research on Shanghai's alleyway houses, Luo Suwen gives a historical and literary interpretation of the term *shikumen*. Luo found that the term was associated with the names for entrances of palaces in ancient China. In ancient China, the standard design of the entrance to an emperor's or king's palace consisted of five layers of gates, and of the entrance to a prince's or

---

24. The terms *lilong* and *longtang* are of exactly the same meaning, but there is a slight difference in usage. *Lilong* is used on both formal and informal occasions while *longtang* is more or less slang. For instance, in post-1949 Shanghai, one of the basic neighborhood organizations based essentially on divisions of alleyway-houses was called "*lilong* residents' committees" not "*longtang* residents' committees."

25. Bureau of Social Affairs, The City Government of Greater Shanghai (comp.), *Standard of Living of Shanghai Laborers* (Shanghai: Chung Hwa [Zhonghua] Book Co., Ltd., 1934), 136. The framework was made of marble or the local red stone produced in Ningbo. Later, in order to reduce cost, these materials were often replaced by bricks. But the term *shikumen* was still popularly used, and it was not considered that the name fell short of reality because the word *shi* (stone) in the Shanghai dialect is commonly used to refer to cement and brick.

5.1. The birthplace of the Chinese Communist Party (the second house from the left). In July 1921 it was a newly constructed ordinary shikumen home in the French Concession. Note that the stone-framed wooden door, the brass knockers, the carved ornaments, and the full brick wall were all standard features of shikumen houses. This row of houses is now the CCP First National Congress Museum, a sacred site in China. From an architectural point of view, it is also Shanghai's best preserved common residential house of the early twentieth century. (Photo by Hanchao Lu)

duke's palace, three layers of gates. Each of the gates bore a special and literary name, but the outmost gate for both emperor/king's and prince/duke's palaces shared the same name: *kumen*. Thus the name of Shanghai's alleyway houses, *shikumen*, means a "stone *kumen*."[26]

Given the fact that the main entrance or the front door of the house was stone-framed, this interpretation is illuminating. Along this line of thinking, however, we may suggest that the outmost door (i.e., the *kumen*) referred not to the front door of individual houses inside the compound but instead to the entrance of the compound itself. Since a typical alleyway house was always

---

26. Luo, *Shikumen*, 18.

built inside a walled compound which had a stone-framed main entrance, it seems more likely that the word *kumen* (or the outmost door) originally referred to the gate of the compound. A newspaper advertisement for shikumen houses, which is among the earliest pieces of information about this type of house, corroborates this. It described the advertised premises as being "inside a *shikumen*," revealing that the name referred to the entrance of the compound rather than the door of individual houses.[27]

This discussion of the term *shikumen* is not offered as textual criticism, but to suggest an important social change that was occurring in Shanghai in the second half of the nineteenth century. After the turmoil of the 1860s, newly built alleyway houses were no longer temporary dwellings for refugees but stable homes for newcomers. Two decades or so after the break down of the segregation of Chinese and Europeans, the foreign concessions in Shanghai gradually gained a reputation as the "model settlements" of East Asia, and the Chinese started to see the settlements as their "happy land" (*letu*).[28] To call the main entrance of these residences "stone kumen" was to imply that these new homes, which were predominantly built in the foreign settlements, were as comfortable as a palace. At the beginning this may well have been commercial puffery, but it was also an instance of the Chinese practice of praising favorite objects with exaggerated artistic or literary expressions.[29] This love-of-home sentiment was further evidenced in the practice of giving each alleyway-house compound a distinctive name. All of the names contained the word *li* or the like (most commonly, *fang*)—words that in ancient China referred to the basic urban neighborhoods, which varied in size from 25 to 100 households.[30] The use of these words, therefore, indicated that the Chinese sojourners in the foreign settlements had started to see these alleyway-house compounds not as temporary lodgings but settled neighborhoods. The word *li* was so commonly used for naming alleyway-house compounds that, by the twentieth century, it became equivalent to "alleyway house."[31]

---

27. *Shenbao*, September 27, 1872.

28. Isabella Bird, *The Yangtze Valley and Beyond* (Boston: Beacon Press, 1987 [1899]), 15, 19.

29. For instance, the dragon and the phoenix were symbols of the emperor and the empress respectively, but the wedding of ordinary people was (and still is) commonly described by others in complimentary terms as a joining of dragon and phoenix.

30. Zhang Jishun, "Lun Shanghai lilong."

31. For instance, Augusta Wagner wrote (*Labor Legislation in China*, Yenching University, 1938): "In Shanghai the two-story *li* or alleyway house is the typical housing unit" (p.50).

A typical name for an alleyway-house compound consisted of two characters plus *li* or *fang*.[32] Names were selected by various methods. An alleyway-house compound could be named after its owner, or things related to the owner (such as his hometown), or local features (such as an old tree), or something that was significant to the owner, and so on. But by far the most common way of naming an alleyway-house compound was to use words considered auspicious or words with good connotations. Among the most common of such words were *fu* (luck), *bao* (treasure), *fu* (wealth), *gui* (noble), *qing* (celebration), *rong* (glory), *an* (tranquility), *chang* (prosperity), *ji* (auspiciousness), *shan* (kindness), *de* (virtue), *he* (peace), *kang* (healthiness), *xing* (flourishing), *xiang* (auspiciousness), and others. Sometimes a character like *yong*, *heng*, *jiu*, or *chang* (all of these characters mean "permanent," "forever," or "long") was combined with a lucky word to express the wish for everlasting happiness. For example, a popular name for an alleyway-house compound was *Yongxing Li*, meaning "Neighborhood of Perpetual Prosperity." A survey found that there were 230 alleyway-house compounds which started their name with the character *De*, 279 with the character *Fu*, and 365 with the character *Yong*.[33]

It was also popular to name alleyway-house compounds with words that contain moral meanings, such as expressions from the Confucian classics. For instance, "*mingde*" (bright virtues or "to understand virtue"), a phrase from the Confucian classic *The Great Learning* (*Daxue*), was borne by seventeen alleyway-house compounds scattered all over the city.[34] Among other popular names in this category were *Airen* (love and benevolence), *Hengde* (lasting virtue), *Huaide* (cherishing virtue), *Huairen* (cherishing benevolence), *Rende* (benevolence and virtue), and so on.[35]

To give a fine name to an alleyway-house compound was a matter of adding a touch of elegance, bestowing a blessing on a new home, and practically, establishing an everlasting advertisement. The names were inscribed and sometimes painted in red on a horizontal stone installed above the often arched entrance of the alleyway-house compound. The characters were written in regular script by a fine calligrapher. Each character was about 2 x 2 feet and could be seen from a distance. The names were also a must for postal service.

---

32. Shi Songjiu (ed.), *Shanghaishi luming daquan* (A complete guide to Shanghai street names)(Shanghai: Shanghai renmin chubanshe, 1989), 401-673.

33. Zheng Zu'an, *Shanghai diming xiaozhi* (A moderate gazetteer of Shanghai) (Shanghai: Shanghai Academy of Social Sciences Press, 1988), 73-74.

34. Shi Songjiu, *Shanghaishi luming daquan*, 540-541.

35. See Shi Songjiu, *Shanghaishi luming daquan*, 401-673, Table of the Names of Alleyway-House Compounds in the City Proper of Shanghai, passim.

Every house inside an alleyway-house compound was numbered but the compound itself was not. Instead the name of the compound was an essential part of the address. A standard home address in pre-1949 Shanghai read, in order, "name of street, plus name of alleyway-house compound, plus number of house."[36] This administrative use of alleyway-house names further strengthened the status of the compound (*lilong*) as an residential unit or a community.

One might think that a walled alleyway-house compound with an elegant name inscribed at its entrance would help create a sense of community among its residents. Such a sense would perhaps be more likely to develop if the alleyway houses had a stable group of residents who came from similar social backgrounds or places of origin. But history did not give much time for alleyway-house residents to build up such a feeling. In the first half of the twentieth century, old shikumen houses underwent a number of changes stimulated mostly by the goal of meeting the needs of residents increasingly diversified in character. New designs of alleyway houses appeared: these new designs did not replace the shikumen but made it outmoded.

From multi-bay to single-bay houses. While the general layout of Shanghai's alleyway houses—i.e., they were built in row—revealed the influence of the West, the interior layout was obviously derived from the traditional Chinese house known as the *siheyuan* (the courtyard house or quadrangle house).[37] The alleyway house consisted of a two-story central part, which contained a living room on the first floor and a master bedroom on the second floor, and wings on each side—a floor plan that could house a large family (parents with their married children) fairly comfortably. A paved and walled courtyard was located in front of the living room between the two wings, providing some space for outdoor activities. A kitchen, a servants' room, and rooms for miscellaneous purposes were located in a single-story detached structure at the back. A flat roof fenced with wooden rails was built on the top of the kitchen and/or the servants' room for drying clothes. In between the two-story front part and the single-story back part of the house, a back courtyard (a long and narrow open-air space) was reserved to provide some privacy on both sides of the residence.

---

36. This can be seen from the correspondence of many well-known figures who resided in Shanghai, including Mao Zedong. In a letter dated 1920, Mao told his friend that his address in Shanghai was "Hatong Road, Minhounan Li, number 29." (The letter is preserved in the CCP's First National Congress museum.) In the 1950s, all residential compounds were given a street number.

37. Werner Blaser, *Courtyard House in China: Tradition and Present* (Basel, Boston, Stuttgart: Birkhauser,1979),5-14; Knapp, *The Chinese House*, 11-13.

These multi-bay U-shaped shikumen houses were built mostly in the late nineteenth century, although a few were constructed early in the twentieth century. One of the earliest multi-bay shikumen compounds survived until the early 1980s. It was built in 1872, known as Xingren Li (Alley of prosperity and benevolence), and located at the core of the British Settlement in Ningbo Road one block north of Nanjing Road and two blocks west of the Bund. The shikumen complex occupied about 3.3 acres of land. The houses were not well maintained, and in the early 1980s the whole complex was torn down to make way for new construction.[38]

Anyone who is interested in the history of Shanghai may have reason to regret the disappearance of the oldest alleyway houses from the city, but practically speaking this type of house was out-of-date due to the mounting pressure of the city's population. The design of the alleyway house as row houses with contiguous walls continued, but the original design was changed in various ways to meet the increasing demand for housing in the limited space of the foreign settlements and their adjacent areas. The U-shaped alleyway house became unpopular in the early twentieth century because it required much space, an important consideration in view of Shanghai's crowded and expensive land. Instead, newly built alleyway houses in the early twentieth century were smaller. The most common way to reduce the size was to remove one of the wings. These single wing alleyway houses were called "two-bay one-wing" (*liangjian yixiang*) houses in order to distinguish them from the old U-shaped two-wing houses, which by then were known as "three-bay two-wing" (*sanjian liangxian*) houses or, in case of a three story structure, "three-up and three-down" (*sanshang sanxia*). The open space between the main building and the kitchen annex was eliminated. The kitchen was connected directly to the back of the house and became known as the "draping room" (*pijian*) or "draping kitchen" (*zaopijian*); the latter is still the word for "kitchen" in the Shanghai dialect. Furthermore, from about the late 1910s on, in many newly built houses wings were totally absent, and what had been originally the central part of the house was built as a single unit known as a "single-bay" (*dan kaijian*), or "one-up one-down" (*yishang yixia*) house (the latter because most were two stories). From then on newly built alleyway houses in the city were mostly two-story single-bay houses.[39]

---

38. Shanghai zhi zui bianweihui (Editorial Committee of the Most, the Earliest, and the Number Ones in Shanghai), *Shanghai zhi zui* (The most, the earliest, and the number ones in Shanghai) (Shanghai: Shanghai renmin chubanshe, 1990), 133.

39. Gao Chao, "Shanghai lilong zhuzhai yan'ge"(The evolution of alleyway houses in Shanghai), in *Shanghai wenshi ziliao xuanji*, no.64 (1990): 222-230; Jia You, "Shanghai longtang mian mian guan"(Various perspectives on the alleyways of Shanghai), in Benshe

Not only were the wings removed and the central part made into a single unit, but compared to the U-shaped shikumen the overall size of the single-bay house was reduced. An average two-story single-bay house occupied a lot of about 4m x 14m. Each floor was about 4m high. A number of alleyway houses built in the 1920s and 1930s were below these standards. Sometimes the lot was reduced to 3.5m x 6.5m, and the front courtyard was deleted. The height of the first floor was reduced to 3.3m, and the second floor to 3.0m.[40] These small and lower ceiling alleyway houses without a yard were called "Japanese houses," a name apparently derived from the notorious Chinese image of the Japanese as "dwarfs."[41] But the name also was connected with the fact that these houses were favorite residences for the Japanese in Shanghai. Many of these houses were built in Hongkou, the center of Shanghai's largest Japanese community. There was yet another name for these structures: "Cantonese houses." It was said that these houses resembled those of Canton. It is perhaps also because, like the Japanese, many Cantonese immigrants in Shanghai lived in this type of alleyway house, in particular, in Hongkou.[42]

However, not all changes in alleyway houses represented a deterioration. Simultaneously with the appearance of single-bay alleyway houses in the late 1910s, some newly built alleyway houses featured modern amenities, mainly, sanitary fixtures (bathrooms with a bathtub and flush toilet) and a gas supply (for cooking and hot water). These houses were called "new-type alleyway houses" (*xinshi lilong*), in order to distinguish them from the old alleyway houses (i.e., the shikumen), which usually did not have modern sanitation or gas.[43] These houses were still built in rows and belonged to the general category of alleyway houses (*lilong*). But they were usually three story houses with a front gate of iron plate, a feature which differentiated them from the "wooden door within a stone framework" (shikumen) type. Some were built in such a style that in the eyes of average Shanghainese (who were, typically, residents of the old-type alleyway houses or shikumen), they were not exactly an "alleyway house" in its classic meaning (i.e., the shikumen), but rather were associated with *yangfang* (foreign houses or Western-style houses). These

(ed.), *Shanghai zhanggu* (Historical anecdotes of Shanghai)(Shanghai: Shanghai wenhua chubanshe, 1984), 89-103.

40. Wang Shaozhou, *Shanghai jindai chengshi jianzhu*, 81.

41. Chen Congzhou and Zhang Ming (eds.), *Shanghai jindai jianzhu shigao* (A draft history of architecture in modern Shanghai) (Shanghai: Sanlian shudian, 1988),163.

42. Wang Shaozhou and Chen Zhimin, *Lilong jianzhu* (Architecture of alleyway houses)(Shanghai: Shanghai kexue jishu wenxian chubanshe, 1987), 59-60; Chen Congzhou and Zhang Ming, *Shanghai jindai jianzhu shigao*, 163.

43. Wang Shaozhou, *Shanghai jindai chengshi jianzhu*, 77; Chen Congzhou and Zhang Ming, *Shanghai jindai jianzhu shigao*, 160-165.

new-type alleyway houses were of higher quality, with a reinforced concrete structure (shikumen houses were of wood and brick), steel-sash windows, waxed hardwood floors, gates of iron wrought, a small front garden, in addition to sanitary fixtures and a gas supply. Garages were also built in the better new style alleyway house compounds, indicating that some of the residents had private automobiles. Consequently, the main lane in such compounds was widened to at least six meters, and the branch lanes to 3.5 meters.[44] Some of these houses had two bays or two-and-a-half bays to meet the requirements of well-off tenants or buyers, but most had a single-bay and were designed to house a single nuclear family.[45]

The shrinkage of alleyway houses indicated an important social change. Although available demographic data on modern Shanghai do not contain precise details on the composition of residents in terms of occupation, there is little doubt that immigrants to Shanghai in the second half of the nineteenth century were mostly well-off merchants, absentee landlords, frustrated bureaucrats and literati, skilled workers, and adventurers.[46] It was estimated that in 1860-1862 at least 6.5 million taels of silver were brought by Chinese immigrants into Shanghai's foreign concessions.[47] Shanghai at that time was seen as a place primarily for business and pleasure. The tide of immigrants who flooded into the city looking for jobs (in particular, factory jobs) had not yet come.

Well-off immigrants who came to Shanghai with their family in tow required large dwellings. As extended families were common in China, it was usual for these people in their hometown to live in a multi-generation household in a big courtyard house or, for better-off families, in a private garden-house (*tingyuan*). After moving into Shanghai's foreign settlements, these people were no longer able to have such spacious homes. But the U-shaped alleyway house was an ideal substitute for the traditional dwellings they used to live in and allowed them in some ways to continue their traditional family life in this "foreign barbarians' area" (*yichang*), as the concessions were called in those days. For an extended family, the wings of an alleyway house

---

44. Shanghaishi fangchan guanliju (Shanghai Municipal Bureau of Real Estate), *Shanghai lilong minju* (Shanghai's alleyway houses) (Beijing: Zhongguo jianzhu gongye chubanshe,1993), 26.

45. Wang Shaozhou, *Shanghai jindai chengshi jianzhu*, 81-83. For twenty detailed samples of these new style alleyway house compounds, see Shanghaishi fangchan guanliju, *Shanghai lilong minju*, 97-145.

46. Zhang Zhongli (ed.), *Jindai Shanghai chengshi yanjiu* (Research on modern Shanghai city) (Shanghai: Shanghai renmin chubanshe, 1990), 53-59, 712-752.

47. G. Lanning and S.Couling, *The History of Shanghai* (Shanghai: Kelly & Walsh, Limited, 1921), vol.II, 26.

could accommodate the married sons in such a way that the young couples could live under the same roof with their parents while still having some privacy. Some earlier alleyway houses, such as those in the Xinren Li compound, had double wings on each side, a backyard, and several annexes behind the backyard which allowed the residents to keep domestic servants.[48] While a well-off family that moved from a traditional town in Jiangnan to a Shanghai shikumen might miss the elegance of their private gardens, they could take comfort in the notion that the alleyway house was a comfortable and pragmatic urban alternative.[49] The resemblance of the early alleyway house to the traditional courtyard house was an architectural invention that catered to people's reluctance to abandon a traditional way of life.

But changes in housing patterns were inevitable when land values skyrocketed in the twentieth century.[50] As noted, Shanghai's real estate dealers soon found that the U-shaped shikumen was less popular than the two-bay one-wing house, and the latter was in turn less popular than the single-bay house. By early in this century, U-shaped alleyway houses had largely been eliminated from the foreign settlements. Alleyway houses built after the 1910s were mostly single-bay structures. The lot of an average alleyway house in the 1930s had shrunk to about one-fourth of that of U-shaped houses built in the 1870s.[51]

Simultaneously, alleyway-house compounds were getting larger. A typical alleyway-house compound in the late Qing contained 20-30 units, although some had less than ten units. By the 1920s, it was not uncommon to see alleyway-house compounds with more than a hundred houses. The construction of the largest alleyway-house compound in Shanghai, Siwen Li (Alley of gentleness), was completed in 1921. It was comprised of over 700 houses in a single walled compound.[52] Any sizable alleyway-house compound always had a main lane no less than four meters wide leading to several branch lanes, each about 2.5 meters wide—wide enough for a rickshaw to pass. As the city was always short of land, developers limited the width of alleys as much as

48. Wang Shaozhou and Chen Zhimin, *Lilong jianzhu*, 6-8.

49. Luo Suwen, *Shikumen*, 17.

50. In the less than seventy years, from 1865 to 1933, the average land value in the International Settlement had increased 26 times, from 1,318 taels per *mu* to 33,877 taels per *mu* (1 acre = 6 *mu*). See Zhang Zhongli and Chen Zhennian, *Shaxun jituan zai jiu Zhongguo*, 35-36.

51. Luo Suwen, *Shukumen*, 21.

52. Shanghaishi Jing'anqu renmin zhengfu (Governement of Jing'an District of Shanghai), *Shanghaishi Jing'anqu dimingzhi* (A gazetteer of Jing'an District of Shanghai) (Shanghai: Shanghai Academy of Social Sciences Press, 1988), 93; Luo Suwen, *Shikumen*, 21. This alleyway-house compound is still densely populated. It is located to the west of Lane 566 in Xingzha Road, Jing'an District.

possible. It was not uncommon to see some back alleys that were only 1.5 meters wide. Narrow alleys were dubbed "one thread of sky" (*yi xian tian*), after famous Mount Lingyan of Suzhou where a narrow chink between two precipitous peaks leaves the sky looking like a piece of thread.[53] Let us step back in time and look at an average single-bay alleyway house, the place called home by the majority of Shanghainese in this century. In 1937, a housing committee of the SMC surveyed Chinese houses in the International Settlement and gave the following description in its report on its "inspection of typical premises":

It is the "li" or alleyway house that is the unit in the Chinese housing system in the Settlement, and it is this type of housing that constitutes the dominant problem. This type of house has a frontage of about 12 feet, and a depth of about 40 feet, or a ground area of about 500 square feet including yard space. Thus, there are approximately 12 to 13 houses to the mow [*mu*, or one-sixth of an acre]. Roughly described, passing through the door in the outer wall is found a small courtyard designed to admit a certain amount of light and air. From the courtyard the main room is entered, which occupies the full width of the building, that is about 12 feet, and it is about 15 feet deep. A door at the far end leads to a wooden stairway. ...Beyond the stairs there is a kitchen and a small back yard. Over the main front room is an upper room of similar size. There is a small back bedroom over the kitchen, and above this again an open space intended for use as drying stage and reached by a steep stair.[54]

Half a century later, houses of this type had deteriorated due to age and generally poor maintenance, and in the building frenzy in Shanghai in the 1990s, they were torn down on a wide scale. Still, today it would not require a thirty minute walk from any place in the city to find such a house, although to locate a well maintained alleyway house compound in its original form would be more difficult. In the recent building binge, the city government decided to preserve a few authentic shikumen house compounds as relics of the type of dwelling that once housed most Shanghailanders. These protected structures have been declared off-limits to builders. Among them is Jianye Li (Alley of establishing careers), a shikumen compound constructed in 1930 in

53. Shanghaishi fangchan guanliju, *Shanghai lilong minju*, 26.
54. "Report of the Housing Committee, 1936-1937," (*Municipal Gazette of the Council for the Foreign Settlement of Shanghai*, vol.30, no.1653, March 30, 1937), 99.

the French Concession.[55] This is a sizable compound, with 260 units lined up in 22 rows and with three major entrances from the street. Our tour could start from any one of these entrances. On the stone arch spanning the entrance were inscribed three big characters: Jian-Ye-Li. Stepping inside, we find ourselves on the main alleyway, about 5 meters wide, which runs directly from the entrance. The length of alleyways varied greatly according to the size of the compound. Some compounds had just a single lane. But more commonly, a compound had a main alleyway plus a number of branch alleyways stretching from both sides of the main lane thus forming an insulated residential compound. Since houses in Jianye Li were identical, we could walk into any unit and quickly get a sense of what all the others are like.

Walking through the two-plank shikumen door of a typical unit, we first come to an open space called the *tianjing* (lit., heavenly well), which was a paved, walled, and almost square courtyard. Courtyards varied slightly in size from compound to compound; in Jianye Li, they were about 10 square meters. The *tianjing* was a place for drying clothes and other outdoor activities. Often flowerpots were placed in the yard. Sometimes a flower bed was built at the corner of the yard. The plants in the yard were perhaps the only greenery that an average Shanghai resident could enjoy on a daily basis in this urban jungle of cement. Stepping forward, through the front yard, we come to a French window beyond which lies the rectangular living room (*ketang*) of about 20 square meters, which is one of the two major rooms of the house. At the far end of the living room is a stairway, located between the living room and the kitchen at the other end of the house. The kitchen is about 10 square meters and could also be entered through a back door.

Directing our feet up the stairs, on the second floor we find a bedroom of exactly the same size as the living room right below it, that is, a rectangular room of about 20 square meters, with front windows facing to the south overlooking the courtyard. Some stylish alleyway houses built after the early 1920s replaced the front windows with a French door through which one could walk onto a small, half-roofed or open-air balcony to get a good view, but Jianye Li was not among them. Retracting our steps to the stairs, we find, halfway down the stairs, a room right on top of the kitchen. This room was known as the *tingzijian* (pavilion room): a den, or a place for study, or a room

---

55. The present-day address of Jianye Li is "Lanes 440, 456, and 496 of Jianguoxi Road." The following description of Jianye Li is based on the author's field study conducted in July 1993. For more information on Jianye Li see Shanghaishi Xuhuiqu renmin zhengfu (Government of Xuhui District of Shanghai) (comp.), *Shanghaishi Xuhuiqu dimingzhi* (A gazetteer of Xuhui District of Shanghai) (Shanghai: Shanghai Academy of Social Sciences Press, 1989), 32, and 191; Shanghaishi fangchan guanliju, *Shanghai lilong minju*, 84-85.

for miscellaneous purposes. A flat roof with waist-high walls was built on top of the pavilion room and served as a deck for drying clothes. If this was a three-story house (which was not too common among shikumen), the third floor would consist of a bedroom of the same size as the living room and a pavilion room of the same size as the kitchen, and the flat roof would be built on top of the third-floor pavilion room.[56]

The shift in popularity from multi-bay to single-bay alleyway houses was also a reflection of changes in the composition of immigrants to the city in the early twentieth century: from more social elite type of immigrants such as rich landlords, merchants, literati, bureaucrats, and the like to more commoner type of immigrants such as shop assistants, clerks, school teachers, artisans, and the like. In view of Shanghai's increasingly expensive housing market, the latter could not afford to have several generations living under one roof. The majority could only afford to keep their immediate family with them in the city. Indeed, it was not unusual for a person to leave his or her entire family back in the village and come to the city alone to pursue the "Shanghai dream." For these people, the single-bay house was a more practical and affordable proposition than the multi-bay house. Furthermore, along with the broader social changes in China brought by the New Cultural Movement and the May 4th Movement (multifaceted and far reaching nationalistic upheavals of the late 1910s and early 1920s to sweep away the old and modernize China), of which Shanghai was a powerhouse, the nuclear family became more common in the city than the multi-generation household. But the housing situation in Shanghai involved more than a change in the composition of the household. In the twentieth century, in the face of a mounting demand for housing, the single-bay house quickly became subdivided into small rooms for rent.

Compartmentalizing the shikumen. All types of alleyway houses were designed to accommodate one family per house. Such a house, even the single-bay house, was a cozy home for a couple with unmarried children. Usually the bedroom on the second floor was for the parents, and the children were accommodated in the pavilion room or, if it was a three-story house, in the third-floor bedroom. There was no dining room in a single-bay alleyway house; the family dining table was commonly put in the kitchen or living room.

However, because of the shortage of housing in Shanghai, alleyway houses were often not occupied as their designers had intended. Instead, alleyway houses commonly housed more than one family. Many houses were remodeled to create more rooms and increase floor space to accommodate tenants. These

---

56. The floor plan described above is the original design. Virtually all houses in Jianye Li had undergone some sort of remodeling to accommodate more rooms and tenants, as I will discuss below.

newly created rooms had their own particular names, which were such common knowledge in the city that it would be hard to find a single Shanghai resident ignorant of the terms. Following is a list of the reconstructions that were most commonly found in shikumen houses:[57]

1) The living room was extended to engulf what was formerly the front courtyard.

2) The living room was divided into a front living room (*qian ketang*) and a back living room (*hou ketang*).

3) The ceiling of the back living room was lowered to allow an additional room to be created between the back living room and the bedroom on the second floor. This addition was called the second loft (*er ceng ge*).

4) Like the living room, the bedroom on the second floor was divided into a front bedroom (*qianfang*) and a back bedroom (*houfang*).

5) The ceiling of the second floor was lowered to make room for a so-called false third floor (*jia san ceng*) or third loft (*san ceng ge*).

The floor area of a single-bay alleyway house that underwent such remodeling could be increased 50 percent, and a house originally designed for a family of no more than 8 or 9 could be remodeled to accommodate 15 to 20 persons, or 4 to 9 families.[58] A 1936-37 survey of housing in Shanghai conducted by the SMC found that virtually every house surveyed had undergone some sort of remodeling. The following account from the SMC report provides a graphic description on how a single-bay shikumen house with a floor area of 718 square feet and 8,077 cubic feet of space housed eight families with twenty-four persons:

The courtyard has been covered over. The main ground floor [living room] has been cut in two by a partition, and a passageway with a storage loft [the second floor loft] added above and on the side. In the front part [the front living room], about ten feet square, live the lessor [the "second landlord"] and his family, five persons in all. He customarily pays the rent of the whole house to the landlord, letting out the rest to sub-tenants ["third tenants"]. In the back portion [the back living room], about 10 ft. by 8 ft., live three persons. The kitchen has been sectioned off and three more live in a 9 ft. x 9 ft. room. Upstairs, the large front room [bedroom] has been divided into two. The front part [the front bedroom] is the best in the house for it has light and air and runs the full width of the house—it is occupied by two persons. The

---

57. See Yu Shan, "Er fangdong yu dingfei yazu" (The second landlords and rent deposits), *Shanghai wenshi ziliao xuanji*, no.64(1990):43-48.

58. Ibid.

back part [the back bedroom], smaller by reason of the passage, is home to three persons. The room over the kitchen [the pavilion room] has its advantages because it is secluded; this also is occupied by two persons. This was originally a two storeyed house, but two lofts [the third floor lofts] have been made in the slope of the roof. The front one has a height of only 5 feet in front, 7 ft. 6 in. at the apex of the roof, and is about eight feet deep; it shelters two persons. The back room, about 10 sq. ft., is right under the roof slope, is only 3 ft. high at the back and is occupied by a single person. What was the drying stage [platform] has been enclosed, and two more people live in it—about 9 sq. ft. [59]

The subdividing described in this report was typical in Republican Shanghai. Investment in old-type alleyway houses (i.e. the shikumen) stagnated after 1935; in the city's most desirable areas few new shikumen compounds were built.[60] Instead, the new-type alleyway houses that we have mentioned (with steel-framed windows, waxed floors, modern sanitary facilities, and a small front garden) were built. But the population continued to increase and the majority of people could not afford the new-type alleyway houses, and so shikumen houses were still in big demand. The solution to the limited availability of and continuing demand for the old-type alleyway house was subdivision, and more and more residents came to live in compartmentalized rooms within a single shikumen. According to the 1937 SMC report, in the International Settlement where most of Shanghai's alleyway houses were located, the numbers of families per house were:

14,310 families living one family to a house
12,874 families living two families to a house
18,945 families living three families to a house
22,764 families living four families to a house (mode)
15,435 families living five families to a house
14,028 families living six families to a house
 7,840 families living seven families to a house
 3,824 families living eight families to a house
 2,061 families living nine families to a house, and
 1,305 families living more than nine families to a house.

---

59. "Report of the Housing Committee, 1936-1937," 99-100. My interpolations (in brackets) are added to indicate the standard local terms for the rooms and tenants.
60. Zhang Zhongli and Chen Zhennian, *Shaxun jituan zai jiu Zhongguo*, 45.

The report indicated that, in some cases, a single alleyway house accommodated as many as 15 families. A concentration of four families or 24 persons per house was the rule in these neighborhoods, which gives an average of 30 square feet or 337 cubic feet per person.[61]

The crowding within shikumen became a favorite topic of literature. A local farce, "The 72 Tenants," played by the well-known comic actors Yang Huasheng and Lu Yang, tells of the life of tenants in a shikumen house. The farce was so well received that the term "72 tenants" became a synonym for sharing rooms in the crowded shikumen houses of Shanghai. The plots of a number of Chinese movies produced in the late 1940s that later became classics, such as *Wanjia denghuo* (Lights in thousands of families) and *Wuya yu maque* (The crow and the sparrows), were based on neighborhood life in crowded shikumen houses.[62]

Second Landlords (*Er fangdong*)

Rooms in a compartmentalized shikumen house were not rented out by the owners but subletted by tenants. Standard lease contracts in Shanghai had a clause prohibiting subletting without the owner's permission, but this rule remained largely on paper.[63] After renting a house from the owner, as long as the tenant paid the rent, there was little interaction between the landlord and the tenant. There was no manager or leasing office on the premises; an owner might just hire a gate guard whose main responsibilities were to sweep the alleyway and collect rent. Nobody was on the site acting on the landlord's behalf to watch for subletting. Actually, subletting without the lessor's consent was permitted by law. According to code 312 of the Civil Law of the Shanghai Mixed Court: "If during the term of the lease the lessee sub-lets the leased thing to a third party, he must (first) obtain the consent of the lessor, unless there is any custom to the contrary."[64] In other words, *custom* prevailed.

It seems that subletting was not a controversial issue in landlord-tenant relations in Shanghai prior to the end of 1920s. By the early twentieth century subletting had already been a common practice, and the expression "second

61. "Report of the Housing Committee, 1936-1937," 98.

62. Shen Weibing and Jiang Ming, *Ala Shanghairen* (We are Shanghainese) (Shanghai: Fudan University Press, 1993), 29; Cao Maotang and Wu Lun, *Shanghai yingtan huajiu* (Reminiscences on Shanghai's movie industry) (Shanghai: Shanghai wenyi chubanshe, 1987), 206-209.

63. Chen Yanlin, *Shanghai dichan daquan* (A complete book of Shanghai real estate) (Shanghai: Shanghai dichan yanjiusuo,1933), 337.

64. A.M.Kotenev, *Shanghai: Its Mixed Court and Council* (Shanghai: North China Daily News & Herald, 1925), 468.

landlord" (*er fangdong*), which referred to tenants who sublet rooms to others, was already in common use. Bao Tianxiao, a well-known journalist and writer, came to Shanghai from his hometown of Suzhou in 1906. Since he planned a long stay, he started to look for a house. He spent three days looking along the newly constructed roads (today's Huanghe Road and Fengyang Road) toward the west end of Nanjing Road where a number of shikumen compounds had been recently built, and finally came across a shikumen compound with a notice pasted on the entrance announcing there was a room for rent. Bao walked into the alley and found the house:

I knocked at the door and stepped in. I saw an eighteen or nineteen year old girl sitting quietly in the living room making shoes. I noticed that she was a pretty girl (and according to psychologists, this very first impression indicated that things were moving forward favorably). I explained my purpose and an old lady came out to greet me. She brought me upstairs to look at the room. This was a two-bay two-story house, and the room for rent was the wing on the second floor. Because this was a new house the walls were clean. The wing faced east and had a window at the back, which made the room cool in the summer. Everything looked fine and I felt satisfied.

When I asked about the rent, the old lady, who was the second landlord, at first did not answer. Instead, she asked me questions about my family, occupation, native place, etc., and I answered accordingly, which seemed to satisfy her. She told me her family had five members. She and her husband had a daughter, who was the girl I just saw, and they also had a son and a daughter-in-law. Although their native place was Nanjing, they spoke the Suzhou dialect because their in-law was a native of Suzhou. She said: "We like a quiet life. Tenants with a big family would bring bustle and we would decline them. You, sir, are an intellectual and, in addition, you are a native of Suzhou. I therefore would not ask for an unfair price—the monthly rent is seven dollars." I agreed with the rent immediately. I paid two dollars as a deposit and asked them to remove the "for rent" notice right away.[65]

A few important points can be gleaned from this account of renting a dwelling in early twentieth century Shanghai. First, it seems that subletting was an accepted and common practice. In the first place, Bao was looking to sublet rather than to rent an entire house directly from the owner. The fact that the Cai

---

65. Bao Tianxiao, *Chuanyinglou huiyilu* (A memoir of the "Bracelet Shadow Tower") (Taipei: Wenhai chubanshe, N.d. [reprint]), 315-316.

family (i.e., the second landlord), posted an ad at the entrance of the compound where they lived indicated that they did not scruple to publicize the subletting in the neighborhood, which further suggested that subletting was not regarded as an infringement on the owner's rights, otherwise the Cai family would at least have tried to post the ad somewhere else. In fact, to post a for-rent sign was the most common way of finding a tenant in Shanghai. Such an advertisement, known as a "call for rent" (*zhaozu*), was customarily a piece of red paper, equivalent to about one quarter of a sheet of 8.5"x11" paper, on which the location and size of the available rental were written by brush. Such notices were often posted at the entrance of the lane, or on the telephone poles in the streets nearby.[66]

Bao regarded the seven dollar rent as reasonable, although it almost equaled a month's income for an average factory worker. The range of monthly wages for workers in one of the major flour mills in Shanghai at that time, for example, was 7.5-10 dollars.[67] In some less desirable areas outside of the central part of the International Settlement, such as Hongkou, the rent for a house let directly by an owner averaged three to four dollars a month in 1906.[68] The Cais' shikumen house, although new, was not located in the best residential area of that time. The rent that the Cai family asked for must not have been merely a share of rent but had to include a profit. In other words, subletting in early twentieth-century Shanghai was already a profitable business.

The Cai family's preference for a Suzhou tenant showed that native place or local origin (*jiguan*) played some role in choosing one's neighbors and tenants. In this story, the fact that the Cais, who hailed from Nanjing, adopted their daughter-in-law's Suzhou dialect suggests a social favoring of people of Jiangnan origins, in contrast to the bias against Subei people that developed in later times in the city.[69] But the preference for having neighbors with the same

---

66. Jia You, "Shanghai longtang mian mian guan," 102; Xia Lingeng, *Jiu Shanghai sanbai liushi hang* (The three hundred and sixty professions in old Shanghai) (Shanghai: East China Normal University Press, 1989), 166.

67. Shanghaishi liangshiju (Shanghai Municupal Bureau of Food Grains), Shanghai gongshang xingzheng guanliju (Shanghai Municipal Bureau of Industry and Commerce), and Shanghai shehui kexueyuan jingji yanjiusuo jingjishi yanjiushi (Economic History Division of the Institute of Economics, Shanghai Academy of Social Sciences](comps.), *Zhongguo jindai mianfen gongye shi* (A history of the flour industry in modern China)(Beijing: Zhonghua shuju, 1987), 323-324.

68. Xu Run, *Xu Yuzhai zixu nianpu* (An auto-chronicle of Xu Yuzhai](Taipei: Shihuo chubanshe, 1977), 234.

69. Although geographically Nanjing is located south of the Yangzi River, by custom people of Nanjing origin were often regarded as "half Subei" people. This may be partly because the Nanjing dialect is sufficiently different from major Jiangnan dialects such as the

local origins was never strong enough to create native-place based segregated alleyway house neighborhoods. Some districts of Shanghai were known for some degree of concentration of people who came from similar native places. For instance, North Sichuan Road in Hongkou was known for its concentration of Cantonese residents. But many others, including Japanese, also lived in the same area. Segregation by local origins (mainly segregation of Subei people) could be found in the city's peripheral shantytowns,[70] but it never existed in the city's vast alleyway-house neighborhoods. Researchers of modern Chinese socioeconomic history have in recent years paid increasing attention to the role of local origin in Chinese society (in particular, in large cities). But in an important dimension of social life in Shanghai—choice of place of residence—local origin was insignificant, at least for the majority of the people. It was rare to see a single alleyway house—much less a whole alleyway-house compound—inhabited by families of the same local origin.[71]

One thing that caused people of different local origins to live together was that, in an environment of mounting population pressure, most Shanghai residents simply could not afford to pick and choose their neighbors on the basis of local origins. The first three decades of the twentieth century saw the most rapid population increase in the city's history. At the turn of the century, Shanghai's population had not reached one million; by 1930, over three million people lived in the city, mostly in the foreign concessions.[72] These three decades were the golden age for Shanghai's shikumen houses. Among the 108 shikumen compounds located in the core of the Nanjing Road area (which, today is known as the Nanjingdong Road Ward) where the first shikumen were built, 98 were constructed between 1902 and 1931.[73] But, as I have suggested, the availability of housing lagged far behind demand and, consequently, subletting became very common.[74] By the late 1920s, second landlords had gradually become the major players in leasing dwellings in the city, and continued to be so in the 1930s and 1940s. As a result, a tenant leasing a room from a second landlords was known as the "third tenant" (*san fangke*) and the owner of the house was called the "big landlord" (*da fangdong*). By the early

---

Suzhou dialect and close to Subei dialects.

70. Emily Honig, *Creating Chinese Ethnicity: Subei People in Shanghai, 1850-1980* (New Haven and London: Yale University Press, 1992), 44-45.

71. Interviews with alleyway house residents, July 14, July 16, and August 6, 1993.

72. Zou Yiren, *Jiu Shanghai renkou bianqian*, 90.

73. Shanghaishi Huangpuqu renmin zhengfu (Government of Huangpu District of Shanghai)(comp.), *Shanghaishi Huangpuqu dimingzhi* (A gazetteer of Huangpu District of Shanghai)(Shanghai: Shanghai Academy of Social Sciences Press, 1989), 211-223.

74. Liu Fengsheng. "Buke siyi de Shanghai yi shi zhu" (The inconceivable clothing, food, and housing of Shanghai), *Shenghuo* (Life), 2,3(November 1926):17.

1930s, these appellations had already become popular and they remained what an informant called a "Shanghai specialty" (*Shanghai techan*) throughout the Republican period.[75]

A key element that contributed to the rise of subletting was the appearance of the so-called take-over fee (*dingfei*) as a requirement for renting. The take-over fee was originally compensation paid by a new tenant to a previous tenant who had left some fixtures or furniture in the house. Because these things were useful to a new tenant but cumbersome for an old tenant to have to move, the payment was a mutually beneficial arrangement welcomed by both parties. The fee was supposedly voluntary, and was usually less than half the original price of the materials left behind. This custom probably started from the late nineteenth century when renting (rather than purchasing) a house had become common in the city. But the nature of the fee gradually changed. By the late 1920s, this kind of courtesy between tenants had already become something belonging to the "good old days," and take-over fees became a standard and non-refundable charge for renting.[76]

To rent a shikumen house in the early 1930s a tenant had to pay the landlord a take-over fee which usually equalled about two to three month's rent. A shrewd tenant saw the take-over fee as an investment, because the rental was not only his own residence but also a business opportunity. After renting the house, he could sublet rooms and out of the rents he collected from the subletting he could soon recoup the take-over fee. After that, the difference between the rent he paid the "big landlord" and the rent he collected from the "third tenants" was a constant source of income. Being a second landlord was therefore a popular business in Republican-era Shanghai.

In addition to the ambiguity of the legal codes regarding subletting in Shanghai's real estate market that I have mentioned above, the city's special situation as a treaty port also contributed to the second landlord practice. According to an early agreement between the Shanghai daotai Gong Mujiu and the British consul George Balfour, rental contracts in the foreign settlement had to be registered with the consulate and endorsed (sealed) by the daotai,

---

75. Wang Weizhu, *Shanghaishi fangzu zhi yanjiu* (Research on house rent in Shanghai)(Taipei: Chengwen chuban gongsi, 1977 [reprint of a 1933 manuscript]); Yu Shan, "Er fangdong yu dingfei yazu;" Luo Suwen, *Shikumen*, 30-31.

76. Zi. "Erfangdong zhi xinji" (The calculation of the second landlords), *Shanghai Shenghuo* (Shanghai life), 3,1(January 1939):16-17. Yu Shan, "Er fangdong yu dingfei yazu"; Du Li. "'Baimayi' yu erfangdong" ("The 'termites' and the second-landlords,") in Tang Weikang et al. (eds.), *Shanghai yishi* (Shanghai: Shanghai wenhua chubanshe, 1987), 275-284.

hence the name *daoqi* (title deed sealed by the daotai).[77] Before 1890, only foreigners were permitted to hold title. A Chinese who wished to purchase land in the settlement thus had to go through a foreign registrant. Later, the provision was abolished but Chinese land buyers still preferred to have their property registered in the name of a foreigner in order to avoid exposure to the corruption and legal ambiguities that frequently occurred under the Chinese authorities. The result was a booming business run by Shanghai's Westerners acting as registrants for real estate actually owned by Chinese. These Westerners, known as "foreign registration merchants" (*guahao yangshang*), charged ten taels of silver as an annual fee. As a result, an alleyway-house compound often had two owners: one, the "registered owner," that is the foreigner under whose name the daoqi was issued, and the other, the "beneficial owner" who was the real, Chinese owner.[78] The ambiguity of ownership made it almost impossible for the real owner to sue because of subletting, for ownership itself may have been legally in doubt. Furthermore, an alleyway-house compound had only one title deed, in spite of the fact that it may have contained dozens of houses. To purchase an individual house within an alleyway-house compound thus involved the compound owner issuing a "certificate of ownership" (*quanbing dan*) indicating that the house was registered as part of the compound but was actually owned by the purchaser. This type of transfer of ownership was widely practiced during the Sino-Japanese War but, since it often involved the "foreign registration merchants" acting on the behalf of Chinese absentee landlords who had left Shanghai at the beginning of the war, it further complicated the issue of ownership.[79] The most important reason for subletting without interference from the owner was, however, that the take-over fee continued increasing in the Republican era and by the early 1940s it was close to the purchase price. Once the tenant paid the fee, it was mutually understood (without being spoken, and never put in writing) that he had the privilege (if not the right) to sublet the house at a profit.

The subletting boom brought brokers into the business. Brokers earned commissions by introducing house owners and renters. But brokers' main

---

77. In January 1930, the name was officially changed to "permanent rental contract" (*yong zu qi*), but the term *daoqi* continued in use until 1949. See Zhang Xiaobo,"Shanghai Daoqi kao" (An empirical study of title deeds sealed by the Daotai), in *Shanghai difangshi ziliao*, vol. 2, 98-107.

78. Ye Shumei,"Shanghai zujie de fangdichan maimai zhidu" (The real estate market system in Shanghai's foreign concessions), in *Shanghai difangshi ziliao*, vol.3, 177-182.

79. Jin Xuan. "Shanghai fangdichan chanquan pingzheng pouxi" (An analysis of real estate title certificates in Shanghai), in *Shanghai wenshi ziliao xuanji*, 64(1990): 31-38; Ye Shumei, "Shanghai zujie de fangdichan maimai zhidu," 180.

interest was not to earn a commission based on the monthly rent but to get a commission on the take-over fee. Brokers in this business were called "termites," an epithet reflecting exactly how people felt about them. Advertisements by *dingwu gongsi* (companies for "taking over" houses) appeared every day in Shanghai's newspapers in the 1940s. Such companies amounted to no more than an office (which was often rented not owned), a telephone, and a notebook to record information about clients. But companies like this were by no means the most obscure ones in the business. In fact, the majority of the "termites" were, to use a popular term in present-day China, "go-it-alone individual enterprises" (*dan'gan geti hu*). Most "termites" conducted their business in teahouses. Two of Shanghai's famous teahouses, Tongyuchun in Nanjing Road and Chunfeng Deyi Lou in the Yu Garden of the old Chinese city, were particularly favored by brokers. A Shanghai resident recalled: "Everyday when dawn broke and the city was still asleep, these teahouses were already full of customers. The great majority of these customers were the 'termite' type of rental brokers. They came here every day just like workers go to their early shifts. Over a cup of tea and a piece of cake, they exchanged information with each other. In the conversations they all attempted to gain as much information as they could and grudgingly gave information to others. But as long as there were no conflicts of interest they liked to exchange information, because more information meant a better chance to have more business, and more business meant a lot of commissions."[80]

The speculation in subletting was greatly stimulated by the wars that occurred in Shanghai and its vicinity in the Republican period. The Wusong-Shanghai War of 1932, commonly referred to by Shanghai residents as the "128" war (January 28, read as "1-2-8"), brought a tide of refugees to Shanghai and contributed to a boom in the subletting business. As an author commented in 1933: "Last year when the January 28 War occurred in the Chinese districts, the Special Districts [i.e. the International Settlement and the French Concessions] ordered a reduction of rents for three months [in order to guarantee affordable housing for refugees]. The 'big landlords' were like 'a dumb person tasting bitter herbs' [i.e., unable to complain]. But the 'second landlords' beamed with a smile—'A Pavilion Room For Rent for $20 a Month,' 'A Third Floor Loft For Rent for $18 a Month'—the paste underneath these posters had not yet dried before these rooms were already gone!"[81]

This wartime housing crush was repeated, with even more severity, in the 1940s. The Sino-Japanese War of 1937-45 and the Civil War of 1946-49,

---

80. Du Li, "'Baimayi' yu erfangdong."
81. Wang Zhuwei, *Shanghaishi fangzu zhi yanjiu*, 50392.

although each at the beginning brought a temporary set-back to commerce in the city, did not end the prosperity of Shanghai. Quite the opposite; the so-called Solitary Island (*gudao*) period (1938-1941) and the mid-1940s were among the most flourishing periods in the city's history. A huge population, rich and poor, poured into Shanghai from everywhere seeking a relatively safe haven. Most of the new alleyway houses with modern facilities were built in the late 1930s and the 1940s, but their numbers were far from sufficient to meet the demand for housing. As mentioned earlier, these new-type alleyway houses were mostly rented or purchased by well-off families. Very few old-type alleyway houses (*shikumen*) were built after 1940, which meant that the majority of the population—which by 1949 was close to 5.5 million—had to jam into the shikumen houses that were built before 1935. Under this situation, the second landlord business boomed. It was in the 1940s that the take-over fee was no longer equivalent to a few months' rent but was close to the purchase price.[82]

A researcher of Shanghai's real estate pointed out in the early 1930s: "The biggest creditors in the market were landlords, and the most serious debts were rents. In our people's daily life, the number one expense is rent for housing."[83] For the common people, the biggest creditors were the "second landlords" rather than the "big landlords." It was estimated that in working-class shikumen neighborhoods, second landlords controlled 99 percent of the rentals.[84] An average factory worker or shop assistant paid 20 to 40 percent of his or her income to rent a kitchen, a pavilion room, or a loft of less than 10 square meters (about 108 square feet): in such a single room the whole family lived.[85] Because of the extreme shortage of housing in wartime Shanghai, Shanghai's second landlords exhausted virtually every possible way to subdivide and compartmentalize rooms for renting. Remodeling, such as adding a number of "lofts" underneath the roof, was common everywhere in alleyway-house neighborhoods. Even a few pieces of tinplate could form a room on the flat

---

82. Ye Shumei, "Shanghai zujie de fangdichan maimai zhidu," 180.

83. Chen Yanlin, *Shanghai dichan daquan*, 327-329.

84. Shanghai jiqiye gongren yundong shi bianshen weiyuanhui (Committee for the history of the labor movement in Shanghai's machinery industry), *Shanghai jiqiye gongren yundong shi* (A history of the labor movement in Shanghai's machinery industry)(Beijing: Zhonggong dangshi chubanshe, 1991), 56-57.

85. Shanghai shehui kexueyuan jingji yanjiusuo (Institute of Economics, Shanghai Academy of Social Sciences), *Shanghai Yong'an gongsi de chansheng, fazhan he gaizao* (The birth, development, and transformation of the Shanghai Yong An Company)(Shanghai: Shanghai renmin chubanshe, 1981), 190-191.

Table 5.1

Subletting in Republican Shanghai

(Samples from an early 1950s survey)

Time of leasing:	Before 1938	1938-1945	1948
Number of tenant households:	383	1,198	568
Number of tenant household leasing as "third tenants":	258	910	482
Percentage of "third tenants":	67%	76%	85%

Source: Adapted from Yu Shan, "Er fangdong yu dingfei yazu."

roof on top of a pavilion room. In some extreme cases second landlords rented their lofts by the bunk (or berth) space, as if they were running a little inn.[86]

For the majority of the people of Shanghai, who could not afford to rent a whole house, the second landlord was a person they generally disliked but could not avoid in their daily life. A comment on second landlords made by a journalist perhaps represented the general sentiment of Shanghai residents: "If you want to figure out who are the most scheming people in Shanghai, the conclusion should be that they are the second landlords."[87] In spite of the ill reputation of the second landlords, money still counted, and many tenants found that being a second landlord was an attractive way of making money. Toward the end of the Republican period when the civil war drove hundreds of thousands of people into Shanghai, even "third tenants" tried hard to sublet their rooms. According to *Shenbao*, it was not unusual in the late 1940s for a third tenant who lived in a wing to divide the room into three (namely, a "front wing," "middle wing," and "back wing"). Typically, the third tenant family lived in the front wing, and sublet the middle and back wings. No wonder in these years when people paid a New Year's visit to friends and relatives (by custom, after exchanging greetings people wished each other well for the New Year), they commonly offered the felicitation, "May you become a second landlord this year!"[88]

---

86. Su Zi, "Shanghairen" (Shanghai people), *Shanghai shenghuo* (Shanghai life), 3, 11 (1939):17-19.
87. Hua Zi, "Erfangdong zhi xinji."
88. *Shenbao*, March 8, 1948.

The Shikumen Mélange

A mixture of residents. Although second landlords were often only grudgingly accepted by the general public and criticized by some indignant intellectuals as an "exploiting class,"[89] they were indeed no more than a group of "little urbanites" (*xiaoshimin*) who sacrificed the comfort of their homes to offset some of their rent, to supplement the family income, or to make a living. Their financial situation was not necessarily better than that of the third tenants who rented rooms from them. It was common for second landlords and their family to live in the less desirable (if not the worst) part of the house (such as the kitchen, loft, or back room) in order to rent out the better parts of the house (such as the front bedroom, front living room, and pavilion room). There was no clear line of class or social rank dividing these landlords and their tenants.

Indeed, shikumen residents came from all walks of life and had widely different backgrounds. Sociologists may have some difficulty in trying to classify them according to conventional sociological criteria. In post-1949 China, the Communists' labeling of these residents according to the Party's standards of social class was purely for the purpose of orchestrating political campaigns, and in no way reflected objective reality.[90] It was precisely the differences among these people (whether differences in class, occupation, local origin, etc.) and the similarity of their residences that characterized Shanghai's alleyway-house neighborhoods. These neighborhoods may not have been a melting pot, but they were certainly, to use another figure of speech, a Chinese wok that was ideal for stir-frying—a place where a great variety of people were tossed together to produce a saute (*chaocai*): it is this I call "the shikumen mélange."

Xia Yan's classic drama, *Under the Eaves of Shanghai* (Shanghai wuyan xia), which describes the lives of a group of shikumen residents in the 1930s, can serve as a vivid showcase of the shikumen mix. A typical single-unit shikumen house located in East Shanghai (Hudong) is the setting of this three-act tragicomedy. According to the author, the drama was based on his personal experience in Shanghai's shikumen houses. He himself had lived under "these kinds of eaves" for more than ten years before he wrote the story in the spring of 1937, intending to tell of the "grief and joy of those small

---

89. Wang Weizhu, *Shanghaishi fangzu zhi yanjiu*, 50391.
90. Examples of class labelling and political campaigns in the PRC can be found in Lynn T. White III, *Policies of Chaos: The Organizational Causes of Violence in China's Cultural Revolution* (Princeton: Princeton University Press, 1989), 10-15, and *passim* on the situations in Shanghai.

figures in this abnormal society of Shanghai."[91] The author's familiarity with the lives of the characters which he created and his intention of reflecting real life in Shanghai give this celebrated work the merit of realism, and it is therefore worthy of discussion in the context of an historical analysis.

The inhabitants of the house in Xia's story are a microcosm of Shanghai's shikumen residents. Lin Zhicheng (aged 36), the "second landlord," who lived in the living room, was a clerk in the payroll office of a cotton mill. An elementary school teacher, Zhao Zhenyu (aged 48), lived in the kitchen with his wife (aged 42) and two children (son aged 13, and daughter aged 5). The pavilion room (*tingzijian*) was rented by a college graduate Huang Jiamei (aged 28) and his wife (aged 24). Huang had been an office worker in a foreign-owned company but had been recently laid off. The bedroom, which was the main room of a shikumen house, was rented by a seaman's wife, Shi Xiaobao (aged 27 or 28). Her husband's occupation often kept him away, and the lonely young lady supported herself as a "half-open" prostitute (or, to use a euphemism applied to this kind of prostitute at that time in Shanghai, a "modern lady"). She occupied the best room of the house for the convenience of her clients. A dark loft underneath the bedroom (the so-called second loft) was the home of a newspaper seller, Li Lingbei (aged 54), who was single and an alcoholic.[92]

Such a variety of residents in a single shikumen house was not merely the result of the exercise of artistic license, but reflected real life in Shanghai's alleyway-house neighborhoods. Within about 50 square meters of floor space, dwellings like this normally housed three to five families, or about a dozen residents of all sorts of backgrounds.[93] A mix of residents in a single alleyway house was evident everywhere in the city, but it was particularly apparent in shikumen neighborhoods. A year after Xia Yan wrote his drama, a school teacher published an essay describing what he called "ten views from a loft," namely, ten households that lived in a compartmentalized single-bay shikumen

---

91. Xia Yan, *Shanghai wuyan xia* (Under the eaves of Shanghai) (Beijing: Zhongguo xiju chubanshe, 1957),88.

92. Xia Yan, *Shanghai wuyan xia*; Biweng, "*Shanghai wuyanxia* jiantao" (A review of "Under the eaves of Shanghai"), *Shanghai shenghuo* (Shanghai life), 4,8 (August 1940):34-37.

93. Four square meters per person was about the average dwelling space for the people of Shanghai in the late 1940s. Up to 1990, four square meters (43 square feet) per person was still a cut-off figure for the allocation of houses in Shanghai. Families with floor space below that figure were classified as "households in difficulty" (*kunnan hu*). See Shanghaishi zhufang zhidu gaige lingdao xiaozu bangongshi (Office of reforming the Shanghai housing system) (comp.), *Shanghai zhufang zhidu gaige* (Reforming the housing system of Shanghai)(Shanghai: Shanghai renmin chubanshe, 1991 [restricted version]), 75-76.

similar to that described by Xia Yan. Using a plain style of writing, the author offered a sort of record of "all mortal beings" in Shanghai's alleyway-house neighborhoods. Here is a sketch of the residents by the order of the rooms they occupied:

1) Front Living Room: a policeman with his wife and two teenage daughters. The policeman, a Shandong native, was also a money-lender; most of his clients were peddlers who lived nearby.

2) Back Living Room: a couple with three children. The couple were teachers in an elementary school inside the alleyway (a so-called "alleyway school"). They became romantically involved when the wife was a student of the husband. But the romance was ruined by being "married, with children." The author complained that the couple often quarreled, the wife cursed and cried, and the children made all sorts of noise.

3) Second Floor Bedroom: shared by two dancing girls and a tourist girl (guide). They stayed home in the morning and worked afternoons or nights. Sometimes they came back home after midnight or at dawn. The author admitted that he often felt aroused by his young female neighbors who lived so close to him in the same house: "Every time I saw them walk up and down the stairs, their breasts and hips undulating like waves, my heart beat faster."

4) Second Floor Loft (between the back living room and the second floor bedroom): a cobbler and his wife, both from Subei. Everyday the cobbler shouldered his bamboo carrying pole and walked to nearby alleyways to ply his trade: repairing and making shoes. His wife just loafed or played mahjong with neighbors. She was quite unaware that her idleness had become a topic of discord for her neighbors, the couple (the school teachers) who lived downstairs in the back living room. The wife blamed the husband for failing to give her a better life, saying the cobbler had a low-class occupation but he nevertheless was able to let his wife enjoy her life.

5) Third Floor Bedroom: a woman in her early thirties who had a full-time live-in maid cum companion. The woman was an opium addict, stayed home most of the time and supported herself by being a mistress.

6) Kitchen: the second-landlord, a man in his fifties, and his young wife who was in her late twenties. The wife, a Suzhou native, was a shrewd woman who dominated their household. The man seems to have spent his leisure time by going to a Suzhou storyteller's theater every day.

7) The Flat Roof: a single man who was a proofreader for a newspaper.

8) Third Floor Pavilion Room: a Suzhou native in her twenties who was stage actress (of modern dramas, *wenming xi*) and her husband, an opium addict who just idled about and was supported by his wife.

9) Second Floor Pavilion Room: four young men who were waiters in a Western-style restaurant. They often dressed in white Western suits and

boasted that their work clothing was "better than what university students wear." These young men and the second floor girls often teased and flirted with each other in the pavilion room.

10) Third Floor Loft: the author, a schoolteacher who lost his job because the elementary school where he taught was bombed by the Japanese during the August 13 incident of 1937. He moved into this shikumen house in the International Settlement and worked as a free lance writer to support his family.[94]

Shikumen houses like this could be found in most parts of the city but they were particularly common in the central and northeast parts of the International Settlement which included the busy commercial center of the city around Nanjing Road and the factory and dock areas in Yangshupu northeast to the Huangpu River. In these areas and elsewhere in the city factory workers were found in shikumen neighborhoods. The majority of Shanghai's factory workers (aside from casual employees) resided in shikumen houses, not in the city's squalid shantytowns. Shanghai's industrial areas like those in Yangshupu and Huxi (West Shanghai) had some concentration of factory worker residents, but even there factory workers lived in shikumen with people of various other callings. Elsewhere in the city shikumen houses were the most common residence of factory workers of all sorts.[95] Pavilion rooms, for instance, were popular among factory workers because of their relatively cheap rent and secluded position in the house.

Pavilion rooms in some way were a symbol of life of Shanghai. This small room of about ten square meters was sometimes jokingly referred as the "immediate supervisor" (*dingtou shangsi*) of the kitchen for it was always built above the kitchen. Like all Chinese houses, the front rooms of an alleyway house (i.e., the first floor living room and the second floor bedroom) were so designed, wherever possible, to face the south so that the main rooms would be warm in winter and cool in summer and have ample light. Thus, the pavilion room at the back of the house often faced the least favorable direction, the north, and could enjoy sunlight only on steamy hot summer days. But the room was located right off the middle landing of the staircase towards the second floor, had its own entrance, and was not adjacent to other rooms. For roughly

---

94. Xiangyu, "Gelou shijing" (Ten views from a loft), *Shanghai shenghuo* (Shanghai life), 2,3 (August 1938): 11-13.

95. Yang Ximeng, *Shanghai gongren shenghuo chengdu de yige yanjiu* (A study of the standard of living of Shanghai labors) (Beiping [Beijing]: Shehui diaochasuo, 1930), 71-73; Bureau of Social Affairs, *Standard of Living of Shanghai Laborers*, 54-56; Zhu Bangxing, Hu Lin'ge, and Xu Sheng, *Shanghai chanye yu Shanghai zhigong* (Industries and workers in Shanghai) (Shanghai: Shanghai renmin chubanshe, 1984 [Originally published by Yuandong chubanshe (Hong Kong) in 1939]), *passim.*

the same rent—seven to eight dollars in a moderately desirable neighborhood in the thirties—most tenants would choose a pavilion room over a back living room or a back bedroom. Consequently, pavilion rooms were known for the diversity of their dwellers in these already very diverse neighborhoods. One could find office clerks of all sorts, factory workers, apprentices, college and high school students, free lance writers, and what might call "intellectual vagrants" of all types such as unemployed or self-employed artists, dramatists, musicians, and so on.[96] The very name, "pavilion room," seems to suggest that the room was small but cozy like a pavilion in a traditional Chinese garden.

This type of room was, in particular, the home for many of Shanghai's educated single youths who were typically from a small rural town and sojourned in the city looking for a career (mostly, in literature, journalism and education). Their small income limited them to renting a pavilion room. One such sojourner recalled that during the eight years that he had lived in Shanghai, except for two years during which he lived in a dormitory provided by his employer, his home was always a pavilion room. He seems to have missed his life there, not only because the pavilion room was the place where he entertained all his lady friends but, more memorably, because of the numerous evenings he spent with young men like himself:

After supper a group of my friends who were lonely would come over to my place to chat. The little room was full of people—chairs and my tiny iron-framed bed were occupied by one buttock after another. We were smoking cigarettes, laughing and wrangling. Everyone felt free, being unrestrained and undisciplined. The topics we talked about were even more unlimited: from the Three and Five Emperors in remote ages to the decline of Xuantong [the last emperor of the Qing]; from Mr. Sun Yat-sen's revolution to the treason of Chen Jiongming; from Mussolini and Hitler to Stalin and Roosevelt; from "Manchukuo" to the Japanese warlords. If we tired of current political affairs, we would shift the subject to the life and folk customs of various places, from Beiping to Nanjing, from Shanghai to Guangzhou, from Hangzhou to Hong Kong, from Suzhou to Yangzhou. And, inevitably, the topic shifted to women. Starting from female students, we would go all the way to concubines, social butterflies, dancing girls, massage girls, prostitutes, waitresses, and country girls. Along this line, the topic would become the "wife issue," and all of us would join in the debate about one's taste in

---

96. Duojiugong, "Shanghai tingzijian jiepou tu" (An examination of Shanghai's pavilion rooms), *Shanghai shenghuo* (Shanghai life), 2,2(July 1938):1-2.

choosing a spouse. Or, we might sigh, stroking the beard on our chin, and feel full of self-pity.

But these young men also felt burden free, being single as they were in Shanghai. Without a family around, the happy gathering often went on after midnight. On a fine night, they would take a stroll in the streets and alleyways nearby and go back to the pavilion room, and the talking would continue. Whenever their pocket money allowed, drink and a potluck meal crowned these gatherings.[97]

It was from this kind of lifestyle that came some of Republican China's finest "literary youth" (*wenxue qingnian*). Recalling them and some of their seniors is like entering a gallery of twentieth century China's most prominent writers: Lu Xun (1881-1936), Mao Dun(1896-1981), Ba Jin (1904-), Yu Dafu (1896-1945), Liang Shiqiu (1903-1987), Zou Taofen (1895-1944), and so on. All had lived and wrote in a pavilion room. Although the room was small and, as one writer put it, "if these people sit and talk in the same room they end up breathing the carbon dioxide that comes out of each others mouths,"[98] it was nevertheless a happy nest for many intellectuals. In 1933, Qu Qiubai (1899-1935), the Communist intellectual and leader, lived in a pavilion room in Number 12 Dongzhao Li (Alley of eastern lights), within walking distance of Lu Xun's home in Number 9 Dalu Xincun (New village continent). Qu's wife, Yang Zhihua, recalled that her husband's friendship with Lu Xun was built in the pavilion room: "Almost everyday Lu Xun paid us a visit. He chatted with Qiubai on various subjects— politics, current news, and literature—and we enjoyed having him as if we had fresh air and warm sunlight in a boundless world. Qiubai was a quiet person, but every time he saw Lu Xun he immediately changed his mood. They talked happily and sometimes laughed heartily, breaking the stuffy air of the pavilion room. We were always reluctant to let Lu Xun leave, but every time after he left, his laugh, happiness and warmth still remained in our little pavilion room."[99] Lu Xun himself was part of this "pavilion room" type of life. All his residences in Shanghai, with one exception, had a pavilion room. He worked the fanciful name of his study in his Hongkou residence, *Qie jie ting*, meaning, the "Semi-Concession

---

97. Si Ying, "Tingzijian de shenghuo" (Life in the pavilion room), *Shanghai shenghuo*, 1,1(March 1937):24-25.

98. Wang Guanquan (ed.), *Huainian Xiao Hong* (Cherishing the memory of Xiao Hong) (Harbin: Heilongjiang renmin chubanshe, 1981), 63.

99. Zhang Qing, *Tingzijian: yiqun wenhuaren he tamen de shiye* (The pavilion rooms: a group of literati and their careers) (Shanghai: Shanghai renmin chubanshe, 1991), 5.

Pavillion," into the title of three of his best-known books (that is, collections of his essays).[100]

Although Lu Xun and other famous twentieth century writers had lived and written some of their best pieces in pavilion rooms, their prestige eventually set them apart from the image that a pavilion room conveys. Shanghai's pavilion rooms had been so powerfully associated with the image of the urban petty bourgeois writer in the Republican period that "pavilion room writer" (*tingzijian zuojia*) and "pavilion room man of letters" (*tingzijian wenren*) became stock phrases. These authors were, typically, sensitive and self-esteemed, scornful of the world and its ways but always part of it, hard working but never quite successful—not unlike those frustrated garret writers and artists in Balzac's world. From this group emerged radical youth who eventually left Shanghai for Yan'an and became Communist revolutionaries. They made such an impact on the intellectual life in the heart of the Communist revolution that, in a speech in Yan'an in 1938, Mao Zedong mentioned the divisions among revolutionary intellectuals in the red areas brought by them. In a humorous tone but appearently addressing a serious issue, Mao spoke of "men from a Shanghai pavilion room" as representative of urban-based intellectuals who had newly come to Yan'an and "men from the hilltops" (i.e., intellectuals with a rural background), and urged these two groups to know their own limitations and respect each other.[101]

Mixing residence with commerce. The mix in alleyway-house neighborhoods was not only a matter of the social composition of the residents but also of the co-existence of residences and various types of businesses. The front row of houses in an alleyway house compound faced the street and was used primarily as premises for business, mostly small shops serving the

---

100. Lu Xun entitled the three collections of his essays *Qiejieting zawen* (Essays from the Qiejie pavilion), *Qiejieting zawen erji* (Essays from the Qiejie pavilion, volume 2), and *Qiejieting zawen mobian* (Final essay from the Qiejie pavilion). The expression *Qiejieting* is a pun. The first character, *qie*, forms half of the character *zu*. The second character, *jie*, forms half of a different character also read *jie*. This latter character (*jie*) combined with the character *zu*, forms the word *zujie*, meaning "foreign concession." *Ting* implies a pavilion room. Hence, Qiejieting cleverly suggests "a pavilion room in the semi-Concession." Why Lu Xun chose this name had to do with where his home was situated. His residence, Number 9 Dalu Xinchun (where he lived from April 1933 to his death in October 1936), was located in Hongkou, at the boundary between the International Settlement and the Chinese district. It was here that some of the controversial "extra-Settlement roads" (*yuejie zhulu*) had been built. Sovereignty over the areas covered by these roads was ambiguous. Hence, these areas could be called a "semi-Concession." The three collections of essays are found in volume 6 of *Lu Xun quanji* (The complete works of Lu Xun) (Beijing: Renmin wenxue chubanshe, 1991).

101. Cited from Zhang Qing, *Tingzijian*, 3.

neighborhood.[102] But various businesses other than small neighborhood stores were also found there. Even in predominately residential areas, businesses were often mixed with residences. Shanghai residents were so familiar with these enterprises in their neighborhoods that "alley factory" (*longtang gongchang*), "alley school" (*longtang xuetang*), "alley store" (*longtang shangdian*), etc. were standard terms in the local dialect.

The Social Daily News (English title of *Shehui ribao*) once published an essay entitled "Inside Our Alley—A Survey Table of Residences," which was actually not a "table" but a description of seven houses, numbering from 24 to 36, in a shikumen lane. The author explained that the people in this little lane had "extremely different backgrounds, which is a token of the complex and mixed conditions in the world's sixth largest metropolis." This lane, for our purposes, can be taken as an example of how residence and commerce were mixed in alleyway house neighborhoods. In addition to regular residents, in this short lane (approximately 100 feet) one could find a tailor shop, a textile mill, a warehouse, and a dormitory for an amusement center.

A couple named Li with three children—the eldest was eleven or twelve—lived in Number 24. Mr. Li, a Suzhou native, obviously had a good income since he worked for the Maritime Customs—any position there was regarded as one of the best in town or as it was put, was like having a "golden rice bowl." Neighbors noticed that the family spent a lot of money to have the house painted when they moved in. Li impressed them as a sweet talker and a "perfect philistine." The "sweet talk" part was linked with a stereotype in Shanghai about Suzhou people who were generally thought to have a "sweet mouth"—Suzhou cuisine is known for being sugary and the Suzhou dialect sounds soft and sweet.

Next door, House Number 26, was the shop of tailor Zhao Shentai. The owner, a native of Changshu, and his wife, a Wuxi native, seemed to have very different personalities. The man was a quiet and private person, seemingly always at work at his tailoring table inside the home; he seldom talked with neighbors. The wife, on the other hand, was fond of gossip and she often, even while she was in the sixth or seventh month of pregnancy, went to neighbors' houses to chat, something considered slightly outrageous in those days. Next to the tailor shop, in House Number 28, was a little textile mill making rayon socks. The factory ran day and night and employed both men and women: men worked in the second floor workshop and women worked downstairs. The neighbors naturally complained of the noise of machines, but they were also

---

102. See Hanchao Lu, "Away from Nanjing Road: Small Stores and Neighborhood Life in Modern Shanghai," *Journal Of Asian Studies*, 54,1(February 1995):93-123.

bothered by the noise of the workers who either hummed various ditties or flirted with each other over the floor in the workshop.

House Number 30 was considered a mysterious nest. Only two women lived there. The younger was sixteen and she called the older woman, who was only about twenty-six or -seven, "mom." Every night the two women donned provocative clothing and went out. Neighbors could not figure out if they were dancing girls or prostitutes. A woman in her late twenties and her elderly maid lived in House Number 32. A man, who looked like a banker, regularly paid the young woman a visit once or twice a week. Neighbors gossiped that Number 32 was but a "little house" for a mistress. As was common in Shanghai, the gossip went, the man probably first met the young woman in a brothel, then fell in love, and eventually payed off the madame to get his favorite. But it looked like the woman was quite discontented with the lonely life in the "little house": she often stood at her back door gazing around, as if she was trying to seduce young men. Ironically, all the neighbors next door in House Number 34 were women. These women seemed to dress in the same sort of modern attire, but in a style that was out of date. Their occupations were unclear. They might be a group of waitresses at an amusement center or night club, although they seemed never to have to work, and they played mahjong all day long.

House Number 36, at the end of the lane, had been used as a storehouse by an electric lamp store that had recently closed. The owner of that store, a successful young businessman, had recently appeared in the newspaper in the "local news" column: his run-away mistress had sued him for mistreatment. Before the lingering lawsuit had reached a conclusion, the young man, badly upset and frustrated, went out for a drive and died in an accident. At the time the essay was published in *The Social Daily News*, the electric lamp store had a new owner and House Number 36 was vacant.[103]

The various non-residential institutions in shikumen neighborhoods included many local schools. Elementary schools located in alleyway compounds were popular because they were convenient for children—the schools were always located within a safe walking distance from home, and students usually did not need to cross the street to go to school. In these schools, the shikumen living rooms and bedrooms were turned into classrooms and the kitchens and pavilion rooms were used as offices. The front courtyard might be too small to serve as a playground but outdoor activities could always extend into the alleyway. A three-bay shikumen house could be transformed into six to nine classrooms, each with twenty to thirty seats. Sometimes walls

---

103. *Shehui ribao*, October 1, 1934.

between a few contiguous shikumen houses were removed to form a sizable school.[104]

"Alley schools" also included institutions of higher education. Shanghai's earliest Chinese-run private university, Datong University, was founded in 1912 in a shikumen compound named Nanyang Li (Alley of the southern sun) in Nanshi.[105] Another school, Daxia University, was founded in 1924 in a shikumen house in Meiren Li (Alley of beauty and benevolence), located a few yards south of Avenue Joffre in the French Concession. One of the founding faculty members recalled that the university office was in a single-bay shikumen inside the compound. A sign was posted on the front door reading "Please Use the Back Door." This was because the landlord lived in the living room on the first floor, and so to enter the house from the front door meant one had to pass through his room.[106] Shanghai University, known for its sociology programs as well as its Communist inclination, was also set in an allway house compound. The writer Mao Dun called Shanghai University "a veritable 'alleyway university'" because it was located in an alleyway house compound (Qingyun Li [Alley of meteoric rise] on Qingyun Road in Zhabei). It was briefly relocated to Ximo Road in the Settlement in 1924, and then it moved to Shishou Fang (Alley of teachers' longgevity), another alleyway house compound on Qingyun Road. The school "had no gate, no sign board, and, of course, no auditorium. The assembly hall was formed by merging two rooms together by removing the wall."[107]

Printing houses and bookstores were also set up in shikumen neighborhoods.[108] In his memoirs, Zhu Lianbao, a publisher who had worked in various presses in Shanghai for half a century (1921-1970), recorded the details of about 600 printing houses and bookstores in pre-1949 Shanghai, of which more than half were set in alleyway houses, mostly in shikumen houses.[109] Shikumen compounds housed some of China's best-known presses and newspapers. Li Boyuan, who was regarded as the forefather of Shanghai's

104. Interview with shikumen residents, July 29, 1995. See also Jia You, "Shanghai longtang mian mian guan."

105. Shen Deci, Fang Jishi, Wang Huaichang, and Dong Dichen, "Huiyi Datong Daxue" (Recalling Datong University), *Shanghai wenshi ziliao xuanji*, 59 (1988):137-142.

106. Ou Yuanhui, "Daxia Daxue xiaoshi jiyao" (A concise record of Daxia University), *Shanghai wenshi ziliao xuanji*, 59 (1988):143-158.

107. Mao Dun, *Wo zouguo de daolu* (The roads I have walked) (Hong Kong: Joint Publishing Co. [Sanlian chubanshe], 1981), 3:196.

108. The bookstores (*shuju*) referred to here were primarily printing houses but they often had a retail sales room.

109. Zhu Lianbao, *Jinxiandai Shanghai chubanye yinxiang ji* (A Record of the presses in modern and contemporary Shanghai) (Shanghai: Xuelin chubanshe, 1993), 2 and *passim*.

tabloids, founded *Fanhua bao* (Prosperity) in April 1901. The office and print shop of the tabloid were located in Yixin Li (Alley of boundless good fortune) on Nanjing Road.[110] The largest press in modern China, the Commercial Press, started business in 1897 in Dechang Li (Alley of virtue and prosperity) on Jiangxi Road in the Nanjing Road area. The next year, the press moved to Shunqing Li (Alley of smoothness and celebration) on Beijing Road, still another shikumen compound.[111] The Liangyou Press, publisher of the most popular pictorial in Republican China, *Liangyou* (Fine companion), which was published for almost two decades and had a circulation of 40,000, was started in 1926 as a small printing house in Hongqing Fang (Alley of great celebration) on North Sichuan Road.[112] In 1929, the Settlement police raided the press of a Communist newspaper, the *Red Flag*, which was produced in an ordinary alleyway house. The living room on the first floor had been turned into a print shop and the rooms on the second floor were used as a dormitory for the printers. This arrangement was seen as perfectly normal in alleyway house neighborhoods. The underground Communist Party thus took advantage of the anonymity of shikumen compounds to produce their secret publications.[113]

The Shanghai Bookstore, the CCP press from 1923 to 1926, was in Zhenye Li (Alley of promoting careers) in the Little North Gate (Xiaobeimen) district of Nanshi, in the midst of a densely clotted alleyway house neighborhood. At the same time, the Mingxing (Bright star) Printing House, a mill that produced numerous Communist publications including the noted journals *New Youth* (Xin qingnian), *Chinese Youth* (Zhongguo qingnian), and *Guide* (Xiangdao), operated downtown in a shikumen house in Xi Fuhai Li (Alley of an ocean of fortune, west) near the well-known Garden Hotel. Its warehouse was yet another shikumen house across the street in Sande Li (Alley of three virtues).

110. Yang Hao and Ye Lan (eds.), *Jiu Shanghai fengyun renwu* (Men of the hour in old Shanghai)(Shanghai: Shanghai renmin chubanshe, 1987),111-112. *Fanhua bao* published a number of novels and other works of fiction that are among the important works of twentieth century Chinese literature, such as Li Boyuan's *Guanchang xianxing ji* (Records of current officialdom), Wu Yuanren's *Hutu shijie* (A muddled world), and Liu E's *Laocan youji* (The travel notes of Laocan).

111. Zhu Lianbao, *Jinxiandai Shanghai chubanye*, 339.

112. *Liangyou*, December 1934 (Number 100).

113. Shanghai Municipal Police Files (Microfilms from the U.S. National Archives), D-627.

From 1927 to 1932, the CCP's masthead journal, *Bolshevik* (Bu'ershiweike) was located in Hengchang Li (Alley of prosperity) in Yuyuan Road.[114] In other ways also the Communists skillfully used Shanghai's alleyway house neighborhoods for their revolutionary agenda. The concessions proved to be a relatively safe place for underground activists because, of course, the Chinese police could not operate openly there. Inside the concessions, the mixed alleyway house neighborhoods, especially with their many schools, printing houses, and bookstores, were ideal for underground Communist activities. In a residential neighborhood where people of all walks of life lived side by side with businesses of all kinds, whatever the Communists did was unlikely to draw attention. To begin with, the First National Congress of the Chinese Communist Party (CCP), which proclaimed the birth of the CCP, was held in a shikumen house in the French Concession on July 23-30, 1921. The house, 106 Wangzhi Road (today the address is 76 Xingye Road), was an ordinary two-story shikumen house located in the middle of a five-house row built in 1920. Number 106 was the home Li Hanjun, one of the founding members of CCP; his elder brother, Li Shucheng, a follwer of Sun Yat-sen who helped found the Tongmenghui (or the United League, the forerunner of the Guomindang), lived next door, in Number 108. The congress, which is described by the Communists as an event that "turned heaven and earth upside down," was held in the living room of Li Hanjun's home. This 18 square meter (194 square feet) room is now a sacred place in China. As early as September 1950, this relic was placed under official protection and completely restored. Today all five houses on Wangzhi Road are the best preserved shikumen in the city. Number 106, a museum of the birth place of CCP, is adorned with a signboard bearing Deng Xiaoping's calligraphy and indicating the name of the museum (see illustration 5.1).[115]

---

114. Wu Guifang,"Jindai Shanghai geming yiji gaishu" (A survey of revolutionary relics in modern Shanghai), *Shanghai difangshi ziliao*, vol.6: 11-31; Gu Yanpei, "Shanghai Shudian jiuzhi" (The relic of the Shanghai Bookstore), *Shanghai difangshi ziliao*, vol.6:49-50; Shanghaishi Changningqu renmin zhengfu (Government of Changning District of Shanghai) (comp.), *Changningqu dimingzhi* (A gazetteer of Changning District of Shanghai)(Shanghai: Xuelin chubanshe, 1988), 125, 170.

115. Zhang Qing, "Zhongguo gongchandang diyici quanguo daibiao dahui huizhi he daibiao sushe" (The relics of the first national congress of the Chinese Communist Party and the lodging accommodations for its participants), *Shanghai difangshi ziliao*, vol.6: 32-36; Shanghaishi Luwanqu renmin zhengfu (Government of Luwan District of Shanghai), *Shanghaishi Luwanqu dimingzhi* (A gazetteer of Luwan District of Shanghai) (Shanghai: Shanghai Academy of Social Sciences Press, 1990), 215-216; Wu Guifang(ed.), *Shanghai fengwu zhi* (Records of Shanghai scenery) (Shanghai: Shanghai wenhua chubanshe, 1985), 113-117.

About one hundred meters north of 106 Wangzhi Road, at 389 Rue Eugene Bard (today the address is 127 Taicang Road), was the Bowen Women's School, founded in 1917 and moved to this location in 1920. The whole school was located in a three-bay two-story shikumen house. The school was used to lodge those who attended the CCP's first national congress. Classrooms were turned into temporary dormitories. On the second floor, Mao Zedong and He Shuheng (representatives of Hunan Communists) were put up in the west wing, and Dong Biwu and Chen Tanqiu (representatives of Hubei Communists) were housed in the east wing. It was not unusual for a school to be used as a domitory in the summer—in fact, the whole group was lodged there as a "group of teachers and students of Beijing University on a summer excursion."[116]

The CCP's Second National Congress was also held in a shikumen house compound. In July 1922, the congress convened in Number 30 of Fude Li (Alley of guided morals) on North Chengdu Road, a compound of 50 two-story shikumen houses built in 1915. A few steps away, in House Number 42, was the Pingmin Women's School, which had a Communist-sponsored work-study program in 1922-23. Students supported themselves by making socks, sewing, and taking in laundry. The CCP held yet another national congress in a shikumen house. The Fourth National Congress was held in January 1925 in a three-story shikumen house located on the north edge of Hongkou. The meeting was held on the second floor and the third floor was used to lodge the participants. According to Zheng Chaolin, a veteran Communist who was the congress secretary, the house was made to look like an English language school, an institution not likely to arouse suspicion in an alleyway house neighborhood. Every participant had an English textbook ready. In case an uninvited visitor came in, it could be claimed that an English class was in session.[117]

If one goes back in time a bit to the New Cultural Movement period (1915-1920) when the Communist ideology was in a ferment in China, more relics of this kind can be found in Shanghai's alleyway house neighborhoods. In 1920, House Number 2 of Yuyang Li (known as old Yuyang Li, Alley of gaining the sun) in Route Vallon (today the address is 100 Nanchang Road, #2), a single-bay two story shikumen house, was the home of Chen Duxiu, the most renowned Communist radical at that time, as well as the editorial office of the

---

116. Zhang Qing,Ibid.

117. Shanghai yan'ge bianxiezu (Writing Group of the Evolution of Shanghai), "Shanghai de geming yiji" (Revolutionary relics in Shanghai), *Shanghai difangshi ziliao* , 6:6-10; Shanghaishi Jing'anqu, *Shanghaihshi Jing'anqu dimingzhi*, 195; Zheng Chaolin, *Huaijiu ji* (Recollections of the past)(Beijing: Dongfang chubanshe, 1995), 94-95.

famous journal he edited, the *New Youth*. Chen and his wife, Gao Junman, lived on the second floor and used the living room on the first floor as the editorial office. It was in this shikumen that Chen and like-minded intellectuals such as Li Da, Li Hanjun, and Chen Wangdao formed the nation's first so-called Communist group (*gongchan zhuyi xiaozu*). The editorial office of a monthly journal of the Communist group, *The Communist*, was also located in the house.[118]

In that year, if one took a stroll from Yuyang Li north to Avenue Joffre, and then turned eastward on Avenue Joffre one could see an alleyway house compound that bears the same name: Yuyang Li. The three black characters, Yu-Yang-Li, were inscribed right on the entrance —as if to show that there was no copyright on names of alleyway house compounds. Customarily, local residents called this alleyway house compound "new Yuyang Li" in order to distinguish it from the old one on Route Vallon. Coincidentally, new Yuyang Li is another important relic in the history of Chinese communism. Inside the compound, in front of House Number 6 there was a wooden board about one foot wide and three feet long inscribed with five characters: *wai guo yu xue she*, "foreign language school." If one checks the September 30, 1920 issue of *Minguo ribao* (The Republic daily), one can find this school advertising its Russian and French programs. However, this alleyway school was in fact a Communist stronghold. Most of the students—the highest enrollment was about sixty—were not recruited via commercial advertisements but through connections with Communist comrades. Among the students one can find the names of many who later became top Communist leaders: Liu Shaoqi, Ren Bishi, Ke Qingshi, Xiao Jinguang, and so on. Their purpose in learning Russian and French was to read Marxist works and prepare for further training in the Soviet Union. In spring 1921, the school sent three batches of student to Moscow.

This two-bay, two-story shikumen house looked identical to the other 32 shikumen houses in the compound, but it seemed as if it was destined to become a historical site. The house was first rented by Dai Jitao (1890-1949), a follower of Sun Yat-sen and a high-ranking official in the Chiang Kai-shek government. In March 1920 when Dai was going to move out, he happened to know that his friend, Chen Duxiu, was looking for a house and therefore he notified him of the forthcoming vacancy. Chen's purpose was to rent a house for Communist activities, since a Comintern representative was in touch with him in Shanghai at that time and they were preparing to found the Chinese

---

118. Yu Jinghai, "*Xing qingnian* bianjibu jiuzhi" (The relic of the editorial office of the New Youth), *Shanghai difangshi ziliao*, vol. 6:46-48; Wu Guifang, "Jindai Shanghai," 11-12.

Communist Party. The house was rented in the name of Yang Mingzhai, an interpreter for the Comintern. In addition to housing the foreign language school, Number 6 was used as the headquarters of the Socialist Youth League (later known as the Communist Youth League) and as the office of the Sino-Russian News Agency (Hua E tongxunshe). The wings on first floor were used as classrooms. When enrollment increased, the living room was also turned to classroom. On the second floor, the front bedroom was used as the office of the Youth League, and the back bedroom and wings as a student dormitory. The pavilion room was Yang Mingzhai's bedroom as well as the office of the news agency.[119]

Since 1950 most of these Communist-related alleyway houses have been well preserved and restored as relics of the revolution. Unintentionally, this has also helped preserve a slice of life in the city in the Republican period. However, cultural institutions such as schools, presses, and bookstores were a less important part of the businesses established in Shanghai's residential alleyway compounds. Most alleyway businesses were purely commercial, such as stores, workshops, warehouses, opium dens, brothels, and other small enterprises. For instance, from the late nineteenth century on, the shikumen compound of Furun Li (Alley of wealth and profit), located a few yards from Nanjing Road, was known for its "three abundances" (*san duo*): an abundance of shops, workshops, and warehouses.[120] Another well-known compound, Baxian Fang (Alley of eight immortals), contained 71 shikumen houses. Rooms on the first floor of the houses were mostly used for businesses, not as residences. Pawnshops alone occupied six of the houses. These businesses were interspersed with the dwellings of Baxian Fang residents, most of whom were street peddlers, small merchants, artists, prostitutes, magicians and other entertainers.[121]

In the Nanjing Road area, both modern, Western-type banks and *qianzhuang* (traditional Chinese banks) were found in shikumen compounds.[122] In the Republican period, Qingyuan Li (Alley of purity and remoteness) and Ruyi Li (Alley of doing as one wishes), among the earliest shikumen

119. Wang Meidi, "Zhongguo zuizao de Qingniantuan zhongyang jiguan jiuzhi"(The relic of China's earliest headquarters of the Communist Youth League), *Shanghai difangshi ziliao*, vol. 6(1988): 43-45; Shanghaishi Luwanqu, *Shanghaishi Luwanqu dimingzhi*, 146.

120. Shanghaishi Huangpuqu, *Shanghaishi Huangpuqu dimingzhi*, 221. The present-day address of Furun Li is 270 Guizhou Road.

121. Shanghaishi huangpuqu, *Shanghaishi huangpuqu dimingzhi*, 250. The present-day address of Baxian Fang is 109 Ninghaixi Road.

122. For information on Qianzhuang, see Andrea Lee McElderry, *Shanghai Old-Style Banks (Ch'ien-chuang) 1800-1935* (Ann Arbor, 1976).

compounds in Shanghai (both were marked on a map published in 1876),[123] were distinguished by a number of financial institutions mixed in with residences. Western-type banks were found in Qingyuan Li along its rows facing Beijing Road; *qianzhuang* were located in the rows inside the compound. In Ruyi Li, banks and business offices actually outnumbered residences.[124] The same was true of Xingren Li, another of the oldest shikumen compounds in Shanghai, located a block north of Nanjing Road. Of the 24 houses of Xingren Li, 20 were used as *qianzhuang*. A single family from Ningbo, the Fangs, once owned three banks inside this compound.[125] Obviously, these shikumen neighborhoods became favorite places for banks and *qianzhuang* because of their convenient proximity to the major commercial and financial centers in the Nanjing Road area. Visitors to Shanghai were impressed by the European-style bank buildings along the Bund; few would have noticed these small institutions set in the back alleyways. But these small banks, numerous as they were, certainly contributed to Shanghai's status as China's foremost financial center.

Shikumen houses were also used for entertainment establishments. In shikumen compounds in the city's busy commercial areas (especially, the Nanjing Road area), opium dens, gambling houses, and brothels were plentiful. It was estimated that by the mid-1860s, when Shanghai was just emerging from under the Taiping threat and was not yet a great metropolis, there were already 1,500 brothels in the city,[126] and by the early 1930s, according to Gail Hershatter's estimate, one of every thirty Shanghai residents sold sex for a living.[127] The vast majority of Shanghai's brothels were operated out of ordinary shikumen houses. For half a century from 1860 to the end of the Qing dynasty, Baoshan Jie (Street of treasure and mercy), a street four blocks south of Nanjing Road, and its vicinity, was the center of prostitution. This part of the Nanjing Road area continued to be a red light district (*hongdeng qu*) or "decency district" (*fenghua qu*) in the Republican era. Shikumen compounds on Baoshan Jie, such as Gongxing Li (Alley of collective prosperity), East Gongxing Li, Gongshun Li (Alley of collective smoothness), and—best-known of all and perhaps most appropriately named—Huile Li (Alley of joint

---

123. The present-day address of Qingyuan li is 288 Beijingdong Road and of Ruyi Li 575 Henanzhong Road.

124. Shanghaishi Huangpuqu, *Shanghaishi Huangpuqu dimingzhi*, 207, 210.

125. Shanghaishi Huangpuqu, *Shanghaishi Huangpuqu dimingzhi* 204-5. The present-day address of Xingren Li is 120 Ningbo Road.

126. Zhang Hong, *Shili yangchang: bei chumai de Shanghai tan* (The foreign concession: the sold Shanghai)(Shanghai: Shanghai renmin chubanshe, 1991), 55.

127. Gail Hershatter, "Regulating Sex in Shanghai: The Reform of Prostitution in 1920 and 1951," in Frederick Wakeman, Jr. and Wen-hsin Yeh (eds.), *Shanghai Sojourners*, 146.

pleasure), were full of brothels.[128] Huile Li, a compound of 4,420 square meters originally built at the end of the nineteenth century, boasted a main alleyway 4.6 meters wide and 85 meters long, four branch alleyways, and, after a remodel in 1924, 28 three-bay, two-wing shikumen houses.[129] The compound was built in a moderately tasteful style: each house had a spacious front courtyard, those houses facing the main alleyway had a balcony, and arches were built at the main entrance as well as at the entrances of branch alleys, with stone inscriptions indicating the direction and number of the branches (such as "East First Branch Alley," "West Second Branch Alley," and so on). Although it was not deliberately built to accommodate brothels, by the late 1920s the compound became a favorite site for Shanghai's higher class prostitution.[130] By 1949, 27 of the houses in Huile Li in all or in part were used as brothels; the only house that was not a brothel was a pharmacy, which perhaps primarily served those suffering from sexually transmitted diseases.[131] This shikumen compound was so well known for its prostitution that the name "Huile Li" was virtually a synonym in Shanghai for "whoring."[132]

Shikumen compounds housing brothels could also be found in many other areas of Shanghai. Along Tibet Road, from its northern end in the International Settlement down to the southern end in French Concession, many shikumen compounds accommodated various types of businesses dealing in vice. For

---

128. Xue Liyong,"Ming-Qing shiqi de Shanghai changji" (Shanghai's prostitutes in the Ming-Qing period), in Shanghai wenshiguan (ed.), *Jiu Shanghai de yan du chang* (Opium, gambling, and prostitution in old Shanghai)(Shanghai: Baijia chubanshe,1988), 150-158.

129. The present-day address of Huile Li is 726 Fuzhou Road.

130. For more information on the ranking of prostitutes in Shanghai, see Hershatter,"The Hierarchy of Shanghai Prostitution, 1870-1949," *Modern China*, 15,4(October 1989):463-498; Tang Weikang, "Shili yangcgang de changji"(Prostitution in Shanghai's foreign concessions), in Tang Weikang et al. (eds.), *Shanghai yishi* (Shanghai anecdotes)(Shanghai: Wenhua chubanshe, 1987),261-274; Xue Liyong,"Ming-Qing shiqi de Shanghai changji"; Ping Jinya, "Jiu Shanghai de changji" (Prostitutes of old Shanghai), in Shanghai wenshiguan (ed.), *Jiu Shanghai de yan du chang* (Opium, gambling, and prostitution in old Shanghai), 159-171; Xie Wuyi, "Minchu Shanghai changji yipie" (A glance at Shanghai's prostitutes in the early Republican period),in Shanghai wenshiguan (Shanghai Institute of Culture and History) (ed.), *Jiu Shanghai de yan du chang* (Opium, gambling, and prostitution in old Shanghai)(Shanghai: Baijia chubanshe, 1988), 172-175; and Christian Henriot, "'From a Throne of Glory to a Seat of Ignominy'," (*Modern China*, 22,2(April 1996):132-163.

131. Shanghaishi Huangpuqu, *Shanghaishi Huangpuqu dimingzhi*, 277.

132. According to household registration records, by the end of 1948 there were 151 brothels in Huile Li, with 200 registered brothel owners, 587 prostitutes, and 374 servants (*jiyong*). A January 1949 survey reported 171 brothels in the compound, that is, about one fifth of Shanghai's brothels at that time. See Yang Jiezeng and He Wainan, *Shanghai changji gaizao shihua* (A history of transforming the prostitutes of Shanghai)(Shanghai: Sanlian shudian, 1988), 213-221.

instance, by the late 1930s in Xiande Li (Alley of all virtues), a shikumen compound on Tibet Road built in 1910, 20 percent of its 52 houses were used as brothels, and many others as opium dens. Mixed in together with these businesses were a variety of residents who hailed from all sorts of places: Yangzhou in Subei, Ningbo in Jiangnan, Guangdong, and some Moslems from various places.[133] Another shikumen compound in Tibet Road, Taiyuan Fang (Taiyaun alley), built in 1929, and close to the famous Shanghai entertainment center, the Great World (*Dashijie*, built in 1917), housed numerous brothels, opium dens, and inns with a shady reputation. Four adjoining shikumen houses inside the compound were remodeled into a theater specializing in Yangzhou opera.[134] A few blocks south, in the so-called Great Road of the French Concession (Fa da malu),[135] was a shikumen compound known as Shengping Li (Alley of peace), built in 1925, where 10 houses out of 32 were used as opium warehouses.[136]

These are merely a few examples of the rather creative use of alleyway houses for non-residential purposes. One could add to the list. By the late 1940s, about half of Shanghai's total of 250 hotels were located in alleyway houses. In 1947, seven of the city's 45 broadcasting stations were set in alleyway-house compounds.[137] Chen Guhai, a veteran journalist, recalled that the China United Broadcasting Station, a radio station that was quite active in Shanghai in 1946-47, was actually set in his home in an alleyway house in New Dagu Road and the broadcasting booth was put right in his bedroom for nine months.[138] Early in 1931, the CCP's central broacasting station was set up in Number 11 Xingqing Li (Alley of joy and celebration) in Moulmein Road; the same house also contained the transmitter.[139] In 1933, the CCP even had an underground radio center in Number 20 Heqing Li (Alley of joint celebration) on Dagu Road to communicate with Moscow. During the Civil War, the CCP

133. Shanghaishi Huangpuqu, *Shanghaishi Huangpuqu dimingzhi*, 231. The present-day address of Xianyi Li is "539 Xizangzhong Road."
134. Ibid, 266.
135. The name "Great Road" referred to Nanjing Road. Thus the street can also be translated as the "Nanjing Road of the French Concession." Today this is Jinlingdong Road.
136. Shanghaishi Huangpuqu, *Shanghaishi Huangpuqu dimingzgi*, 267. The present-day address of Shengping Li is "396 Jinglingdong Road."
137. Jia You, "Shanghai longtang mian mian guan."
138. Zhao Yuming, *Zhongguo xiandai guangbo jianshi* (A concise history of broadcasting in modern China) (N.p.: Zhongguo guangbo dianshi chubanshe, 1995), 219-222.
139. The compound was also known as Ji'an Li (Alley of luck and peace). It was built in 1929 and contained seventeen two-story shikumen houses. Its current address is Lanes 111-121 North Maoming Road. Shanghai yange bianxiezu, "Shanghai de geming yiji;" Shanghaishi Jing'anqu, *Shanghaishi Jing'anqu dimingzhi*, 148.

radio station was located in yet another alleyway house: Number 15 Lane 107 Huangdu Road, in Hongkou. Li Bai, the radio operator, secretly worked on the third floor of that house for three years until he was arrested on the spot in December 1948.[140] All sorts of wholesales offices, public bathhouses, fortune tellers, restaurants, clinics, lawyer's offices, and sometimes even government bureaus could be found in the alleys. A local saying described the multifarious use of alleyway houses as "performing a Buddhist [or Daoist] rite inside a snail shell" (*luosi ke li zuo daochang*). This was sometimes not a metaphor but virtually a reality: according to a directory of the Shanghai Buddhist Association (*Shanghaishi Fojiao hui*, founded in June 1929), by the late 1940s many of the city's 285 Buddhist temples were located in shikumen alleys.[141] By setting up a few religious statues and a table for joss sticks and candles, a living room or wing room of a shikumen could be transformed into a Buddhist temple where worship and rituals were conducted in all their proper forms.

Conclusion

Shanghai has long been regarded as the epitome of modern China's commercial culture, and modern Shanghainese (*Shanghairen*) have been stereotyped as astute, resourceful, calculating, quick-witted, adaptive, and flexible (always ready to compromise but not budging an inch unless it is absolutely necessary).[142] It seems legitimate to name such a culture after the city, hence the term *Haipai* (the Shanghai school or the Shanghai type), in contrast to the supposedly rigid, tradition-bound and orthodox *Jingpai* (the Beijing school or the Beijing type).[143] The Shanghai type, even in its original

140. Shanghai yange bianxiezu,"Shanghai de geming yiji," 10; Shanghaishi Hongkouqu renmin zhengfu (Government of Hongkou District of Shanghai)(comp.), *Shanghaishi Hongkouqu dimingzhi* (A gazetteer of Hongkou District of Shanghai)(Shanghai: Shanghai Academy of Social Sciences Press, 1989), 311. Li was executed by the Guomingdang on the eve of the Communist's take over of Shanghai in May 1949. His devotion to the secret radio station made him a nationally renowned hero and was made the subject of a popular movie, *The Eternal Electric Wave* (*Yongbu xiaoshi de dianbo*).

141. You Youwei, *Shanghai jindai Fojiao jianshi* (A concise history of Buddhism in modern Shanghai)(Shanghai: East China Normal University Press, 1988),136-37, 171.

142. For a fine scholarly discussion of the characteristics of modern Shanghainese, see Yue Zheng, *Jindai Shanghairen shehui xintai* (The social mentality of modern Shanghainese) (Shanghai: Shanghai renmin chubanshe, 1991).

143. The term *Haipai* was originally created in the late nineteenth century to refer Shanghai-style painting and Shanghai-style Peking Opera. Later, the term was used in literary circles, and it was hightlighted in a debate in 1933 and 1934 between hinterland-based writers such as Shen Congwen and Shanghai writers. Since the 1930s the terms *jingpai* and *Haipai* have become broadly defined terms to refer to the general cultural

meaning as a school of literature, was part of a broadly defined commercial culture. As Lu Xun pointed out, "*Haipai* is just the helper of commerce," whereas "*Jingpai* is the hack of officialdom."[144]

The shikumen story illuminates the degree of commercialization in the daily life of Shanghai's people. In it we may find at least part of the roots of Shanghai's extraordinary commercial culture. Shanghai—specifically the houses built in the city's core along Nanjing Road—was the birthplace of China's first modern real estate market. Commerce so deeply penetrated into people's daily life that in many alleyway-house neighborhoods tenants became a type of merchant by subletting space to others. Shanghai's commercial culture, according to Lu Xun, reflected the city's character as a foreign concession where "merchants were abundant."[145] In the so-called second landlords, we see a type of merchant whose business primarily grew out of what might be called their living arrangement. The unconventional but common second-landlord/third-tenant phenomenon was a way in which people coped with life in the city, either in search of success or merely survival.[146] It was also a showcase of Shanghai as a land of opportunity: one could earn a living—or by certain standards even make a fortune—by simply renting part of one's dwelling. People who could not afford or were unwilling to pay the "take-over fee" could rent any size of room in any type of alleyway house and thus, in search of the "Shanghai dream," sojourn in this "golden land" (*cunjindi*). Out of these living arrangements welled a deep sense of commerce which was destined to help shape the mindset of the people of Shanghai. Such a mindset was further "commercialized" by the co-existence of commerce and residence in the city's alleyways. Millions of shikumen residents lived with businesses operating literally under their very noses. These businesses—stores, workshops, factories, banks, pawnshops, opium dens, brothels, teahouses, bathhouses, inns, schools, temples, and so on—were located right inside the same alley where they lived. The influence of commerce upon the people of Shanghai was thus intimate and certain.

---

differences between Shanghai and the "hinterlands" (represented by Beijing). See Yang Dongping, *Chengshi jifeng: Beijing he Shanghai de wenhua jingshen* (The monsoon of the city: the cultural spirits of Beijing and Shanghai)(Beijing: Dongfang chubanshe, 1994), 69-117.

144. Lu Xun, *Lu Xun Quanji* (The complete works of Lu Xun)(Beijing: Renmin wenxue chubanshe, 1991), vol. 6, 302.

145. Ibid.

146. Tahirih V. Lee, "Introduction" to "Coping with Shanghai: Means of Survival and Success in the Early Twentieth Century — A Symposium," *The Journal of Asian Studies*, 54,1(February 1995):3-18.

In a nation where commerce had long been despised, such influence was deemed to be corrupting. As early as 1861, Wang Tao (1828-97), who came to Shanghai in 1849 and worked as a translator for a British-run press there for twelve years, wrote in his diary, "Shanghai is a place of corrupted social values, and the corruption is indeed due of the search for profits (*lisou*)."[147] Wang was one of the few reform-minded intellectuals of his time and was regarded as the one of the pioneers of introducing Western culture in modern China, yet in private he did not hold Shanghai and commerce in high regard; we can imagine how still more unfavorable was opinion of Shanghai and its commercial culture among the conservatives. In spite of the commerce-based prosperity of the city in the modern times, commerce continued to be criticized as the cause of the deterioration of the general social climate. "In Shanghai, people only care about the value of gold and silver and do not know the origin of elegance and vulgarity." "The general social mood is so bad that everybody places great value on profit and takes personal reputation lightly. Commerce and the market are the place where the will of the people is worked out." Comments like these were frequently encountered in local newspapers and other publications, and presumably they were common in people's daily conversations.[148] By orthodox, Confucian standards then, Shanghai's commercial culture was corrupt. The Communists also condemned that culture, and saw it as a part of, to use Bergère's words, "the model of development inspired by the West of which the city had become the symbol":[149] thus they sought to eradicate it.

The Communists were certainly right in relating Shanghai's commercialization to the West. But in so doing they obviously, on purpose or not, underrated the Chinese initiative in the process. In the shikumen story, as we have seen, Western innovation and influence may have served as the first motive power (in the sense of getting the ball rolling) but the later development and innovation were almost entirely Chinese. *Haipai* culture, although it became distorted, continued to exist in the decades after 1949. This is an indication of the persistence of a tradition rooted neither in the Chinese superstructure, nor in an alien culture brought by foreigners, but in the quotidian life of the city's people. When the Communists finally awoke to the

---

147. Wang Tao, *Wang Tao riji* (The diary of Wang Tao) (Beijing: Zhonghua shuju, 1987), 116.

148. Wodusheng, *Huitu Shanghai zaji* (Pictorial Shanghai miscellanies)(Shanghai, 1905), *juan* 3; *Shenbao*, October 31, 1904.

149. Marie-Claire Bergère, "'The Other China': Shanghai From 1919 to 1949," in Christopher Howe (ed.), *Shanghai, Revolution and Development in an Asian Metropolis* (Cambridge: Cambridge University Press, 1981), 1-34.

importance of Shanghai and declared that the city would serve as the "dragon head" (*longtou*) of the nation's modernization program, they were recognizing a culture that had been condemned and denied for decades.[150] The people who can carry on the *Haipai* tradition will be—it is predictable—the survivors among the alleyway-house residents, their descendants, and the newcomers who have joined this vigorous and all-embracing culture.

---

150. In his famous 1992 "Inspection Tour of the South" (*nanxun*), Deng Xiaoping admitted that his major mistake was not to include Shanghai in the special economic zones at the beginning of the reform. "Otherwise," Deng maintained, "the situation of reform and opening to the outside in the Yangzi River Delta, the entire Yangzi River Valley and even the entire nation would be different." See *Deng Xiaoping wenxuan* (Selected works of Deng Xiaoping) (Beijing: Renmin chubanshe, 1993), vol. 3, 376.

Part III
The Fate of Shanghai's Commercial Culture in Wartime

Selling Fantasies at War: Production and Promotion Practices of the Shanghai Cinema, 1937-1941

Poshek Fu

Film came to China in 1896. Soon after the Lumiere brothers' first public exhibition of motion pictures at Grand Cafe (Paris) in December 1895, Shanghai audiences were amazed to see "real people" on the screen set up inside Xu Garden. In less than two decades, this nascent, most westernized cultural production became a major medium of commercial culture in China. It is no coincidence that Chinese cinema radiated out from Shanghai, which boasted the best organized studio system, the most elaborate distribution network, and the largest number of cinemas and production companies. The Shanghai film industry was, as Robert Snyder describes the vaudeville industry in Times Square, like an octopus with tentacles reaching all urban centers in the country.[1] Its productions reached as far as Mukden and Kunming.

Like film industries elsewhere, Chinese cinema was dominated by Hollywood during the "golden age" of silent film. But with the introduction of talkies in 1931, a national cinema began to take shape and to challenge Hollywood. Between 1933 and 1936, as Japan intensified its aggression, two of the industry's giants, Mingxing (Star) Studio and Lianhua (United China) Productions, captivated the audiences with such classics as Sun Yu's *Da Lu* (Great path) and Yuan Muzhi's *Malu tianshi* (Street angel) which demonstrated the political commitment and technical coming of age of Chinese filmmaking.

---

1. Robert Snyder, "Vaudeville and the Transformation of Popular Culture," in *Inventing Times Square: Commerce and Culture at the Crossroads of the World*, ed. William Taylor (New York, 1991), 134.

The budding cinema was ravaged by the eight years of the War of Resistance (1937-1945) during which Shanghai's film industry was "decentered." The Japanese occupation of the city generated an exodus of filmmakers into the interior, creating a new locus of patriotic filmmaking in Chongqing (along with Yanan and Hong Kong). According to conventional film history, the wartime capital, Chongqing, became the new "center" of Chinese cinema, although it had produced mainly documentaries and newsreels due to a lack of filmstock and studio equipment. And Shanghai, with its motion picture industry operating under Japanese rule, was marginalized as a suspicious other. Thus the war created an aberration, a lacuna on Chinese screen, with patriotic fervor but little cinematic achievements on the one hand, and "trivial," "poisonous" entertainment on the other. Chinese cinema came to life again only after 1945 when creative talents such as Bai Yang, Zhao Dan, and Zhao Junli returned to liberated Shanghai and revived the "tradition" of progressive filmmaking.[2]

The cinematic landscape of wartime Shanghai was actually more intricate than this stereotypical account would allow. Especially during the period known as the *gudao* (solitary island, 1937-41), when the foreign concessions, claiming neutrality in the hostilities, remained intact outside the surrounding sphere of Japanese domination, the city witnessed a boom of filmmaking. Despite the dismal business condition, over two hundred feature films were made in less than four years. Yet underneath this burst of productivity lay a fundamental predicament that the film makers failed to overcome in the end: how to find a formula to accommodate the political agenda into commercial interests. The failure explained in part, I believe, the marginalization of Shanghai cinema in official discourse.

The political predicament of the motion picture industry was reflective of the predicament confronting everyone in the solitary island. Life in Shanghai increasingly took on a tone of banality as the occupation wore on. A sense of political weariness prevailed. For the humiliation and indignation of having to live under the enemy remained overpowering and at times demanded outlets for expression. The film industry, far from being able to "manipulate" popular taste, had to try to "read" audience preference by way of box-office trends

---

2. See, for example, Cheng Jihua and Li Shaobai, *Zhongguo dianying fazhan shi* (A history of the development of Chinese cinema) (Hong Kong, 1958), and Feng Min, *Zhongguo dianying yishu shigang* (An artistic history of Chinese cinema) (Tianjin, 1992). For a fresh, stimulating study of the postwar cinema, see Paul Pickowicz, "Remembering a Holocaust: Post-war Film Portrayal of the War of Resistance," paper presented at the Centennial Symposium on Sun Yat-sen's founding of the Kuomintang for revolution, Taipei, November, 1994.

(surely its "reading" was invariably shaped by the industry's ideological positions).[3] It trod warily between providing simple pleasure on the screen and trying to articulate patriotic sentiments. Thus this chapter studies the social conditions of film production by analyzing the various strategies with which the *gudao* industry struggled (and failed) to come to terms with the predicament inherent in the wartime situation.

* * *

The Battle of Shanghai (August-November 1937) devastated the film world there. Since all of the major studios, including Mingxing Studio and Lianhua Productions, were located in the war zone, they were either destroyed or seized by the Japanese military. At the same time, inflamed by patriotic zeal, many filmmakers, actors, and such actresses as Zhao Dan and Chen Bo'er left the occupied city to resettle in the Chinese hinterland. Others, like the famous stars Hu Die and Lu Ming, took refuge in British Hong Kong.[4] But the majority of the film people stayed behind, apprehensive about the uncertain times ahead.

By December 1937, as the war shifted westward toward Wuhan and Shanghai slowly recovered from the ravages, a few filmmakers started to look for ways to reconstruct the business in order to survive the war. Zhang Shankun, owner of Xinhua (New China) Movie Company, whose studio was destroyed during the battle, rented a small lot in the International Settlement neighboring Huxi to make two low-budget comedies—Bu Wancang's *Qigai qianjin* (Beggar girl) and *Feilai fu* (Unexpected fortune). Both films turned out to be box-office successes. This unexpected "fortune" gave Zhang the confidence to release in April 1938 a big-budget period drama, *Diaochan*, featuring "movie king" Jin Shan and Gu Lanjun.

The movie, which had begun production in mid-1937 as a part of Xinhua's prewar expansion plan, was only 80% complete when the war started. For completion, Zhang rented studio space from Nanyue Productions in Hong Kong, where elaborate historical sets could be staged, and he flew such stars as Jin Shan and Gu Eryi there from Wuhan, while shipping the remaining crew and all kinds of shooting equipment from Shanghai. This high-profile, expansive move (publicized as "costing over Ch.$10,000 in on week," which

---

3. For a succinct critique of this "manipulationist" approach initiated by the Frankfurt School, see Elizabeth Traube, "Secrets of Success in Postmodern Society," in *Culture/Power/History*, ed. Nicholas Dirks et al. (Princeton, N.J., 1994), 558-560. See also Graeme Turner, *Film as Social Practice* (London and New York, 1992), Ch. 6.

4. See Huang Tianshi, *Yiduan bei yiwang de Zhongguo dianying shi* (A forgotten phase of the history of Chinese film), n.d., 2-3.

meant half of the average production cost of a pre-war film),[5] which came to be the signature of Zhang's show-biz style, was turned into a publicity stunt: big stars, big budget, and great style. *Diaochan* opened in the Grand Theatre on Nanjing Road, the plushest cinema in Shanghai, hitherto devoted to first-run Hollywood motion pictures. Eye-catching posters of *Diaochan* were posted in the windows of every major department store on Nanjing Road and an alleged Ch.$20,000 worth of advertisements were placed in all Chinese and English newspapers in town. The well-designed publicity and the nationalistic pride as the first Chinese movie exhibited in the Grand Theatre made it an instant hit.[6] *Diaochan* later opened in New York's Metropolitan Music Hall to critical acclaim which was then fed into the publicity drive to enhance the prestige of Xinhua.[7]

The success of *Diaochan*, along with the demise of Mingxing and Lianhua, convinced Zhang that it might be time to build a movie empire. In fact, life in *gudao* had become "normalized." From the middle of 1938 onward, as the economy moved into a state that contemporary observers called "abnormal prosperity," the entertainment business thrived to the dismay of many intellectual resisters.[8] The huge influx of war refugees from the lower Yangzi Delta region (that brought the total population of the solitary island from 1.5 million in 1937 to about 5 million in 1938) brought not only cheap laborers to fuel the manufacturing machine but also rich landlords and small-town merchants who swelled the ranks of avid consumers as the occupation wore on. Since there were few venues for relaxation in the nervous, over-crowed city, going to the movies became the most popular family entertainment in *gudao*. According to studio executive Su Yadao, all the cinemas were sold out even when only old movies were shown. Hollywood distributors (e.g. MGM and Paramount) took advantage of the "boom" by increasing their imports while demanding larger shares (60% rather than the original 40%) of box-office returns from exhibitiors. Distribution agents in Shanghai representing southeast Asian markets (led by Tianyi Company) also resumed buying Chinese movies in great quantities.[9] Thus Zhang's decision to expand Xinhua, thereby beginning the story of the Shanghai cinema under the occupation.

---

5. See Wang Qi, "Yinian lai zhi xinhua" (Xinhua in the last year), *Xinhua huabao* 4:1 (January 1939).

6. See Wang Qi (1939).

7. See *Xinhua huabao* 4:1 (Jan. 1939).

8. For an example of the resisters' criticism of the "immoral and shameless" Shanghai, see Kong Lingjing et al. (1939).

9. Su Yadao, *Lunjin yinhe* (Chinese cinema) (Hong Kong, 1982), 89-92.

It is indeed difficult to overestimate the impact of Zhang Shankun (1905-1956) on the movie industry of wartime Shanghai. A native of the Zhejiang city of Nanxun, Zhang was arguably the most visionary, colorful, and controversial producer Chinese cinema has ever produced. He was the only college graduate among his colleagues and was a successful businessman before entering the movie industry. After graduating from Nanyang College he was hired by Huang Chujiu to carry out publicity for his tobacco company. He proved to be a business prodigy, reaping big profits for Huang. In 1933, after the death of Huang, Zhang took over the management of the Gongwutai Theatre next to the Great World Amusement Palace on Avenue Edward II and turned it into a profit-making venture by applying movie techniques to Beijing Opera.[10]

With the money from Gongwutai Theatre, he started Xinhua Movie Company in 1935, hoping to capitalize on the expanding film business. Overshadowed by Mingxing and Lianhua, Xinhua remained a tiny, insignificant company until the immense success of *Yeban gesheng* (Singing at midnight), a horror classic by Maxu Weibang, in mid-1937. This catapulted Zhang into a major player in the crowded Shanghai show business. He soon approached financiers with an ambitious plan for building Xinhua into a movie empire. The war shattered his dream, but only temporarily. It ended up providing Zhang a once-in-a-lifetime opportunity to dominate Shanghai cinema.[11]

Following the commercial success of *Diaochan*, Zhang started recruiting all the creative talent remaining in the solitary island. These artists were now unbound by their former contracts. Zhang signed contracts with, for example, the superstars Yuan Meiyun and Chen Yanyan and the veteran directors Bu Wancang and Zhu Shilin. He also put on the payroll such second-line stars as Mei Shi and Liu Qiong who soon became top leading men in *gudao* where few actors remained. To expand Xinhua's production capacity while avoiding dependence on the Hong Kong studio, Zhang secured a long-term lease of Dingxiang Park in the International Settlement bordering Huxi which, along with many lakes and bamboo groves, could hold five stages at the same time. Boasting capital of Ch$500,000, Xinhua was becoming a movie empire in wartime Shanghai.[12]

---

10. Chen Dieyi, ed. *Zhongguo yingtan juren* (The giant of Chinese cinema) (Hong Kong, 1958), 3-33; Huang Ren and Ai Yi, "Yingxi danwang Zhang Shankun chenfu lu," (The ups and downs of movie king Zhang Shankun), *Shijie ribao* no. 3 (1996).

11. See Gongsun Lu, *Zhongguo dianying shihua* (A popular history of Chinese cinema) (Hong Kong, 1960), Vol. I, 122-126; Su Yadao, 1982, 69-100.

12. Wang Qi, 1939; Gongsun Lu, 1960, Vol. I, 125-126; Toshida Massatoshi, "Hen shuru Shanghai Shina eiga kakusha," (Chinese production companies in Shanghai), *Eiga hyoron* no. 16 (March 1941).

Zhang's success drew on many competitors. In late 1938, for fear of Xinhua's move toward monopoly, the cinema tycoons Liu Zhonghao and Liu Zhongliang formed Guohua (China) Production with start-up capital of Ch.$300,000. Guohua did not have its own production crew, instead it had a long-term contract with Zhang Shichuan's Mingxing Studio, which was unable to resume operation on it own due to financial insolvency. Under this arrangement, Mingxing would make films under Guohua's name and for its exhibition circuit. Among the company's few major stars was the former radio personality, "Golden Voice" Zhou Xuan. Soon afterward, Yan Chuntang's Yihua (Chinese arts) Motion Picture Company which had been founded in 1932 and closed for one year since the outbreak of the war, reopened with capital of Ch.$300,000. Because almost all its former stars had fled to Xinhua, it had to fill its ranks with starlets and by constantly scouting for new talent to keep the company competitive.

Besides these three majors, there were at different times as many as twenty other production companies. But all of these independent producers were small-time players with minuscule capitalization (average Ch.$40,000) and production capacity. Most of them did not have actors under contract, but borrowed stars and rented studios from the majors after collecting enough money to start a project. For example, in late 1938 the famous restauranteur Bian Yuying started Yuandong (Far East) Movie Company, and he contracted out production work piecemeal from it to Mingxing and made profits by adding soundtracks to some of its silent films (e.g. the tragic romance *Baiyun ta* or *White Cloud Pagoda*). Guangming (Brightness) Productions, on the other hand, was founded in February 1938 by Shen Tianyin, a well-connected production manager of prewar Yihua who, in order to make a living after losing his job, secured loans of Ch.$50,000 from financiers of various backgrounds and brought together a production crew consisting entirely of his former Yihua colleagues. Their only film was shot at a studio rented from Yihua.[13]

This plethora of production companies led to an "abnormal boom" in wartime Shanghai's movie business. Between 1938 and 1941, solitary island saw the opening of seven new cinemas, among them four first-run Chinese and Hollywood venues (Astor, Jindu, Guolian, and Roxy), which brought the total of *gudao* cinemas to 28 (compared to about 40 in Greater Shanghai before the war). Besides Jindu, which was owned by the Liu brothers, all the other new first-run venues were financed by recent migrants who tried to succeed in the

---

13. See *Wenxian* 1:4 (January 1939), Vol. I, 6-8; Ni Na, "Huanying Chen Yunshang lai Hu" (Welcoming Chen to Shanghai), *Xinhua huabao* 3:3 (December 1938); Toshida Massatoshi, 1941.

booming show business. For example, Shi Tingpan, the famous proprietor of the Astor Theatre (1939) on Avenue Edward VII, just a few blocks from the Great World, had previously been involved in the exhibition business of Suzhou; and the major financier of Guolian House (1940, others included Zhang Shankun and Yan Chuntang) on Yu Xiaqiang Road was a cinema tycoon from pre-war Nanjing. This outside capital contributed further to the "abnormal boom."[14]

* * *

The boom was "abnormal," as was the general economy of the time, because the market structure and the business conditions of wartime Shanghai were not conducive to the well-being of its movie industry. To begin with, because of the war, all of the major markets except Southeast Asia were now largely closed.[15] The Japanese blockade made marketing into the hinterland under Chinese rule both dangerous and costly, while the occupied areas were either economically devastated or under firm control by various Japanese-sponsored movie studios. Hence Shanghai and the overseas Chinese communities in Southeast Asia became the major outlets for *gudao* productions. But Southeast Asia had been a comparatively small and scattered market, saturated with fierce competition from small-budget Cantonese movies from Hong Kong. This made the local market more important that ever, yet Shanghai remained as before the war under the domination of Hollywood motion pictures which displaced Chinese productions to the margin of the cinema industry, appealing mainly to the less educated and more tradition-bound petty urbanites and recent refugees. On the other hand, Shanghai remained dependent on Western markets for filmstock and all kinds of shooting equipment. Along with general inflation, the war had disrupted the trade (e.g. Agfa film ceased to be available after 1938), making production costs spiral upwards with a 300% increase in 1940. Thus while a foot of raw film cost $0.23 in 1937, it rose to $1.30 in early 1940.[16]

---

14. *Dianying shijie* 2:1 (January 1940); *Xinhua huabao*, 5:5 (May 1940); *Dianying shenghuo* no. 14 (July 1940).

15. Hong Kong remained accessible, but Mandarin productions had only limited appeals to the predominantly Cantonese audiences there until the aggressive marketing strategies of Shaw Brothers in the early 1960's. For a study of the Hong Kong film industry during the war, see Poshek Fu, "Patriotism or Profit: Hong Kong Cinema during the Second World War," in *Early Images of Hong Kong and China*, ed. Law Kar (Hong Kong, 1995).

16. See *Xinhua huabao* 5:8 (August 1940); *Dianying shijie* 2:1 (January 1940); *Shenbao*, June 30, 1940; *Dianying shenghuo* no. 8 (April 1945).

Along with this change in market structure and rising costs, there was also threat of political terrorism. Although Japan could not control the foreign concessions for fear of provoking the Western powers into war, it instead recruited Chinese gangsters and former Nationalist turncoats to terrorize the city. These Japanese agents challenged the authority of the Shanghai Municipal Police and engaged the underground Nationalist secret services in a "terrorist war." Bombings, kidnappings, and assassinations became part of the everday life in Shanghai and people of any or even no political inclination fell victim to the terrorism. As a mass medium that was "bathed in the purple glow of luxury," the movie industry became an easy target.[17] In fact, Japan began as early as 1938 to try to infiltrate Shanghai's film industry; as a result rumors of which company was a cover for Japanese agents and who were "traitors" terrorized all people involved in filmmaking.

Actually the Japanese had made little headway in influencing the movie business until 1940. Before then the only Chinese filmmakers the Press Bureau of the Central Expeditionary Army in Shanghai succeeded to recruit were the Taiwan-born modernist writer Liu Na'ou and his long-time associates, Wang Tianshi and Tianzuo, both movie administrators with the GMD Central Studio who had been out of work since the fall of the city. Liu and the Wang brothers approached Shen Tianyin to fund Guangming's production, Li Pingqian's *Chuhua nu (Camelia)*, in the guise of "overseas Chinese money." They then shipped a copy of the film secretly for exhibition in Japan in November 1938, which became an instant scandal back home. This forced Shen to repeatedly try to explain his innocence and apologize and finally under public pressure, to close his new company.

About the same time, Liu Na'ou helped arrange a secret meeting between the Press Bureau chief and Zhang Shankun in which the latter was asked to accept Japanese capital in Xinhua. Zhang refused the offer and, fearing retaliation, went into hiding for two weeks. To avoid further harassment, he followed the example of the city's foreign-published Chinese press (*yangshang bao*), which astutely sought freedom of expression in the neutrality of the foreign powers, by registering his company as an American firm.[18] Also, in mid-1938, after failing repeatedly to press the Mingxing Studio owners Zhang Shichuan and Zhou Jianyun into submission, the Japanese military burnt down

---

17. The quotation is from Margaret Thorp, *America at the Movies* (New Haven, 1939). For terrorism in *gudao* Shanghai, see Frederic Wakeman, *The Shanghai Badlands: Wartime Terrorism and Urban Crime, 1937-1941* (Cambridge, 1996).

18. For the development of *yangshang bao*, see Poshek Fu, *Passivity, Resistance, and Collaboration: Intellectual Choices in Occupied Shanghai, 1937-1945* (Stanford, 1993), ch. 1.

its newly built studio in Fenglingqiao. Consequently Mingxing closed.[19] The press in unoccupied China as well as Hong Kong enthusiastically reported both incidents as a show of "patriotic defiance." The *yangshang* strategy of Zhang Shankun was hailed in particular as marking a "success of passive resistance against the enemy."[20]

This new business environment presented the Shanghai film industry with a fundamental predicament. The industry struggled to avert Japanese harassment as well as to profit from the "abnormal boom" (not knowing how long it would last) by "trying to give what the audience wanted." At the same time, in a wartime situation in which nationalist sentiment prevailed, it felt the industry faced political issues: how to balance political demands with commercial imperatives and how to continue to "sell fantasies" in a semi-occupied city?

Caution characterized the film industry's initial response to the predicament. In the first year of the semi-occupation, all the majors and independent companies trod cautiously by releasing films only of the low-budget popular genre. Even after the commercial success of *Diaochan*, all of the 18 films produced in 1938 by Zhang Shankun, who had the reputation of risk-taking ambition, were adventure fantasies, comedies, and tragic romances billed for box-office safety. A few examples: Wu Yonggang's *Wudi wushutuan* (An invincible martial arts troupe), Bu Wancang's *Qingtian xuenei* (Tragic love; a remake of a Ruan Lingyu's silent classic *Lian'ai yu yiwu*, or *Love and Responsibility*), and Yang Xiaozhong's *Diyu tanyan ji* (The search for beauties in hell). A spokesman for Xinhua explained this lack of "serious" product as a result of the "hostile circumstances."[21]

Despite such attempts at justification, this production trend enraged the community of critics who sought to police the Shanghai cultural world, molding it into a bastion of patriotic propaganda. Between 1938 and 1939, these critics assailed the movie business for making what the enemy rather than the audience wanted and thereby weakened the Chinese people's spirit of resistance. As fifty-one writers and literary supplement editors (including Ke Ling and the Communists A Ying and Yu Ling) raged in an open letter to the motion picture industry: "Unfortunately . . . Shanghai cinema which had had a history of magnificent achievements and a glorious mission before the war became after the emergence of *gudao* a miserable situation in which all sorts of monsters and ghosts and immortals (yaoshen-guiguai) run wild without fear

---

19. See Huang Tianshi, 13-18; *Wenxian* 1:4. For rumors see also *Yilin* no.48 (Dec. 1939) and *Xinhua huabao* 4:1 (January 1939).

20. *Yilin* n. 50 (March 1939).

21. Wang Qi (1939).

... [We see that] as romantic love between humans and ghosts. And they claim that these films are intended to fight feudalism or to punish evil-doers in order to reward the good. Actually they are (whether consciously or not) helping the enemy in poisoning (*mazui*) the minds of our fellow compatriots."[22]

This fierce assault oversimplified the social conditions of filmmaking. Cinema was both an art form and a risky business. In wartime Shanghai as in Hollywood, motion-picture production was capital-intensive, especially taking into account all the pre-release publicity and advertising which added substantially to the cost.[23] Yet there was no guarantee of profitable returns. The cinema industry did not know how long the boom would last, nor could it predict the market with certainty. In order to reduce the risk in production financing, especially in their first year of operation, all major studios and independent companies organized their release plans around genres of proven box-office records. Also, apart from Japanese threats, they tried to avoid political subjects for fear of harassment by the foreign settlement's Film Censorship Boards, whose rejection would cause serious financial damage.[24] Thus the preponderance of formulaic pictures in 1938.

* * *

At the time of war, when the country was swayed by intense nationalism, and national consciousness was permeated by what Paul Fussell calls a "versus habit," a perception structured by a "gross dichotomy" of "us" versus "them,"[25] the scathing criticism of the movie industry took the moral high ground. This pressure intensified the *gudao* filmmakers' sense of predicament. They sought an effective narrative formula that could combine patriotism with entertainment value. This new formula was to be developed—by chance—by Zhang Shankun.

In mid-1938, Zhang Shankun took a business trip to Hong Kong where he signed an up-and-coming Cantonese star Chen Yunshang (Nancy Chen) and

---

22. "Shanghai ge bao fukan bianzhe jinggao Shanghai dianyingjie," *Wenxian*, v. 3, 14-15.

23. For two rich discussions of the Hollywood studio system and market strategies, see Tino Bilo, *Grand Design: Hollywood as a Modern Business Enterprise, 1930-1939* (New York, 1993).

24. For fear of Japanese intervention, and in response to the rising tide of political terrorism and deterioration of social order in the solitary island, the Film Censorship Boards of both the International Settlement and the French Concession became adamant about banning any motion picture exhibiting overt political messages and violence and "sexual provocation." Thus, to the chagrin of the Shanghai audience, James Cagney's hit *Angels with Dirty Faces* and all Hollywood news reels were banned in 1938. See *Xinhua huabao* 4:4 (April 1939) and 4:6 (June 1939).

25. Paul Fussell, *The Great War and Modern Memory* (New York, 1975), ch. 3.

persuaded Ouyang Yuqian, a famous dramatist now living in exile, to write for Xinhua. Ouyang's new script turned out to be a costume melodrama, *Mulan congjun* (Hua Mulan joins the army), featuring the famous woman warrior Hua Mulan who replaced her feeble father to defend the country against foreign invasion during the Tang dynasty (618-907 A.D.). The story projected an idealized image of patriotism and feminine devotion at a time of turbulence, beautifully interweaving a political theme with a romantic narrative intended to increase its box-office power. Directed by Bu Wancang, who had created many outstanding period pieces since the 1920's, and starring Chen Yunshang and Mei Xi, *Mulan congjun* became a wartime classic.

Mulan congjun premiered on Chinese New Year's Day, February 16, 1939, at the Astor Theatre, which itself opened that same day. It came to be one of the highest-grossing pictures in Chinese cinema, running for 85 days of full houses, including subsequent-run playoffs. Moreover, the picture was universally welcomed by local critics as a wartime masterpiece, a "paean to nationalist spirit, expressing the indignation of the Chinese people here and now."[26] This broad popularity resulted as much from the brilliant cinematic portrayal of Hua Mulan as from the successful promotion campaign orchestrated by Zhang Shankun that revealed the advertising and marketing strategies of the industry.[27]

As with Hollywood, Chinese cinema in *gudao* Shanghai was centered on the star system, which worked not only to structure a film studio's relations with its employees (e.g., exclusive contracts) but also, and more importantly, to mobilize audience engagement and identification with the screen. Indeed the commercial culture surrounding Shanghai cinema was predicated on the drawing power and popular fetish of its (particularly female) stars. Hence, studio publicity, with and promotion campaign as a vehicle, was built around the appeal of its performers.[28] And "a star was not born," as W. Robert La Vine reminds us, "but made."[29] Chen Yunshang was indeed a star made and marketed by Zhang Shankun's Xinhua into a pop icon, the "queen of *gudao* cinema." It is on this star-making strategy that we now focus.

---

26. The quotations are from *Xinhua huabao* 4:3 (March 1939).

27. Because this paper will focus on the business side of Shanghai cinema, I shall not proceed to analyze the film here. For a cultural-political reading of it, see Poshek Fu, "Projecting Ambivalence: Chinese Cinema in Semi-occupied Shanghai, 1937-1941," in *Wartime Shanghai*, ed. Wen-hsin Yeh (London, 1998).

28. For a fine study of Hollywood promotion practices in the 1930's and 1940's, see Bilo (1993), 143-77.

29. Robert W. La Vine, *In a Glamorous Fashion: The Fabulous Years of Hollywood Costume Design* (New York, 1980), 27.

6.1. Hua Mulan (played by Chen Yunshang) as a military hero(ine). This pose became the centerpiece of the publicity campaign for the film *Mulan Joins the Army*. Courtesy of Dr. Hans Tang and Nancy Chan.

Since Chen Yunshang was little known outside Hong Kong, Zhang Shankun began a huge promotion campaign long before her arrival in Shanghai in order to make a star of her. Xinhua dispatched stories to fan magazines, tabloids, and gossip columns in major newspapers calling attention to the various offers Chen Yunshang, who was both "extraordinarily beautiful" and fluent in English, was receiving from Hollywood majors. Yet, on Zhang Shankun's insistence, she came to Shanghai to play in Xinhua's new picture before leaving for Hollywood. Moreover, the story proudly continued, Chen was no Anna May Wong, she was a fervent patriot making a point in her contracts with both Paramount and MGM that she would not feature in anti-Chinese racist productions. In other words, both Western recognition and national pride characterized Chen Yunshang's film career. Of course, all this was promotional gimmickry.[30] This promotional strategy in fact projected and reinforced the ambivalent psychology of many Shanghainese during the war: politically patriotic yet culturally pro-western. It also revealed the film company's construction of female identity which, in effect, echoed the hybridized image and commercial aesthetics of "beautiful lady" depicted in "calender poster," (Meinu yuefenpai) of the times.[31] Chen Yunshang often posed either in Western fashion (including swimming suits), but displaying a traditional mode of facial and body expression, or in Chinese *qipao* with a broad energetic smile typical of what the press described of a "Hollywood star." And she was invariably described by the Xinhua publicist as a "modern Chinese beauty" representing a rare blend of Chinese femininity and virtues and modern Western womanhood—refined and delicate, yet outgoing and independent.[32]

Besides appealing to the potential audiences' nationalist and modernist sentiment, which concurred with the political theme of the movie, Xinhua manipulated conventional promotion devices such as star photos to market its protegee. Like their American counterparts, Shanghai fans were voracious collectors of "glamour photos" of movie stars. Film magazines like *Dianying shenghuo* (Movie life) and *Dianying shijie* (Movie world) competed for circulation by printing as many recent and high-quality photographs of movie stars as possible, and the bulk of the letters to the editors consisted of requests for stars' photos or addresses. To satisfy the demand, portrait studios such as

---

30. See Huang and Ai (1996), 27.

31. See Wu Hao et al, ed., *Duhui Modern* (Calendar posters of the modern Chinese woman) (Hong Kong, 1994).

32. See Tan Zongxia, *Chen Yunshang zhuan* (A biography of Chen Yunshang) (Hong Kong, 1996), 116-136.

Shanghai Xinyi Meishu Gongxi began to compile a huge collection of Chinese and Hollywood star photos of different sizes and qualities for sale. Also for publicity purposes, distributors and production companies often handed out star photos or fancy special issues (*tekan*) filled with these much sought-after souvenirs.

In order to launch Chen Yunshang's debut, Xinhua arranged for her to come to Shanghai on Christmas Eve. Soon after her arrival, Zhang Shankun took her to a Christmas ball at the luxurious Paramount Club, where glossy photos of the star were being given out. They were also distributed in 16 other top night clubs in town. For the next three days, accompanied by Zhang and other top Xinhua administrators, Chen visited the four major department stores on Nanjing Road, the site of Shanghai's commercial culture, as well as several other night clubs in the neighborhood where "some patrons began to recognize her."[33] When she began work at the studio a few days later, news reporters chased her around for stories. Thus a new star, the future Hu Die from South China, was soon to be born.[34]

Before the film's release, following common practice in movie publicity, Xinhua placed advertisements on all local newspapers. Probably unsure of the commercial appeal of a political subject, the publicists chose to follow the convention of stressing the spectacle, stars, and genre of *Mulan congjun*. For example, on genre: "An absolute unique/solemn, ebullient, soul-stirring/great historical costume drama." And on the star:

"Ms. Chen Yunshang will soon return south,
this is her only performance [here].
Going all out, putting her whole soul in it,
this is a performance of consummate skill."[35]

Colorful posters were put all over town, while an empty lot next to the Sun Department Store between Nanjing and Yu Xiaqing Roads was rented to set up a life/human-sized image of Hua Mulan in military uniform (the same image as that on the newspaper ads and posters to attract the passersby).[36]

To maximize the drawing power of the new star, Zhang Shankun signed a contract with his friend Shi Tingpan, owner of the newly completed first-run house, Astor, for the film's release. Hence the premiere gala coincided with the

---

33. Ni Na, "Chen Yunshang yizhou jian" (Chen Yunshang in one week), *Xinhua huabao* 4:1 (January 1939).
34. For this quotation see Ni Na (1939).
35. For these ads, see *Shenbao* Feb 14 and 15, 1939.
36. Interview with Tong Yuejuan by Fu Poshek and Law Kar, Hong Kong, July 3, 1994.

cinema's opening ceremony which was attended by many social dignitaries and members of the business elite including Yu Xiaqing and Wen Lanting. As a result, a huge prominent crowd was drawn to the premier. In order to lend to the event a social cachet, the opening-day was promoted as the "day of Hua Mulan joins the army" benefit, with the stars Chen Yun Shang and Mei Xi performing on stage before each show and part of the proceeds going to refugee relief. Following the premier gala came 84 days of full houses.

A star had indeed been born. Zhang Shankun's well-orchestrated publicity campaign interwove patriotic concern with mass appeal and created a perfect correspondence between his protegee's screen persona and her carefully constructed off-screen personality, thus launching Chen Yunshang into stardom overnight and reaping huge profits for Xinhua. Overcoming the predicament created by the contradiction between high-minded purpose and the profit motive, Zhang Shankun became the "Number One" of the *gudao* film business.

* * *

Hoping to repeat this success, Xinhua duplicated the same narrative formula for Chen Yunshang and focused its production on historical drama. Besides repeating Chen's role as a woman warrior in such vehicles as *Qin Liangyu* and *Fei Zhen'e ci hu*, the company released a series of high-budget period pieces with patriotic themes in 1939 and early 1940 that included the three critically acclaimed films: Wu Yonggang's *Yue Fei* (starring Liu Qiong), Zhang Shankun's *Ge Nengniang* (Gu Lanjun) and Bu Wancang's *Xi shi* (Yuan Meiyun). Other production companies also tried to follow suit. Thus the marketplace of 1939 and 1940 was crowded with heroes and heroines dedicated to moral purity and national freedom. For example, the independent companies Hezhong (Solidarity) shot *Xiang fei* (d. Zhu Shilin) and Minhua (People's China) made a reputation in releasing the high-budget and well-crafted *Kong Fuzi* by Fei Mu, while the major Yihua produced Wang Cilong's *Jing Ke ci Qin wang* (The assassination of the Qin Emperor by Jing Ke) and Wang Yuanlong's *Taiping Tianguo* (Kingdom of heavenly peace).[37]

But by early 1940, historical dramas began to show signs of saturating the market. Both of Xinhua's high-budget vehicles *Yue Fei* and *Ge Nengniang* (a transcription of A Ying's 1939 patriotic stage hit *Mingmo yiheng* or the Sorrow of late Ming), for example, were box-office flops in spite of critical acclaim.

While the film community was debating on how to revitalize the historical genre, the unexpected box-office success of the independent Zhongguo

---

37. Surely this flurry of historical films was a result of both political imperative and market value. For an analysis of the political reasons, see Poshek Fu (1998).

Lianmei (China United) Productions' costume romance Wu Cun's *Liang Shanbo yu Zhu Yingtai* (The butterfly lovers) started a new genre cycle: *minjian gushi*, folktales and popular fiction.[38] There were three main reasons for the popularity of this costume genre. First, in 1940, the Shanghai market aside, Southeast Asian audiences preferred costume dramas, especially those with light-hearted, familiar stories and memorable musical numbers. As distributors would pay as much as 10,000 for a copy, which accounted for anywhere between 1/3 and 1/10 of the production costs, the industry followed its audience. Guohua turned out to be the biggest beneficiary of this new production trend, because of the shrewd leadership of veteran director Zhang Shichuan, who was reputed to be the industry's best producer of popular romance while its superstar Zhou Xuan was a mesmerizing singer. So as to increase the copy fee, Guohua put in a total of ten numbers in Zhou's *Xixiang ji* (Romance of the western chamber),whose theme song *kaohong* was to become the No. 1 hit in Shanghai as well as in Southeast Asia.[39]

Second, patriotic historical drama was politically risky. As the director Zhu Shilin explained, his *Xiang fei* had to undergo several reviews and many cuts before release. *Minjian gushi*, with its narrative emphasis on romance and formulaic twists of fortune was safe. Third, at a time of rapidly rising costs, the genre required little capitalization; it involved only adaptation of available folklore and popular fiction, and above all, smaller investment because of demonstrably less lavish sets and props than historical films. It was this combination of low-cost, dependable market, and political safety that resulted in an accelerated race in the industry. Overlap of production (or *shuangbao an*, "twins," as it was know in the trade) was as common as sloppy craftsmanship due to the pressure of the time. In 1940 alone there was a total of four "twins," involving all three majors. The most notorious one was that between Guohua and Yihua in May of 1940: they jockeyed to be the first to finish *San xiao* (Three smiles). The result was appalling: Yihua (starring the new star Li Lihua) finished it in six-and-a-half-days! To the surprise of the industry, however, both pictures did well at the box-office.[40] After several bad investments, Zhang Shankun, who had been trying hard to project an image (after *Mulan congjun*) of a serious filmmaker deeply concerned for the "naional cause," could not afford to remain aloof and jumped in the race, making nine pictures simultaneously in 45 days![41] Even his "woman warrior"

---

38. Zhonghua Lianmei was founded by 16 leaders of the industry who included Zhang Shankun, Yan Chuntang, and Bian Yuying. See *Xinhua huabao* 5:2 (February 1940).

39. Su Yadao 1982, 93.

40. Ibid., 103-7; and *Zhongguo yingxun* 1:9 (May 1940).

41. *Dianying shijie* no. 17 (October 1940); *Zhongguo yingxun* 1:15 (June 1940).

Chen Yunshang was recast into a trite role of a maudlin, acquiescent girl in the folk romance *Bi yuzhan* (Green jade hairpin). Zhang Shankun felt compelled to justify his change of production strategy in terms of political necessity, insisting on the "educational function" of his films, on a front-page advertisement he put in all the city's major newspapers: "Our company is dedicated to . . . making movies of meaningful themes and keeping in touch with social needs in order to fulfil the principle of combining entertainment with education . . . [The trend we now follow of making *minjian gushi* movies] is certainly a step backward. But it might in fact be valuable as a strategy of gradually introducing this important medium to the audience who are more familiar with local operas and, especially women, with *tanci* (storytelling)."[42]

The predominance of *minjian gushi* melodrama drew vilification from the film critics. They accused the industry of political "retrogradation" (*kai daoche*), giving rein to "feudal" sentiments that jettison the "heroic" tradition of Shanghai cinema. For example, in an interview with a pro-Guomindang magazine, Chen Yunshang (not without self-interest) took up her screen persona to chastise the production trend as a disgusting mimicry of Hong Kong movie making, which had an (undeserved) reputation in Shanghai for poor craftsmanship and backward politics.[43] A film critic went so far as accusing: [All our films] are like digging out dead persons from graves . . . sending forth a stale smell of decay, celebrating superstitions and feudalism, disseminating the Japanese policy of pacification."[44]

However, by 1940 the industry had very little maneuvering room to develop new narrative formulae and promotion campaigns. It was subjected to the worst business conditions before the onset of complete occupation in 1941. The "abnormal boom" seemed to be coming to an end. As severe inflation drove up production costs, the market was rapidly contracting. Starting in 1940, Shanghai was able to sell some pictures to the southwest. But, as evidenced by the mass burning of *Mulan congjun* as a "traitorous" product in Chongqing in early 1940, the prevalent prejudice of identifying residence in Shanghai with complicity made it a restricted outlet. Then the departure of many refugees as partly a result of economic pressures led to a decrease in Shanghai's audiences, and the outbreak of the European war raised concern over Southeast Asia's economic stability. In desperation, with Zhang

---

42. *Shenbao* June 30, 1940.
43. See *Yilin* no. 69 (March 1940).
44. *Dianying shijie* no. 13 (June 1940).

Shankun's lead, the industry began to export their products into the occupied areas around central China.[45]

In order to cut costs, moreover, in late 1940 the film industry came to a binding agreement that all companies had to limit their newspaper advertisements to a certain length.[46] But as the very success of *Mulan congjun* shows, movie sales depended on carefully planned promotion and publicity. This cost-cutting move would certainly affect box-office earnings. No wonder the Yihua boss Yan Chuntang complained in a rare interview that he would have been a millionaire, if he had put all his money in speculation rather than into the "bottomless pit" of movie making.[47]

In addition to all these financial problems, censorship became ever more stringent after 1940, when the solitary island was plagued with mass unemployment and political incidences of foreign powers' increasing concessions to Japanese demands. Although there has never been conclusive proof of any casual relation between movies and social behavior, the Film Censorship Boards of the foreign concessions, like governments everywhere, found the film industry an easy scapegoat and banned any picture that it thought would provoke the Japanese or damage "social morale." For example, Guohua's 1940 highly publicized social melodrama *Hei tiantang* (Dark paradise), starring Zhou Xuan, which added some elements of social commentary into its generic structure, was reviewed three times and release was permitted only after the scene on denouncing commodity speculation was cut. Xinhua, on the other hand, was prohibited from shooting an exploitation film based on a true story of prostitution for it would expose the violence and brutality of the city's night life.[48]

By early 1941, the popularity of costume drama subsided. The industry had to come up with a new narrative strategy to draw crowds. Under all the financial and political restraints, as well as the audience's and distributors' demand for *shizhuang* (modern) genres, it initiated a new tide of tragic romance and melodrama, mostly transcriptions of a 20th century popular fiction and stage drama. There were significant differences of production emphasis, however, between movie companies. Among the three giants, Guohua and Yihua emphasized entertainment value, adapting mainly from Mandarin Duck and Butterfly novels (by authors such as Zhang Henshui and

---

45. For the marginalization of Shanghai cinema and the controversial sale of film into occupied areas, see Poshek Fu (1998).

46. *Dianying shenghuo* no. 19 (December 1940).

47. Cheng Da, "*Yinhai zuotan*" (A symposium on cinema), *Shanghai shenghuo* 4:5 (May 1940).

48. *Zhongguo yingxun* 1:19 (July 1940).

Cheng Xiaoqing) and justifying their release plan with the familiar anti-feudal rhetoric. Xinhua tried to maintain its reputation as the industry's "Number One" by including also famous May Fourth works. After making profits from such farces as *Xianxia da guniang* (Village girl) starring Yuan Meiyun, for example, it produced Cao Yu's *Yuanye* in mid 1941. The Big Three were also interested in acquiring the movie rights to Ba Jin's popular classic *Jia* (Family). Xinhua won the race but before it was able to shoot it, Japan extended its occupation into the foreign areas of Shanghai. *gudao* disappeared and along with it, its film industry.

* * *

This paper demonstrates that the *gudao* film industry, except for *Mulan congjun* and several other historical films, did not succeed in overcoming the predicament created by the contradiction between patriotic engagement and commercial needs. This is actually a classic dilemma in world cinema (how to choose between social/artistic purposes and box-office appeals), and it was intensified in Shanghai by the exigency of the Japanese occupation. Shanghai filmmakers were under greater pressure to find an effective production and marketing strategy that could be both entertaining and politically engaged, but not unlike others elsewhere, they failed. In fact, even with the marketing genius of Zhang Shankun and the patriotic persona of Chen Yunshang, it proved impossible to duplicate the success of *Mulan congjun*. Was it because the Shanghai audience had become more anxious about their jobs or food bills than anything else when the occupation became "normalized?" Or, as happened everywhere in the world, did the audiences' tastes simply shift over time in ways that no one could ever predict or control?

It would be an oversimplification of history, nonetheless, if we see only the failure of the *gudao* film industry to overcome the political predicament. A remarkable aspect of the industry was its ability to survive and grow against all the adversity: limited markets, small capitalization, political pressures, ever increasing production costs, as well as the uncertain combination of resourcefulness, strong leadership, and marketing and advertising ingenuity. Nonetheless, the industry was successful not only in providing employment and creative outlets for many stars, directors and technicians, but also in sustaining the growth of Shanghai's commercial culture by producing over 200 films in less than four years. It refused to give up and allow Shanghai to become a cinematic wasteland. Thereby it laid the ground work for the postwar reconstruction of Chinese cinema.

Milk for Health, Milk for Profit:
Shanghai's Chinese Dairy Industry under
Japanese Occupation

Susan Glosser

Alien as it was, milk[1] became the focus of great entrepreneurial energy when, in the 1920s, a group of foreign-educated Chinese businessmen began promoting it as the key to China's revitalization. But milk-entrepreneurs faced several challenges. Milk itself was so foreign as to be literally indigestible. Given that most consumers were probably lactose-intolerant, promoters had to work hard to convince potential consumers of the nutritional advantages of drinking milk. The industry as a whole also continually faced formidable difficulties in ensuring the cleanliness and profitability of their product. In their efforts to surmount these problems, the industry members formed dairy associations. The most powerful of these organizations, the Shanghai Dairy Association (SDA), left records that offer a unique perspective on Republican

---

Research for this paper was done in part with dissertation research support provided by the Committee for Scholarly Communication with the People's Republic of China. The author would like to thank all the participants of the conference "Inventing Nanjing Road: Commercial Culture in Shanghai, 1864-1949" for their comments and criticisms. Special thanks go to Carlton Benson, Marie-Claire Bergère, Alan Cole, Kevin Czapla, Sherry Fowler, and the anonymous reader for the Cornell East Asian series for their careful readings and suggestions. I very much appreciated the alacrity with which the staff at the Shanghai Municipal Archive supplied these files and their assistance in copying out some of the documents. I am grateful to Mark Tam, Director of the Hoover Institute's East Asian collection and Olga Katz, Specialist in Interlibrary Loans at the Hoover Library, for making it possible for me to reproduce a photograph from the East Asian collection. Finally, whether he wants it or not, Frederic Wakeman, Jr. deserves credit for getting me thinking about this fascinating question. Of course, his responsibility ends there; he is not responsible for any crudities or infelicities the reader may find.

1. "Milk" refers to cow's milk unless otherwise indicated.

commercial culture. As major Chinese dairymen emerged in the 1920s, they abandoned their affiliations with Chinese producers and joined forces with the large foreign-operated dairies under the umbrella of the SDA. Later, this association took in stride the obstacles created by Japanese occupation. In a time of food shortages, milk was highly valued by those who could afford it—free foreigners, Japanese hospitals, and wealthy Chinese.[2] The Association took advantage of wartime demand for milk and used it to maintain enough leverage to convince the Shanghai Municipal Government to allow them to continue production during occupation. Their successful appeals to the Shanghai Municipal Government illuminate the process of negotiation and compromise that kept businesses afloat during occupation and ultimately lead us to consider the issue of collaboration and its relationship with commercial culture.

Milk—A Key to Darwinian Success

Chinese entrepreneurs not only competed for foreign customers, but also tried to create a new market by encouraging their wealthy and well-educated compatriots to adopt the Western habit of drinking milk. They touted milk's superior nutritional properties and its digestibility. For example, Hu Jiafeng of the Qingdao Municipal Government wrote, "Recently, among those who talk about public health, not one fails to take milk to be a superior nutritional product. They say milk is rich in nutrients, easy to digest, appropriate for young and old."[3] In their milk promotions, dairymen demonstrated a thorough knowledge of modern production and sanitation, a fervent desire to expand the industry, and a firm conviction that increased milk consumption meant better health. Family and women's magazines and newspapers like *Dagong bao* and *Shenbao* began to carry ads for fresh and powdered milk. The 1930s and 40s even saw a small boom in educational books about milk and other dairy products.

Milk promoters used the logic of Social Darwinism to persuade the Chinese to drink milk. Like many groups that attempted to effect social,

---

2. I am grateful to Frederic Wakeman, Jr. for bringing this point home to me. He also called my attention to the novel, *Au Bonne Buerre*. Set in wartime France, it vividly illustrates the immense importance which dairy products assumed in the scanty diet caused by wartime shortages. For another interesting, if precious, account of food shortages in occupied France see Alice B. Toklas, *The Alice B. Toklas Cook Book* (New York: Harper & Brothers, 1954), 203-22.

3. Hu Jiafeng [of the Qingdao Municipal Government], Preface, *Niuru ji qi zhipin zhi yanjiu* (A study of milk and its products), Jin Cishuo, ed. (Shanghai: Commercial Press, 1936). See also the first page of the introduction of this text.

political, or cultural change in Republican China, dairy entrepreneurs presented milk-drinking as the key to China's success in the evolutionary struggle to survive. For example, the introduction to *Milk and Its Products*, published first in 1937 and reprinted in 1947, began like this:

"Survival of the fittest," this is the universal law of evolution. Under the power of modern science, an unscientific people will find itself behind the times and conquered. Food is the people's heaven. We no longer eat the raw flesh and drink the blood of wild animals. Naturally, food must also be "scientificized." What is a scientific food? It is economical, sanitary, and nutritious. In this light, milk and its products meet these requirements. No wonder it has become an important daily food for Westerners. Because milk is a valuable food, we must proffer encouragement so that the Chinese dairy industry quickly expands. There must be milk for each person to drink. We do not want to let it become [only] a food supplement for rich people! We must also be able to supply ourselves. We do not want to import dairy cows and dairy products from abroad every year.[4]

Such presentations identified milk with Western modernity and science—the keys to Darwinian success. Milk's association with science and contemporary Western societies made it modern. The nutritional knowledge which revealed the body's "need" for milk's nutrients and the technical expertise which rendered it safe to drink made it scientific.[5]

In their discussions of milk consumption, scientific "experts" drew explicit comparisons between Chinese and Western nutritional knowledge. For example, the author of the preface to *Milk Research* reported that:

milk is an important part of the European and American diet. Through the promotion of nutritional experts, it has become a necessary beverage. In contrast, with regard to food, our people only ask that their three meals a day be tasty and plentiful. In a country as scientifically

---

4. Wu Xinfa, Introduction, "*Niuru ji qi zhipin* (Milk and its products)," Wu Xinfa, ed. (1936 Reprint. Shanghai: Zhengzhong shuju, 1947). Wu's valuation of milk and his ambitions for the milk industry were shared by the leaders of the dairy industry. See for example, You Huaigao's (Yu Tse-mai) views on the subject, as treated in Susan Glosser, "The Business of Family: You Huaigao and the Commercialization of a May Fourth Ideal," *Republican China* (Spring 1995).

5. See, for example, Xu Fuqi, "Preface," *Niuru yanjiu* (Milk research), Minzhi shuju, 1929. Booklets on milk were published by experts who wished to share their knowledge about milk products, their nutritional value, and their preservation.

backward as China, there are very few who know about nutritional value or how to handle food in a way that does not destroy its nutrients.[6]

T. M. Yu, president of the SDA from January 1942 to mid-July 1945,[7] believed illiteracy and the failure to drink milk were the two most pressing problems facing China. According to his statistics, the small number of foreigners in Shanghai accounted for three-quarters of family milk consumption.[8] Even when writers laid claim to the historic practice of milk drinking, they did so with an eye to recovering lost vigor. According to one Chinese account,

> In the thirteenth century when Yuan Taizu, Genghis Khan, conquered a large part of Europe, his soldiers all carried dried milk as part of their provisions. . . . As for Chinese consumption of milk . . . although there is no clear record, we can hypothesize that this was an ancient fact. In the provinces of the north east and north west there are still people who live the ancient life of nomadic herding. They . . . drink milk and eat meat to live. Probably the people in the provinces in these parts . . . changed from herding to agriculture and so gradually tended to use plants as their food. Today, because of custom and superstition, few people consume milk.[9]

Arguments promoting milk consumption present one of the most literal interpretations of Social Darwinism found in the Republican period. Entrepreneurs avidly promoted milk as the epitome of what it meant to be scientific and modern. It was as if milk drinkers could absorb into their very bones that which was responsible for Western wealth and power.

---

6. Gu Xueqiu, "Preface," *Niuru yanjiu* (Milk research) (Shanghai: Zhonghua shuju, 1940).

7. Shanghai Municipal Archive, S118.1.3, S118.1.4. All materials which begin with the number S118 can be found in the Shanghai Municipal Archive. Hereafter the citation will only list the file number and a description if appropriate. In *pinyin* Yu's family name is rendered as You. I have retained the spelling which he himself used for the convenience of the reader. When using English, Yu transliterated his name as Tse-mai. He signed his Shanghai Dairy Industry correspondence, which was written in English, T. M. Yu. When writing in Chinese in his capacity as the editor of *Family Weekly* (*Xiao jiating*) he used the pen-name Huaigao.

8. *Jiating xingqi*[Family weekly, *JTXQ*] 1.2 (November 24, 1935): back page.

9. Wu Xinfa, *Niuru ji qizhipin*, 2-4.

The Chinese were not alone in their belief in the redemptive powers of milk. Milk production and consumption had been promoted in Japan since the Meiji Restoration.[10] Japanese occupation forces in Shanghai cared enough about milk production to track the capacity of the city's pasteurization plants.[11] Although milk promotion in the United States has not equated milk with modernity, it has portrayed it as indispensable to a sound mind and body. That dairy entrepreneurs so aggressively tackled the challenge of marketing milk to a traditionally non-drinking population demonstrates the vitality of Shanghai's commercial culture. These men understood their product and their potential customers. In their advertising and promotional literature they skillfully chose a language that would sell their product.[12]

Consumption

The introduction of *A Study of Milk and its Products* claimed that "in recent years, in every great city in China, the consumption of milk has risen daily."[13] The increase in demand was due, in part, to the growing foreign population. In addition, the prevalence of Western candy stores, ice-cream shops, and bakeries accounted for a large portion of milk consumption. But experts and entrepreneurs claimed that the Chinese population created some of the demand too. Wu Xinfa attributed this increase in demand to "the influence of Western customs and scientific knowledge" which resulted in rising Chinese consumption of Western foods.[14] Another author claimed that

10. See for example, Sasaki Rinjiro, "Gyunyu oyobi gyuseihin" (Milk and milk products) in *Gendai shokuryo taikan* (A general survey of modern foodstuffs) Ryoyukai, ed. (1929), 518-521, and Nagasaki Kemeto, *Junbyaku no kideki—gyunyu hyakunen no ayumi* (The pure white trail—a hundred-year history of milk) (Tokyo: Shimin shoren, 1976), 15-57.

11. See for example, Shanhai-shi sei kenkyu kai, "Kobukyoku keihi setsuyaku tokubetsu i inkai hokoku no kensa: Kobukyoku gyosei seiri ni tai suru 2, 3, no shian" (A report and investigation of the special committee on expenses and frugality of the Office of Public Works: the second and third draft of the executive of the Office of Public Works) (1942), 23. This report was marked "Top Secret." Similar information is published in Noguchi Kimniro, *Shanhai kyodo sokaikobukyoku* (Office of the Shanghai International Concession) (Shanhai: Nikko shoin, 1940), 68.

12. Although an occaional critic complained that wealthy mothers used cow's milk to free themselves from the burden of breast-feeding, the modern issues surrounding the promotion of infant formula in developing countries appear not to have been an issue in this time and place. The Chinese hinterland simply lacked the transportation, marketing infrastructure, and buying power to make such an undertaking attractive to milk companies.

13. Ji Cishuo, "Introduction," *Niuru ji qi zhipin zhi yanjiu* (Shanghai: Commercial Press, 1936), 1.

14. Wu, Xinfa, *Niuru ji qi zhipin*, 4.

with the rising standard of living, few mothers[15] wanted to bother with breast-feeding and began to rely on canned or powdered milk instead.[16]

Although no direct studies of milk consumption have emerged, milk advertising targeted those Chinese familiar with Western customs and interested in the new "scientific" approach to nutrition and hygiene.[17] Despite the industry's ambition to supply all Chinese with milk, the beverage remained prohibitively expensive.[18] During occupation the SDA argued that milk was an "essential commodity" (like bread, cooking oil, and sugar) and should, therefore, be exempted from the four-percent retail tax. The Shanghai Special Municipality government disagreed: "Milk is clearly not the same as a daily food necessity for most people and there can be no exemption from the tax."[19] All this suggests that milk played an insignificant role in the average Chinese diet.[20]

Still, dairy entrepreneurs actively polished their image and promoted their industry. Yu insisted that in contrast to the "uneducated class of people" who had operated Chinese dairies in the first decade of Republican China, the businessmen of the 30s and 40s were "a highly educated class" and "persons of high integrity."[21] Yu also organized milk-drinking "movements" in which he delivered milk at discounted prices to students, office workers, and infants.[22] In October 1943, the SDA resolved to establish a publication board for a bi-monthly magazine, *China Dairy Journal*.[23] The SDA also operated its

---

15. Although the text uses the term for parents (*fumu*) here and elsewhere contexts indicates that this should be read "mothers."

16. Xu Fuqi, *Niuru yanjiu*, "Preface," 1.

17. Chinese pharmacology had long recognized the role which foods play in health. Although dairymen did not directly attack this indigenous nutritional tradition, their emphasis on "scientific" nutrition was probably intended as an implicit criticism of this approach to foods.

18. In 1935, daily delivery of a pound (about a pint, or .550 liters) of milk cost six silver dollars per month. (*JTXQ* 1, no. 3 [November 24, 1935]: back page). At this time a live-in servant's wage averaged about five dollars per month.

19. Secretary General, First District Administration, Shanghai Special Municipality, to the SDA, February 1944, S118.1.19, 002.

20. Anecdotal evidence suggests that most Chinese consumed milk only indirectly through ice cream and pastries.

21. Yu Tse-mai, SDA to Director of Public Health, First District Administration, Shanghai Special Municipality, March 11, 1944, S118.1.20.

22. "Riyong pin qianshuo—niunai,"*JTXQ* 1.4 (December 15, 1935): 13.

23. Y. Z. Lee, William Luke, Daniel C. Fu, Captain K. E. Peterson and T. M. Yu [You Huaigao] formed the editorial board. (Executive Committee Meeting, May 13, 1944, S118.1.4, 015.) Whether the publication ever made it to press is unknown. I have been unable to locate a copy.

own promotional department.[24] When the Public Health Department staged a health exhibition at the Race Course on 1 June 1944, the SDA mounted a photo exhibit, distributed promotional literature, and sold milk at a reduced price.[25] Late in 1944, the SDA gave St. John's University 700,000 *yuan* to help its Agriculture Department establish a dairy.[26]

A Statistical Sketch of the Dairy Industry Before Occupation

Just as our information on consumption is scanty and impressionistic, statistical information on the dairy industry is sparse and probably imprecise. Nevertheless, it affords us a sense of the industry's scale and the sizable role which Chinese dairies played in it. Before 1923, most Shanghai dairies operated in the foreign concessions.[27] The Shanghai Municipal Council reported that in 1923 slightly more than half of Shanghai's forty-two licensed dairies operated in the concessions and the Western district. The same report shows Western and Chinese dairies jockeying for control of the market. Chinese and foreign dairies raised almost equal amounts of cattle. Chinese dairies outnumbered Western dairies more than two to one, but, as Table I shows, they also averaged less than half as many cows per dairy.[28] In the next decade, the number of licensed dairies almost tripled. In 1933 the Shanghai Municipal Council licensed 28 dairies[29] while the city government of greater Shanghai licensed eighty-eight.[30] In 1935, sixty-five small dairy farms were gathered in Pudong and other outskirts of Shanghai.[31] Meanwhile, Chinese dairies maintained a dominant position in the industry, accounting for 1,800 of the city's approximately 3,000 head of dairy cattle in the early 1930s.

Dairy production was not, however, limited to Shanghai. In 1936, Nanjing counted thirty farms milking a total of five to six hundred head of cattle. Qingdao, Beijing, Tianjin, and Hankou reported forty to fifty dairy farms apiece. Excluding Mongolia, there were 10,000 head of dairy cows in all of

---

24. Y. Z. Lee was head of the department in January 1945. (S118.1.1, 020 back.)

25. Executive Committee Meeting minutes, May13, 1944, S118.1.4, 015.

26. SDA to St. John's University's Department of Agriculture, c. December 1944; Shen Siliang, University president to the SDA, January 12, 1945, S118.1.22, 006-009.

27. "Rupin gongye gaikuang diaocha baogao shu" (Report on the investigation into the circumstances of the dairy industry) c. 1952, S118.3.1, 1-5.

28. Annual Report of the Shanghai Municipal Council, 1923, Appendix no. 5, p. 159.

29. *Shanghai shi tongji, buchong cailiao* (Statistics for the Municipality of Shanghai, supplementary materials) (Shanghai Civic Association, 1934), 109.

30. *Shanghai shi tongji, buchong cailiao*, 108.

31. *Shanghai nianjian* (Shanghai yearbook) (Shanghai: Shanghai shi tongji guan, 1935), 50.

Table 7.1

Industry Profile

	Chinese	Japanese	Western	Korean	Total
Cows	676	119	640	42	1,477
%	46%	8%	44%	3%	
dairies	26	3	11	1	41
%	63%	7%	27%	2%	
Cows/dairy	26	40	27	42	36

Source: Annual Report of the Shanghai Municipal Council, 1923, appendix no. 5, 159.

China producing 30,000,000 pounds of milk a year.[32] Shanghai was the undisputed leader in milk production, accounting for 12,000,000 pounds per year compared to the 1,000,000 pounds in annual production reported by Nanjing and Canton.[33]

A Brief Organizational History

The organizational history of the Shanghai dairy industry presented here has been pieced together from fragments of organizational documents and from two investigative reports based on interviews which the Chinese Communist Party (CCP) conducted with members of the industry in 1952 as part of the Party's effort to inventory and reorganize Shanghai's businesses after the civil war (1945-1949). The interviewees brought their own agendas to their meetings with CCP investigators—the wealthier, larger dairies seem to have tried to use the CCP to settle old scores with the smaller grade-C dairies. Thus, this narrative is not the final word on the organizational history of the dairy industry. It does provide, however, the outlines of the organizational divisions which reflected the market-place tensions and political ambiguities of the 1930s and 1940s.[34]

---

32. At the time, a good milk cow produced about 5,000 pounds of milk per year for three years. "Memorandum on depreciation of cows," S118.1.17, 107.

33. Wu, Xinfa, *Niuru ji qi zhipin*, 16.

34. Unless otherwise noted, the information for this section comes from the following two sources: "Rupinye di guoqu he xianzai" (The milk industry past and present), December 1952, S118.3.1, 6-11, and "Rupin gongye gaikuang diaocha baogao shu" (Report on the

Chinese dairymen formed their first cooperative association (*lianyi hui*) in 1924 in response to the Shanghai Municipal Council's legislation of stiffer regulations governing the production and processing of milk. In April of the previous year, the Council appointed the Pure Milk Supply Commission to

> investigate the conditions governing the supply of milk in Shanghai, and its vicinity, and to make such recommendations to the Council as the Commission may consider desirable and practicable for the purpose of safeguarding the purity of the milk sold, and improvement in the conditions of its delivery to residents in the Settlements and on roads beyond limits under the Council's control.[35]

Both Chinese and foreign-owned dairies sometimes operated under shockingly unsanitary conditions. A Shanghai resident offered the following description in 1939, fifteen years after the Shanghai Municiple Council had begun a concerted effort to police the dairies. We can well imagine that like conditions prompted 1920s legislation to sanitize these "cesspools of disease."[36]

> Right next door to the apartment house where I live, there is a Dairy (sic) licensed to sell grade A milk. This Dairy is foreign-owned and under foreign supervision. Yet, from what I see at least four time daily, when passing this establishment, I am rather surprised that there are very few epidemics here due to the dirty methods used in obtaining and distributing milk: the house itself (or rather a bunch of old dilapidated shacks) is dirty inside and out; the various shacks, where the different departments of the Dairy are located, in addition to containing machinery etc., are used for the night as sleeping quarters for the Chinese staff: the staff itself (both Chinese and foreign) are unkempt (*sic*) to the extreme, and are usually dressed in white overalls, which are dull-gray from dirt.[37]

---

investigation into the circumstances of the dairy industry), c. December 1952, S118.3.1, 1-5. The former appears to have been the official version of the earlier report. For the most part the history reiterates the report word for word. The history differs in that it offers a clearer narrative and drops the allegations of collaboration.

35. Annual report of the Shanghai Municipal Council, 1923, 146.

36. "Shanghai Milk Supply: The Problem of Dairies Beyond Settlement Limits," *The North-China Herald*, Shanghai, January 13, 1923, 92.

37. "Shanghai's Milk: Question of Pasteurization," *The North-China Herald*, Shanghai, October 4, 1939, 18. Indeed, contamination of milk continued to present a serious threat to health. In September 1939, the *Municipal Gazette* reported that of seventy-nine milk

The Pure Milk Supply Commission recommended a panoply of regulative measures. It urged the Council to create a Municipal Incinerator for the disposal of the carcasses of diseased cattle. It suggested the appointment of a Veterinary Surgeon responsible for certifying the health of all cattle in licensed dairies. It proposed that milk be graded according to cleanliness and quality and made a number of recommendations about building codes and sanitary practices.[38]

Members of the Chinese dairy industry met the stepped-up regulations with an innovative plan to form a cooperative. Apparently, small dairies located in the International Settlement encountered problems of contamination most frequently when they purchased milk from small suppliers. The association, led by T. M. Yu, a graduate of Cornell University's Department of Agriculture, planned to eliminate this problem by establishing a central dairy in Pudong where suppliers could stable and milk their cattle. The complex was to include pasteurization facilities, a bottling room, refrigeration and a distribution center. Through these efforts the association hoped to "keep milk where producers will reap the profits, . . . the Chinese dairyman may retain the control of the industry, . . . the public will be able to purchase their needs at the price most reasonable, and . . . the duplication of delivery routes" will be eliminated.[39] Although the realization of this project has not yet been documented, it is suggestive of the degree of ambition, cooperation, and organization which characterized entrepreneurs in the Chinese milk industry.

At the beginning of the Sino-Japanese War (1937-1945), the dairy industry formed the Shanghai Dairy Association (*Shanghai niuru chang lianhehui*). Although the precise date of its formation is uncertain, association documents suggest that it was established in 1939. In 1942 another dairy organization, the Shanghai Dairy Industry Association, was formed. Given the chronology and later reports, it seems likely that this merged with, or was in fact the same as, the SDA.

The picture is further complicated by the fact that on 24 December 1942, the Shanghai Japan-China Dairy Industry Association was created (*Shanghai rihua ruye lianhehui*). Strangely enough, this organization's constitution noted that the organization would officially be known as the Shanghai Dairy

---

samples gathered in August, forty were found to harbor unacceptable levels of bacteria. ("Letters to the Editor," "Shanghai's Milk: Question of Pasteurization," *The North-China Herald*, September 27, 1939, 537.)

38. Annual report of the Shanghai Municipal Council, 1923, 147-171.

39. "Shanghai News: A Chinese Effort to Solve the Milk Problem," *The North-China Herald*, January 27, 1923, 237.

Industry Association.[40] Although this nomenclature may have been used in an attempt to down-play Japanese intervention, it is possible that these two organizations were for all intents and purposes one and the same. The articles of the two constitutions were very similar and in some places identical.[41] The constitution of the "Chinese" SDA noted that all organizational documents would be written in Chinese and Japanese.[42] (At the same time, English served as the organization's *lingua franca*: the Association wrote its correspondence, including that between the Chinese and Japanese, in English.) T. M. Yu, a prominent member of the SDA, served as a member of the preparatory committee for the Japan-China version of the Association.[43] The SDA included Westerners and Japanese as well as Chinese members. In the early 1940s the Grade C dairies split from the SDA and formed their own association. At some point their organization became known as the Shanghai Dairy Business Guild (*Shanghai niuru shangye tongyegonghui*). Whatever the reason for the split, enmities between the two groups survived for a decade. The industry was not reunited under one association until 1952.

Although documentary evidence for the Guild is extremely sparse, meeting minutes and correspondence for the Shanghai Dairy Industry Association have survived and are held in the Shanghai Municipal Archives. These materials document much of the Association's activity under occupation, including its careful negotiations with the Shanghai Municipal Council and the Japanese authorities. These sources not only provide insight into the intricacies of operating a business under occupation, but also challenge us to confront the issue of Chinese collaboration with the Japanese. The narrative related here raises questions about how historians interpret the actions of those immersed in the economic and political dangers of wartime Shanghai.

---

40. Article 1, S118.1.6.

41. The organizations' goals differed. The "Chinese" SDA "formed with the object of taking cognizance of and controlling all matters affecting the Dairy Industry in Shanghai, China, and generally all matters touching its welfare, and of interest, protection and benefit to the Dairies. Its operations are confined to its members only and shall extend to all matters within the scope of its objects properly submitted to it" (Article two, S118.1.6, pp. 012-013). The Shanghai Japan-China Dairy Association intended to "plan the members' enterprise, promote its development and hope for the friendship and good will of its members" (Article three, S118.1.6).

42. Article 30, S118.1.6. In the English version of the constitution, English was also listed as an official language. Article 23, S118.1.6, 012-103.

43. Minutes from the preparatory meeting for the establishment of the Shanghai Japan-China Dairy Association December 29, 1942, S118.1.6.

The Industry under Occupation

Japanese occupation confronted the dairy industry with new challenges. A large proportion of Chinese dairy farms were located in Zhabei. During the Japanese attack on Shanghai from August to November 1937, this district "received the heaviest concentration of fire ever laid on one piece of earth until then in history."[44] Presumably, many farms were destroyed and those that survived relocated. The stupendous rate of inflation must have cost the dairies some of their customers as the prices of staples like rice and oil soared.[45] At the same time, production was often hamstrung by shortages of power for pasteurization and refrigeration, glass for bottling, and even rubber for delivery cart tires. At the same time, like entrepreneurs in other industries, some dairymen capitalized on the prosperity of the International Concession where the economy flourished during the four years between Japan's takeover of the Chinese parts of the city and its occupation of the entire city immediately after the start of the Pacific War in December 1941.

Before the start of the Pacific War, the Japanese envisioned an ambitious plan to control China's economy, although they expended more effort in North China than they did in Central or South China.[46] The Shanghai Japan-China Dairy Industry Association may have been a product of this plan and Japan's initial "military management" of Foreign Concession industries after December 1941.[47] After the beginning of the Pacific War all of Shanghai came under Japan's jurisdiction. It was, however, at this moment that Japan began to loosen its control of China's industries. By the spring of 1943, Chinese entrepreneurs found themselves more fully in control of their own businesses.[48] Parks Coble has observed that particularly after the start of the Pacific War, the Japanese made greater efforts to gain the economic and political participation of Chinese elites in the occupied area. This reflected both the greater economic and military strains on Japan with the larger war and the desire of some in the Japanese camp to lend credibility to the puppet regime in Nanjing.

---

44. Frederic Wakeman, Jr., *The Shanghai Badlands: Wartime Terrorism and Urban Crime, 1937-1941* (Cambridge: Cambridge University Press, 1996), 6.

45. Frederic Wakeman Jr. reports that "if the cost of living of Shanghai workers in 1936 is indexed at 100, then in March 1941 the price of foodstuffs was 774; of rent, 385; of clothing, 503; of fuel, 636; and of miscellaneous goods, 599" (Ibid., 54).

46. Parks Coble, "Chinese Capitalists in the Lower Yangzi Area during the Sino-Japanese War, 1937-1945," (unpublished manuscript), 10.

47. Wang Ke-wen, "Collaborators and Capitalists: The Politics of 'Material Control' in Wartime Shanghai," *Chinese Studies in History* (Fall 1992): 47.

48. Wang, 47.

7.1. A Chinese farmer drives a valuable Holstein calf through a street clogged with Shanghai residents fleeing to the International Concession in 1937. Courtesy, Hoover Institution, Stanford, California.

SDA records confirm that Chinese dairymen remained in charge of day-to-day administration.[49] Businessmen used this increased control over their enterprises to fight for the supplies they needed. SDA correspondence shows the Association to have been a vigorous advocate that fought for the electrical power, fuel, rubber, and glass that the industry needed. The industry's ability to survive and even flourish under these arduous conditions speaks for the vibrancy of Shanghai commercial culture.

As war-time shortages deprived many city residents of adequate nutrition, milk became particularly valuable to those who could afford it.[50] The Shanghai Municipal Council created a dual price system which allowed children under ten years of age and invalids in the Settlement to obtain regular supplies (probably daily) at authorized prices.[51] Registration for milk at authorized prices began 3 February 1943. The council required residents to show their police identification card or citizen's certificate. Invalids had also to show a medical certificate. Foreign parents had to produce a birth certificate and Chinese parents were required to present a *baojia* certificate showing the number and age of their children.[52] The Shanghai Municipal Government did not initially ration milk. Instead, it asked the dairies to "voluntarily" agree to use up to seventy percent of their milk production to fill the "supply orders" issued by Council or French authorities to children under the age of ten, invalids, and hospitals.[53] In July 1944 it rationed milk to hospitals and to

---

49.   Whether dairy industry leaders joined the Commerce Control Commission (*shangtonghui*), established by Wang Jingwei and the Japanese in Shanghai is unknown (Wang, 49).

50.   Even the side effect of lactose intolerance—diarrhea and vomiting—may have been worth milk's nutritional benefits.

51.   T. M. Yu to Secretary General, First District Administration, Shanghai Special Municipality, February 11, 1944, S118.1.19, 003.

52.   Notification No. 6255, by order of S. Ozawa, Secretary, Council Chamber, published in the *Evening Post*, February 1, 1943, S118.1.17, 125. Efforts to control prices of "essential commodities sold by retail" began October 18 and 20, 1941 when the Municipal Council asked the Consular Body to approve a bye-law which would empower the Shanghai Municiple Council to set such prices. ("S.M.C. to Curb Profiteering; Control of Retail Prices," *The North-China Herald*, October 22, 1941.) The French Concession had introduced a price control system at least a year earlier. (*North-China Herald*, March 6, 1940, 372.)

53. Shanghai Municipal Council, Commodity Control Department, Distribution Section, Assistant Commission to K. Asano Esq., Japanese Dairymen's Association, Shanghai Nyugyo K. K. 12 The Bund, and T. M. Yu Esq., Shanghai Dairies' [*sic*] Association, 1477 Bubbling Well Road, Shanghai, March 17, 1943, S118.1.17, 003-004. At this point, there were supply orders for 14,000 pints. This represented sixty percent of Grade A dairies' production and fifty percent of Grade A and Grade B dairies' combined production. The Council anticipated under-registration and estimated that the final demand might reach

children under twelve months of age and guaranteed these groups a thirty percent discount.[54] The Council decided that milk was "essential" for these two groups only. Milk remained plentiful if expensive and those who were willing to pay the price could readily obtain it.

At least some SDA members happily complied with the Council's request that dairies fill Shanghai Special Municipality supply orders. In August 1943 Shanghai Dairy Farms and Liberty Dairy wrote the Commodity Control Office of the Shanghai Special Municipality:

> Herewith enclosed we are sending you a statement showing figures on the amount of milk daily produced in our dairies and daily supplied to the consumers as against your "Supply Orders." Since our supply has not yet reached the 70% mark we shall be willing to make up the difference by taking in more orders from you. Our only request is that when you issue new orders you give them out slowly or gradually so that it will give us more time to discontinue supplying milk to those consumers who have no "Supply Orders" from you.[55]

At a time when the rising price of milk probably forced many consumers to stop buying milk, dairies found attractive the stability of the Council's supply orders. Three months later, a little over half of Liberty Dairy's and Shanghai Diary Farm's net production of 2,250 pasteurized pints went to fill supply orders for the Shanghai Special Municipality.[56]

The Association continued, however, to voice resistance to the dual price system. Although it conceded "that the dual price system is advantageous to the public in that it will help a group of consumers to whom milk is their essential food enjoy a low price for milk," it also predicted that such pricing would create a black-market in milk. Because of the high black-market prices, they feared that delivery coolies might buy unlicensed milk at a cheaper price

---

seventy percent.
54. Clipping, *Shanghai Times*, July 12, 1944, S118.1.17, 094.
55. August 28, 1943, S118.1.13, 090.
56. The China Milk Powder Co., Ltd. [an agent for Liberty Dairy and Shanghai Dairy Farm] to the Milk Office, Economic Department, First District Administration, Shanghai Special Municipality, Shanghai, November 30, 1943, S118

or steal milk by diluting bottled milk with water.[57] In fact, newspapers frequently reported just such incidents.

Inflation and wartime shortages continually threatened to devour the dairies' profits. In the fall of 1935, an average dairy cow, one that produced about twenty pounds of milk a day, cost 500-700 *yuan*.[58] In July 1943 that same cow cost 50,000 *yuan*.[59] In 1944 alone milk prices increased almost tenfold in eight months. In March 1944, a pint of grade A milk cost 18 *yuan*.[60] By December it cost 145.[61] Prices increased even more dramatically on the blackmarket. One dairy owner estimated the December black-market worth of a pint of Grade A T. T. milk to be 280 *yuan* instead of the 152 *yuan* dictated by price controls.[62]

The SDA had to petition the Economic Department of the First District Administration, Shanghai Special Municipality, to raise prices.[63] When petitioning for a price increase, the dairies submitted detailed reports of production costs. To ensure that members submitted accurate accounts, the SDA engaged a chartered accountant to review members' statements before sending them on to the First District Administration. A member who submitted a faulty statement received a stern letter reminding him of the importance of accuracy:

The accountant has pointed out irregularities that he has found in your statement for October. We shall appreciate your making it a point *to*

---

57. SDA to unknown (probably Shanghai Municipal Council), c. March 1944, S118.1.17, 037. Dairymen routinely blamed their delivery men for the problem. Under the law, the licensee was held responsible for the condition of the milk his company delivered. The law provided for fines, revocation of license, and imprisonment. The Association tried unsuccessfully to convince the Director of Public Health in the First District Administration to revise the law. (Yu Tse-mai, SDA to Director of Public Health, First District Administration, Shanghai Special Municipality, March 11, 1944, S118.1.20.)

58. "Riyongpin qianshuo: niunai" (Brief introduction to everyday products: milk) in *JTXQ* 1.2 (December 8, 1935), 13.

59. SDA, memorandum on the depreciation of a cow, S118.1.17, 107.

60. Clipping, *Shanghai Times*, July 12, 1944, S118.1.17, 094.

61. Yu Tse-mai, President, SDA to O. Hirano, Commodity Distribution Department, Shanghai Special Municipality, Shanghai, December 8, 1944, S118.1.17, 064.

62. K. E. Petersen, Managing Director, The Shanghai Milk Cupply Co., Ltd. to The Executive Committee, SDA, December 22, 1944, S118.

63. SDA to R. Ohkubo, Economic Department of the First District Administration, Shanghai Special Municipality, January 5, 1944, S118.1.17, 103. Some evidence suggests that later in 1944, the SDA began to fix their own prices. It is possible that they fixed the prices within limits set by the authorities. See Yu Tse-mai, President, SDA to O. Hirano, Commodity Distribution Department, Shanghai Special Municipality, Shanghai, December 8, 1944, S118.1.17, 064.

make necessary corrections in your next statement. We also enclose a copy of *directions for filling in your statement* and wish that you will be guided accordingly . . . You are doubtless aware that the Administration will base their decision for any increase in milk prices upon your statement. For this reason, it is highly important that the figures in your statement should be accurate and represent the true fact.[64]

Although the SDA often expressed concern when the Department refused to allow a price increase, the public seemed to believe that the Council allowed the dairies to charge what the market could bear.[65] At the same time, SDA members avoided price wars by agreeing on minimum prices. The grade-C dairies also cooperated in setting a minimum price.[66] But these efforts did not completely equalize economic opportunity for Association members. Within the Association itself, economic exigencies differed. A minority of dairies received "official support" (whether in subsidies or reduced prices is unclear) which allowed them to avoid black market prices for fodder and other necessities. Dairies which did not receive such support urged the SDA to push for milk prices that accommodated black market gouging for fodder and other necessary supplies.[67]

Above and beyond its efforts to work within the system established by the Shanghai Municipal Council Authorities, the SDA pursued a variety of tactics to encourage the profitability of their farms. In an Association meeting late in October 1944, T. M. Yu, the SDA's president, set a four-point agenda to cope with the problems confronting the Shanghai dairies. He recommended that the dairies appeal to the authorities for help in securing allotments of fodder, take a loan from a government bank for the purchase of fodder, persuade the authorities to eliminate price controls on milk, and launch a publicity campaign to convince the public of the necessity of higher milk prices.[68]

The correspondence between the SDA and the Japanese authorities and the Shanghai Municipal Council reminds us that the occupation government did function. For example, customers accused the dairies of profiteering; as the price of milk soared, the dairies forced customers to add to previously paid deposits. One man complained to the Food Control Department. In February

---

64. SDA to "Dear Member," November 27, 1943, S118.1.17, 106.
65. See, for example, clipping, *Shanghai Times,* July 12, 1944, S118.1.17, 094.
66. Meeting minutes, April 11, 1944, S118.1.4, 006.
67. K. E. Peterson, Managing Director, The Shanghai Milk Supply Co. Ltd. to the SDA, December 22, 1944, S118.
68. S118.

1944 he paid a $1,600 deposit in Central Reserve Bank notes[69] to have thirty quarts of milk delivered a month. In May his dairy demanded an additional deposit of $1,000. In August they billed him for $1,400 more. He accused the dairies of using the deposit moneys to purchase cows. Because of the rising cost of cattle, by the time the dairies returned the deposits, they would have "earned" one of every three cows free and clear.[70] The Council subsequently set a maximum of $200 for cash deposits.[71]

Wang Ke-wen has suggested that most Shanghai merchants preferred to deal directly with the Japanese rather than look to Wang Jingwei's administration for support of their businesses during wartime.[72] Although the dairy business' relationship with the Wang regime is unknown, the SDA's interaction with Japanese representatives of municipal authority is well documented. Although one could hardly say business ran as usual, the SDA worked closely with the Japanese to keep their businesses profitable. All aspects of the dairy business, from fodder and electricity to allotments for rubber bicycle tires and permission to raise prices depended on the good will of the men who headed various departments. T. M. Yu, president of the SDA, maintained that good will through frequent correspondence and face to face meetings with O. Hirano of the Shanghai Municipal Council's Commodity Control Division. The three areas to which Yu devoted most of his attention were pricing, electricity, and supplies. Hirano apparently occupied a powerful and strategic place in the administrative structure. Yu channeled many of his requests through this man.

5th July 1943

Dear Mr. Hirano,

In the name of our Association I wish to write thanking you, and through you, the Council most heartily for the great relief to the dairies. Our members are particularly grateful to you for the great part you have played in bringing this about. It is most fortunate that we have in the

---

69. Commonly referred to in the English press as CRB. Wang Jingwei issued these notes in the areas of his alleged control early in 1942. They replaced Chongqing's currency, *fabi* or "legal currency" at a rate of two to one. (Wang Ke-wen, "Collaborators and Capitalists: The Politics of 'Material Control' in Wartime Shanghai," *Chinese Studies in History* [fall 1992], 43.)

70. W. Holzapfel, P.O. Box 1169, c/o Lehol Trading Co., 17 Canton Road to the Food Control Department, Shanghai Special Municipality, First District Administration, Foochow Road, (undated - c. March 1943?), S118.1.17, 54-55.

71. Circular No. 52, April 13, 1943.

72. Wang, 57.

Council an important man like you who understands our difficulties and is willing to help us out.

May I take this opportunity to tell you that as far as the Chinese dairies are concerned we, much encouraged by the recent increase, would all pledge ourselves hereafter to so improve our management and other things as to cut down production costs so that in the future we do not need to ask for increase more than necessary. This is one way of expressing our gratitude and reciprocating your kindness for the help thus given us.

Yours sincerely,
T. M. Yu[73]

The above letter is a typical example of Yu's assiduous efforts to maintain a cordial relationship with this powerful man. By early August the SDA, in spite of its president's promises to reduce production costs, requested another price increase. At least in this particular instance the SDA worked closely with the "Japanese Dairymen's Association" (JDA). President Yu informed the Japanese Dairymen's Association that he had written a joint letter to the Commodity Control Department.[74] After a conference with the Japanese Dairymen's Association, the two groups visited Hirano to discuss the price increase.[75] T. M. Yu continued to work with Hirano in negotiating price increases throughout the war.[76] At a General Meeting in February 1945, Yu reported that he, W. T. Wong, and Y. Z. Lee "called on Mr. Hirano and had a talk with him regarding increasing milk prices. The visit was quite satisfactory."[77]

The Japanese military controlled the Western District Power Company of Shanghai and acted as trustee to the Central China Electricity & Waterworks

---

73. S118.29.

74. Yu Tse-mai, SDA to The President, Japanese Sales Association (who was present), August 2, 1943, S118.1.17, 15.

75. Yu Tse-mai, SDA to O. Hirano, Commodity Control Department, Shanghai Municipal Council, August 5, 1943, S118.1.17, 033.

76. See, for example, Yu to Hirano, Economic Department, First District Administration, Shanghai Special Municipality, July 29, 1944 and Yu to Hirano, Commodity Distribution Department, Shanghai Special Municipality, October 28, 1944, S118.1.17, 062. Yu continued to meet with Japanese authorities after the war. On September 1, 1945 he met with "Japanese Embassy Authorities" to discuss milk prices. (SDA circular no. 75, August 30, 1945, S118.2.3).

77. General Meeting minutes, February 26, 1945, S118.1.4, 051.

Company, Ltd. When Yu[78] ran into trouble with the Power Company, he appealed to Y. Tashiro, Vice-Chief of the Health Department, to have electricity restored.

23 August 1943

Dear Sir,

   I must not fail to ask your help this time as we have failed to report to the Power Company that the two dairies, the Liberty Dairy and the Shanghai Dairy Farms, have been approved by your Department to carry on the joint pasteurization in order to save power and coal. As a matter of fact, the Liberty Dairy, which has been doing the work of the two dairies, naturally uses more electricity while the Shanghai Dairy Farms, which only stores a part of surplus milk, naturally uses [a] comparatively small amount of electricity, Now we have received a bill from the Power Company levying a heavy fine on the Liberty Dairy due to the fact that its consumption of power has exceeded the allotment for the two recent months. The only way to convince the authority of the Power Company is to ask your kindness to testify to the fact that we have mentioned above. Therefore we are enclosing herewith a statement for the electricity consumption of the two dairies for your reference. I am sure you will help us out this time because I remember vividly that during our past meeting you once promised to help the dairy members whenever they are in trouble.

Yours faithfully,
The China Milk Powder Co., Ltd.
Agent for Liberty Dairy
Shanghai Dairy Farms
General manager[79]

Hirano later promised to arrange a meeting between Yu and Tashiro.

27th September 1943

Dear Sir,

---

   78. Yu owned Liberty Dairy and either owned or was involved in the management of Shanghai Dairy Farms.
   79. To Y. Tashiro, Vice-Chief of Health Department, First District Administration, Shanghai Special Municipality, S118.1.15.

I must thank you for your kindness that you have promised to help me in arranging an interview with Dr. Tashiro. On account of its serious nature, would you be kind enough to arrange it as soon as possible? I am waiting for your telephone message. This interview will probably take up about half an hour of your valuable time, but, however, it will bring the two Associations more closely to the Administration, and the public will be very much benefited. I thank you.

Yours faithfully,
T. M. Yu[80]

Sufficient electrical power remained a problem, but Hirano appears to have given the dairies continued assistance. Early in 1944, electricity was allotted at 55% of 1943 usage. Because the dairies frequently exceeded their limit they received warnings and paid heavy fines. In May, the Director of the Economic Department (Hirano held a position in this department at this time) wrote the Japanese Embassy at the SDA's request. He insisted that the present allotment was insufficient to allow the dairies to operate through the summer. He claimed that "dairies are everywhere classified as an essential service. This is especially true in Shanghai at present, because dairies, in cooperation with the Administration, are supplying milk to children, hospitals, and invalids, who can not do without milk."[81] The letter proved effective. A month later Hirano received an effusive letter from Yu:

Dear Sir:
We shall never forget your assistance, as a result of which the dairies in Shanghai have recently obtained an increase in their power allotment. Without your invaluable assistance, our members, not having sufficient electric power for pasteurization and cold storage of milk, would find themselves in a very difficult situation to continue their business during the hot summer months. A timely increase in the power allotment, therefore, solves a most serious problem for our members and saves them no end of worry and trouble.
The purport of this letter is to express, on behalf of our members, our heartfelt thanks and appreciation for your kindness and favor so

---

80. Yu Tse-mai, President, SDA to Hirano, First District Administration, Shanghai Special Municipality, Present, September 27, 1943, S118.1.17, 008.
81. Director, Economic Department, First district Administration, Shanghai Special Municipality to the Japanese Embassy, Shanghai, May 2, 1944, S118.1.17, 079.

willingly and generously given. We can hardly find words adequate enough to express our sentiment in this regard.

Yours faithfully,
(signed) T. M. Yu
President,
Shanghai Dairies Association[82]

Yu appealed to Hirano again in December 1944. Central China Electricity and Waterworks had cut off electricity to factories that produced neither "war materials" nor "daily necessities." Hirano had helped Sunshine and Scotch Dairies regain their power. Yu wrote Hirano requesting that he lend his "valuable assistance" to the rest of the SDA dairies without power. Attempting to stimulate some sense of obligation, he wrote: "As these dairies continue to cooperate with you in supplying milk to invalids and children above twelve months of age, we hope that our request would receive your favorable consideration."[83] The dairies operated through the end of the war. We may assume that Hirano again effectively intervened on the SDA's behalf.

Yu also contacted Hirano about procuring supplies at cheaper prices. When the SDA learned that Japanese dairies had been allotted third-grade flour for their cows, Yu requested the same treatment for SDA dairies. In a letter to the Supplies and Distribution Section of the Economic Department, he reported that the SDA had "brought the matter up to Mr. Hirano, in our recent interview with him. He has kindly promised to give it his favorable consideration."[84]

Yu also turned to Hirano to settle labor disputes. When the men who rented their cows to SDA dairies refused to accept six *yuan* per pound [of milk] Yu asked Hirano to "render some immediate help to the dairies in this matter." Yu assured Hirano that he thought the six dollar cap on the price of raw milk "just and fair." He suggested Hirano send a circular explaining to both the dairies and the men who rented out their cows that the Economic Department had fixed this price.[85]

---

82. Yu to Hirano, June 7, 1944, S118.29.

83. Although Yu does not put too fine a point on it, his use of "invalids" may be read as a reference to wounded Japanese soldiers in hospital. (Yu, resident of SDA to Hirano, Economic Department, First District Administration, Shanghai Special Municipality, December 12, 1944, S118.1.17, 067-068.)

84. Yu, President, SDA to Supplies and Distribution Section, Economic Department, First district Administration, Shanghai Special Municipality, April 4, 1944, S118.1.13, 022.

85. Yu to Hirano, First District Administration, Shanghai Special Municipality, September 13, 1943, S118.1.17, 009.

Making the Transition

In mid-summer, 1945, as Japan's future began to look grim, the executive board of the SDA resigned en masse. On 21 July 1945 the Association met again to elect new officers.[86] T. M. Yu was made President Emeritus.[87] In anticipation of the impending Nationalist victory, the Association commissioned twenty vases inscribed with a narrative relating the hardships suffered by the dairy industry under occupation.[88] Concerned about possible interpretations of their war-time behavior, occupation participants began to shape the past before it had even begun.

Sometime later that summer, the SDA threw a farewell party in honor of their Japanese intermediary, O. Hirano, and presented him with an Eversharp pencil as a token of their appreciation. The accountant entered the expenses for the party and gift just below a record of "Payment to the Puppet Income Tax Bureau In Settlement of Income Tax for Association Members for the Period from 1940-1943."[89] Meanwhile, the SDA bank account shrank considerably. As of 31 October 1945 the Association held $30,447,360.29 in its bank account. On 31 December 1945 the accounts showed a total of only $39,703.62.[90] SDA members moved quickly to protect themselves against the accusations of collaboration and the reprisals and confiscations they might suffer after Japanese defeat.

Did the members of the SDA suffer real hardship during the war? The statistics are sparse but suggestive. Yu's connections served him well. Before the war, Liberty Dairy had 120 head of cattle.[91] By August 1943, Yu had increased his herd to 130 and reported a daily production of 1,200 pounds. By January 1944, Yu added another fourteen cows and boosted production to 1,700 pounds per day.[92] Other dairies also managed to expand. In February 1944, Model Dairy announced that its daily production had increased to 600 pints and predicted that within a month production would climb to 1,000

---

86. General meeting, July 14[?], 1945, S118.1.4, 81.

87. Memo, SDA to Yu, August 21, 1945, S118.1.1.

88. S118.

89. The SDA spent 78,900 (1,100 less than was collected) on the party and 51,900 on the pencil. "Statement of Receipts and Expenditures for the Period from December 31, 1944 to October 31, 1945", and "Statement of Receipts and Expenditures for the Period from 28 February to March 31, 1945", S118.2.9.

90. "Statement of Receipts and Expenditures for the Period from December 31, 1944 to October 31, 1945, S118.2.9.

91. "Riyongpin qianshuo: niunai" (Brief introduction to everyday products: milk) in *JTXQ* 1.2 (December 8, 1935): 13.

92. S118.1.13, 39, 42, 59, 60.

pints.[93] Early in 1944, Liyuan Dairy announced that it had doubled its capital from $500,000 to $1,000,000.[94] Certainly some dairies withstood the occupation better than others. As fodder became increasingly scarce, dairies butchered and sold some of their cows in order to buy feed for those remaining. In February 1945 Liberty and Shanghai Dairy Farms, Yu's enterprises, butchered only nine percent of their cows (20/234). In the same month Culty reduced its herd by 13 percent (52), leaving it with 363 head. Meanwhile, Lucerne was forced to sacrifice almost half its herd, butchering forty of its ninety cows. Nevertheless, many dairymen hung on through the end of the war, a period when most of Shanghai's factories were forced to close down due to a lack of resources.[95]

Perhaps more revealing of how the SDA dairies fared during occupation is their longevity. Attendees at each general meeting were supposed to sign in. Compiling membership information from these sign-in sheets is, however, difficult. Some weeks members used the Chinese names for their dairies and other weeks they used the English equivalent. At other times they signed in using their personal names, again in either English or Chinese. Moreover, a single entrepreneur might operate more than one dairy. Thus, with the exception of core members who attended consistently, it is extremely difficult to track Association membership.

Although occupation strained the industry, it did not ruin it. In December 1946, the Department of Sanitation reported 61 dairies supporting 2,514 head of cattle and producing a total of 37,427 pounds of milk daily. The industry had lost about 500 head and ten to twenty farms. The war did affect the geographical distribution of dairy farms. Before the War of Resistance, most Chinese farms stood in Zhabei and the southern part of the city (*hunan*). In post-war Shanghai, one third of Chinese farms had moved to Pudong. The rest gathered in Huxi, Fahua, and Caojing. The distribution of herd size remained roughly the same. In post-war Shanghai only seven percent of farms possessed over one hundred head of cattle. Forty-eight percent of farms raised twenty head or fewer.[96]

---

93. Yu Tse-mai, President, SDA, to the Milk Office, Economic Department, First District Administration, Shanghai Special Municipality, February 2, 1944, S118.1.13, 83.

94. Liyuan to SDA, January 8, 1944, S118.1.13, 84.

95. Wang, 55.

96. Xu Tianxi, *Shanghaishi nongye gaikuang* (The situation of the agricultural industry in Shanghai) (Shanghai: Shanghai yuanyi shiye gaijin xiehui congkan di 21 zhong, 1947), 19.

Who Tells the Story?

Grade A and B diaries of the SDA may have dominated the occupation bureaucracy, but after the war they found themselves outmaneuvered by the C dairies' Shanghai Dairy Guild. The dispute may have been sparked by the C dairies dissatisfaction with the SDA's plan to raise prices eight times in 1947.[97] On 17 October 1947, the day when the SDA announced its sixth price increase, the C dairies struck out on their own. In *Xinwen bao*, one of Shanghai's most popular newspapers, they proclaimed the formation of the Dairy Trade Guild (*Niuru shangye tongyegonghui*), appealed to the Nationalist government to maintain reasonable prices, and, in the words of the SDA secretary, "libeled the Shanghai Dairy Association."[98] Two days later the Guild published another announcement in *Xinwen bao*. Guild members petitioned the government to divide the industry into two associations, asked the Sanitation Department to sanction the Association, and wrote a public letter to the Shanghai Municipal Trade Association (*Shishanghui*) recounting the history of the dispute. The Municipal Trade Association tried to negotiate a reconciliation between the two associations but failed. On 22 October the Guild took out yet another advertisement. This time it accused the SDA of participating in the Japan-China Dairy Industry Association, declared the SDA an illegal organization, and asked the government to dissolve the SDA. Although the SDA did participate in the Japanese Association, the Guomindang took no disciplinary action. Instead, it continued to urge the Guild and the Association to reunite. Somehow amidst the brouhaha the Guild finagled an official registration with the Bureau of Social Affairs.[99] The SDA toyed with the possibility of changing its name to the Shanghai Dairy Guild (*Shanghai niuruchang tongyegonghui*) in another attempt to register with the Bureau of Social Affairs,[100] but ultimately abandoned the idea.[101]

If the C dairies made life uncomfortable for the SDA under the Nationalists, Association members lost no time in turning the tables when the Communists came to power. By June 1950, prominent members of the SDA maneuvered themselves onto the preparatory committee of the new Shanghai

---

97. The SDA scheduled eight increases for that year. The inflation under the KMT made that of occupied Shanghai seem mild in comparison. By December 1947 the SDA planned to raise the price of Grade A milk to 26,000 *yuan*. "Shanghai niuruchang lian hehu 36 nian gongzuo gaikuang" (The circumstances of the SDA in 1947), S118.1.7, 15-19.

98. "Shanghai niuruchang lian hehu 36 nian gongzuo gaikuang" (The circumstances of the SDA in 1947), S118.1.7, 15-19.

99. "Rupinye de guoqu he xianzai," 10.

100. General meeting minutes, January 16, 1946 [?], S118.1.1, 5.

101. SDA announcement, July 3, 1948, S118.1.1, 6.

Dairy Product Industry Guild (*Shanghaishi rupin gongye tongyegonghui*), an organization that operated under the auspices of the Shanghai Association of Industries (*Shanghaishi gongshangye lianhehui*). This group, which included the elder statesmen of the SDA, Yu Tse-mai and Li Bolong, was charged with investigating the "transference of public property" between the Japanese and the Shanghai Dairy Trade Guild.[102] On 5 July 1950, the first official meeting of the Shanghai Dairy Product Industry Guild was held at 1477 Nanjing Road, the former headquarters of the SDA. In May 1950 the Shanghai Association of Industries invited 153 dairies to participate in the preparatory meeting. Guild members refused to join and held out for a year and a half. On 1 February 1952, the Shanghai Association of Industries announced that the dairy associations had once again been united within one organization, the Dairy Industry Guild (*Rupinye tongyegonghui*).[103]

Of Collaborators and Commercial Culture

When is it appropriate to apply the label "collaborator?" Where do we draw that line? In the cultural world, Poshek Fu has written about the psychological and artistic tensions produced by the decision to defy or cooperate with Japanese authorities. In the world of business we have Parks Coble's careful studies of the various strategies Chinese businessmen adopted when confronted by the facts of Japanese occupation.[104] Yet, has the historiography grappled with the true import of Chinese cooperation and collaboration? Castigation does not make for very useful or interesting history. But at the same time, does history fulfill its responsibility to the past if it ignores the moral significance of decisions to cooperate with the Japanese? After all, occupation was not just another bump in the road to a smooth-running and profitable business. It was qualitatively different than the other obstacles which Republican businessmen faced.

The Milk Industry files at the Shanghai Municipal Archives raise three questions. Were these Chinese businessmen valiantly struggling to support the Chinese nation by sustaining Chinese businesses under adverse conditions? Were they, at best, apolitical actors who only sought to pursue business as usual? Or were they opportunists, willing, even eager, to exploit every possibility in hope of increased profits? Responses to these questions are

---

102. Memo from the *Shanghaishi gongshangye lianhehui choubei hui*, June 22, 1950, S118.4.007, 3.

103. "Rupinye de guoqu he xianzai," 10.

104. Parks Coble, "Chinese Capitalists and the Japanese: Collaboration and Resistance in the Shanghai Area, 1937-1945," paper presented at the Luce-Berkeley Seminar on Urban Culture and Social Modernization of 20th Century China, Berkeley, December 2-3, 1994.

undoubtedly individual, subjective, and highly charged. It is perhaps useful to approach these questions in light of the entrepreneurs' vision of themselves as promoters of health and modernity. The ads for milk which promised improved health and vigor cannot be dismissed as the simple products of cynical advertising. T. M. Yu wrote about his industry with an almost messianic enthusiasm. Yu and others envisioned a revitalized China powered by a commercial economy.

But at the same time, precisely because their program for social and national reform was driven by pursuit of profit, the rhetoric of milk promotion—or any other—was vulnerable to manipulation. It allowed the men of the SDA to justify their cooperation with the Japanese as an effort to provide milk to those who needed it, children and invalids, even as the supplies went to Japanese allies and the Japanese themselves. It also allowed them to commemorate their wartime role as embattled caretakers of the weak and ill. Thus, an examination of the dairy industry before and during occupation leads beyond the issues of collaboration to an examination of the interaction between politics and enterprise in Republican China. As the film 'The Sorrow and the Pity' has so eloquently demonstrated,[105] it is precisely this ability to offer a perfectly reasonable rationale to explain one's toleration or cooperation with occupying forces that makes the issue of collaboration so knotty and frightening. After all, people rarely admit that they collaborated out of pure, calculating self-interest.

Study of the dairy industry under occupation also reveals a strong and flexible commercial culture. In many ways these entrepreneurs do seem to have treated the Japanese occupation as just another challenge to their ability to produce and market their product. As they navigated the economic and political mazes of occupation, industry members affiliated themselves with others of similar economic rather than political interest. Such decisions point to the existence of a well-developed commercial culture that ordered itself according to the universals of profit and market share rather than those of loyalty and nationalism.

---

105. Again, I have Frederic Wakeman, Jr., to thank for calling my attention to this important film.

Afterword

Nanjing Road, Broadway and the Roots of International Corporate Commerce

William R. Taylor

These explorations into the development of consumer commerce in early twentieth century Shanghai provide important evidence about the more general nature of commercial culture. The very existence of the British concession area in Shanghai brought new elements into play. Extensive foreign investment not only attracted capital to Shanghai but also innovative ideas and new mechanisms for fostering consumption on an international scale. These elements in their workings can be seen as early strains of what by the end of the century would become multinational global commerce

During the 1920s and 1930s, Nanjing Road in Shanghai, as the foregoing essays point out, became the focus of a commercial culture similar in many ways to its counterparts in New York and other Western cities. Centrally placed geographically within the foreign settlement area of the city, the road became the hub or radiating center of an expansive new commercial culture. Its "take off" at the end of the 1910s seems to have been ignited by Western products such as the cigarette, commercial institutions originating in the west, such as the department store, and the presence of an entrepreneurial elite from abroad. All of these elements, when combined with a sophisticated and eager local population already schooled in a long tradition of native commerce, introduced a veritable revolution in consumption practices.

The process through which these changes took place, as it is described in the previous chapters, is fascinating to anyone familiar with consumer development elsewhere. While there is still much that remains to be unearthed about the situation in Shanghai, Nanjing Road as revealed here encourages comparisons with the development of commercial culture in New York and elsewhere. Both the similarities and the differences are instructive. The differences, moreover, are profound. It is these differences that make the comparison between Shanghai and commercial centers in the west so interesting and, in the context of the future development of international commerce, so significant.

The key to consumer development everywhere was aggregation and outreach: concentration of population and systematized means for reaching out and stimulating desire for goods and services. Beneath the blossoming and somewhat chaotic commercial development taking place in Shanghai today, it is possible to detect the skeleton of this older "antique" commercial culture dating from the prewar period. Along the Bund, in what was once the British concession area, one can still find the faded monumental structures of banks and other commercial institutions that fired this earlier development. Along the length of Nanjing Road itself, intermixed with new high-rise buildings, some of the original stores and theaters still stand, partly concealed behind new facades and garish new signs.

This older commercial world, to judge from what one learns in these chapters, appears to be in many ways similar to that of New York in the same period. While the scale of commercial activity clearly differed, the basic ingredients were present in both cities: a burgeoning urban population, street lighting, supportive municipal government, the beginnings of a transportation system with ferries and street cars, a clustering of banks and other commercial institutions along the river on the Bund. By the twenties department stores, theaters, newspapers, radio stations, advertising agencies and other instruments of publicity had developed in the vicinity of Nanjing Road, much as they had along Broadway in New York in the area known as Times Square. In both cities consumers from the hinterland appear to have been drawn into this new economic maelstrom.

While the overall configuration is similar in both cities, the particular features of New York commercial culture are important to note. Before anything approaching a consumer society could develop in New York City a number of changes had to take place. At the opening of the nineteenth century, cities were widely viewed as pestilential, dangerous, and seductively wicked places. Those people who lived in cities, for the most part, did so out of necessity. The kind of amenities that were to characterize urban life in the next century—theaters, restaurants, hotels and places of public recreation were very limited.[1] Major literary figures assailed cities as a violation of Nature. A steady barrage of anti-urban rhetoric flowed from pulpits all over the United States.[2]

---

1. For an overview of New York commercial culture, see "Introduction," William R. Taylor, ed. *Inventing Times Square. Commerce and Culture at the Crossroads of the World* (New York, 1991).

2. Morton and Lucia White, *Writers Against the City* (Cambridge, Mass., 1961).

Protestant clergy still preached against most forms of urban entertainment, theater, dancing, and self indulgence of every kind. Respectable people kept to themselves, barricaded from street life behind copiously draped brownstone facades. An ethic of saving and prudent expenditure disciplined commercial life. Very little disposable income remained for most working people after the necessities of life were met. The very term "consumption" retained a pejorative meaning until well into the next century. Economically, manufacturing and retailing were still largely undifferentiated, as in previous centuries, confined to shops of skilled craftsmen such a hatters, drapers, and artisans in the luxury trades, who sold out of the shop/residences where goods were fabricated. Some vestiges of an older apprentice system still remained.[3]

During the nineteenth century, a number of new elements slowly shifted this older paradigm. The first important change came with the rapid expansion of commerce into the port of New York after the opening of the Erie Canal in 1825. The opening of the canal made possible easy and cheap water transshipment into the hinterland of goods arriving in New York harbor, which quickly outdistanced other eastern seaboard cities as America's principal port. New York itself rapidly became a major manufacturing center and native products began to outdistance imports in many consumer markets. The growth of railroads at mid-century further enhanced New York's prominence. The corresponding increase in trade was reflected in the expansion of commercial activity. Broadway assumed its role as the main artery north into Westchester from the shipping facilities at the base of Manhattan. As the century progressed, it blossomed as the site of commercial institutions of every kind. Probably the most important agency of the new commercial culture, William Leach argues, was the department store, which appeared virtually simultaneously in every Western nation at the end of the nineteenth century. These stores concentrated consumption under a single roof and quickly became the leading edge of an emerging consumer culture. New York stores such as Macy's and Gimbels achieved this role by their central location, the amenities they offered to shoppers, especially women, by exhibiting goods in novel and attractive ways, by their aggressive advertising, and by promoting consumption through their support of parades and other civic functions that drew large crowds to their central locations. By the end of the century Wall Street, running perpendicular to lower Broadway, assumed its place as the financial headquarters of the nation and a major center of world finance. Its investment banks and stock exchange provided the capital that fired the revolution under way.[4]

---

3. Taylor, *Inventing Times Square,* 83-98, 16-50.
4. Ibid., 99- 115.

Another important element in this new commercial climate were the industries that provided entertainment and pleasure to New Yorkers and others doing business in the city: the theaters, restaurants, hotels, dance halls, and night clubs. According to Lewis Erenberg, these important institutions, especially as they were promoted by a burgeoning and inventive publicity industry, did more than anything else to change the older attitudes toward cities and to encourage a new sense of cities as exciting and interesting places. They also produced a much-noted change in manners, as middle-class women took up ballroom dancing and began to appear in public, often unaccompanied, even at night in the new jazz clubs and speakeasies.[5]

In the nineteen twenties, Edward Bernays, drawing on his experience in war propaganda, helped create an entirely new publicity industry that was devoted to promoting urban goods and services in ways and on a scale unknown to previous advertising. A tourist industry, using tie-ins with railroads, hotels, and theaters, advanced the novel idea that cities were interesting places to visit. Finally, a new industry devoted to innovative technology in signs and lighting revolutionized the appearance of cities at night. Times Square as "The Great White Way" accordingly became a world renowned symbol of the new urbanism. Meanwhile, from the center of the entertainment district, newspapers, new urban-oriented magazines like the *New Yorker* and, by the 1930s, national network radio carried new images of New York across the country. Finally, in the 1920s the newly created Department of Commerce concentrated its efforts on providing government support for the new consumer industries. In the words of investment banker Paul Mazur, "a staggering machine of desire" had been created.[6]

This situation as it developed in New York, despite the similarities that have been noted, differed in one essential respect from what was happening in Shanghai. This difference was structural and derives from the British imperial system of doing business on an international scale. The key element in the imperial system was imposition by force of trade agreements that brought concessions from China as it had elsewhere. These concessions were both in territory and in trade. The existence of a concession area populated by Englishmen and other foreigners doing business, when combined with the volume of British goods flowing in from abroad, dominated the development of commercial culture in Shanghai. Despite the ingenuity with which Western commercial products and strategies were adapted to Chinese tastes, almost everything that happened in Shanghai bears some mark of imperial coercion.

---

5. Taylor, 158-177.
6. Ibid., 99-115.

The differences from New York were partly a matter of timing. New York itself, of course, was part of a former British colony with a century and a half of experience in the British imperial system, but by the end of the nineteenth century, the crucial moment for commercial culture, the disparities of the imperial system had ceased to characterize what happened there. For much of the nineteenth century, for example, British publishing houses had dominated the book market in the United States. It was Charles Dickens, not Herman Melville that most Americans read, but by the closing decade of the century New York publishers had virtually banished books of British origin and imposed a copyright agreement to protect American authors from pirating abroad. The War of 1812 was fought over an embargo of British goods. English efforts to intervene in behalf of the Confederacy during the Civil War badly misfired and further weakened England's position as a trading partner. But the central feature of commercial development in New York was not the shrinking of British imports but the growing dominance of goods of native manufacture and the novel ways in which these American goods were marketed and promoted.

While London developed a consumer culture similar to that of New York at much the same time, no one saw New York commercial culture as derivative or questioned the originality and native ingenuity that produced the explosive development there. Indeed, nothing anywhere can compare with the heady growth and distinctiveness of commercial culture in New York. The presence of foreigners in New York in no way undercut, and probably enhanced, the original character of what happened there. Americans of English origin along with others foreigners played important roles in New York commercial developments, as they did in Shanghai, but their roles differed from that of their counterparts in Shanghai. Alexander Stewart, one of New York's most innovative retailers, was a Scotch-Irish immigrant. Edward Bernays, the creator of New York's public relations and publicity industries, was Viennese and a nephew of Sigmund Freud. Joseph Urban, the genius behind New York theatrical design, who created almost singlehandedly a style of modernism for New York entertainment, was also Viennese and worked for the Hapsburg monarchy in Vienna for the first half of his career, to cite only a few conspicuous cases. As in the case of Shanghai, practically everyone of any consequence in New York commercial life came from somewhere else. The important thing was what the economic maelstrom of New York did with their talents. Scholars, accordingly, do not ask the questions about New York that historians here are asking here about Shanghai.

By contrast, the entire system for doing business in the concession area appears to have been imported from abroad, along with most of the infrastructure. It seems clear that the models for development in the concession areas of Shanghai were devised initially to serve the needs of foreigners living and doing business in the city. It was from these models for the most part that Chinese adaptations were devised. Practically everything in the settlement areas was imported: the form of municipal government, business practices, such as Western accounting, real estate development and corporate organization, public utilities such as street lighting, electricity and running water, and many amenities of everyday Western life such as soap, towels and cosmetics. Local Chinese merchants resisted for a time Western styles for advertising and displaying goods in stores, but eventually these models, as shown by Wellington Chan, appear to have prevailed.[7]

To say this is not to question the striking similarities between New York and the concession area developments in Shanghai. When one considers the fundamental differences between the situation in Shanghai and that in New York, it is amazing how striking these similarities are. The very fact that commercial culture more or less simultaneously would take much the same form in both places says something about the universality of the changes in consumption taking place in the early twentieth century. These similarities extend from infrastructure and the physical layout of both commercial areas, to the character of particular institutions, to aesthetic features of changes taking place and matters of attitude. Some of these similarities have already been mentioned. As major port cities, for example, both Shanghai and New York were natural centers of commerce and therefore exposed to foreign influences, with the differences already noted. Nanjing Road and Broadway as commercial arteries and axial foci, however, appear to have concentrated commercial activities and clustered commercial institutions such as department stores in similar ways. Real estate development and, in particular, the development of distinctive types of mass housing for the working population characterized both cities. New York created a type of row house adjacent to Broadway early in the nineteenth century. This type of house, built on speculation, was also subject to second and third tier leases, like the *shikumen*. It seems to have served a function similar to the *shikumen* and its later variants described by Hanchao Lu. At the end of the century, still another type of housing, the multi-storied so-called dumbbell or railroad tenement was characteristic of the worker housing adjacent to upper Broadway and Times Square in what was known as Hell's Kitchen and the Tenderloin districts. As in the case of Shanghai, these areas were also centers of prostitution, vice and gambling from the turn of the century into the 1930s. In Times Square itself, the theater and film industries were the focus of all of the new media strategies for publicizing entertainment

---

7. Taylor, "Introduction," *Inventing Times Square*, xi-xxvi.

as on Nanjing Road. A Shanghai figure like the film mogul Zhang Shankun with his showbiz style, discussed here by Poshek Fu, could have walked out of a story by Damon Runyon. In both cities, the department store was the center of a developing consumer culture, and in both cities department store entrepreneurs, as described by Wellington Chan and Western historians such as William Leach, recognized the importance of links to other institutions of a kind discussed by Habermas in his *Structural Transformation of the Public Sphere*. Both cities developed insular characteristics and experienced estrangement from the culture in the hinterland. The anti-urban attitudes in the United States and the condemnation of luxury and self-indulgence fostered by the Protestant clergy seem to have been matched in Shanghai by Confucian ideas of disciplined austerity and by the agitation of groups like the Guomintang New Life Movement, as described by Carlton Benson. Both cities developed distinctive identities to combat these negative assessments. Shanghai's *Haipai* persona and New York's "New Yorker," both originally pejorative labels, became proud self-designations for citizens in both cities. Similarly, a distinctive image of the modern woman, propagated by all the media, was a central feature of modernist ideology: the American "flapper" and the Shanghai cover girl discussed by Carrie Waara. The similarities, of course, are not exhausted by these examples, but it seems to me that these are some of the most striking. What seems most significant about the Shanghai version of commercial culture, however, was not its similarity to New York's but the subtlety and ingenuity with which foreign products and business practices were adapted to very different local Chinese needs. In merchandising, graphic arts, advertising, magazine publishing and film interesting cultural amalgams with a distinctive Shanghai style or *Haipai*, as it was called, were produced. Such developments gave Shanghai commercial culture a truly indigenous character, one that appears to have been widely recognized. It is these amalgams that probably deserve some attention. Some of the following examples have been discussed in earlier chapters, but they warrant further mention here in a somewhat different context.

These examples suggest that in the waning days of the old imperial trading system, strategies were being devised that foreshadowed international trade as it would be practiced under a system characterized by a free, or at least less coercive, exchange of goods. Experience has shown that as products move across national boundaries and into foreign markets, steps must always be taken to link them in some fashion to the consumer culture of the market nation. The early marketing experience of the British American Tobacco Company is a particularly interesting example, in view of the importance overseas sales have assumed today in the profitability of the industry. According to Sherman Cochran's account here, the failure of an initial advertising campaign that utilized techniques and images from its campaigns in the United States apparently led the company to shift strategy, to import state of the art lithography machinery and to found a training school to supply commercial artists. An experienced Chinese commercial artist was then employed to devise advertising with local appeal. One result was the creation of a poster campaign that tapped the Chinese convention of the New Years Calendar Poster. The iconography of these posters, while directed toward promoting the company, was designed to include patriotic motifs and other conventional details. A prominent feature, according to Sherman Cochran, was a woman wearing the classic *qipao* but also wearing Western shoes, signaling a break with the tradition of bound feet—a perfect traditional Chinese/modern Western hybrid. These calendars were then distributed to commercial establishments everywhere in advance of the Chinese New Year. The success of the campaign set the pattern for the company's future marketing strategies and clearly reflected one new direction in promoting foreign products. Its tactics were soon being adopted and adapted by other companies. To adopt a term from the film industry, *subtitling* seems to be the process at work in this example. The product, namely the cigarette, has not been altered, only the script used to promote it. In this instance, the power exercised is one of corporate hegemony rather than an older imperial authority. This process of subtitling would soon be adopted to promote a myriad of other corporate products in foreign markets.

Another development in product adaptation was the devising of a cover for current periodicals that featured a young Chinese girl. Art periodicals during the 1920s and 1930s, according to Carrie Waara, devoted considerable discussion to the effectiveness of using the figure of an attractive and confident young woman, according to the writers the very essence of Chinese modernity, as a cover girl on popular periodicals. She points out that such portrayals, in the way they represented women, appeared to draw upon a classical tradition of Chinese court painting. This strategy, in other words, also combined Western and Chinese cultural elements. Here the imported item is a promotional strategy, namely the magazine cover girl phenomenon, common in promoting goods in the West. In this instance, however, the import itself has been adapted to Chinese culture, in what the film industry might call *dubbing*, the insertion of indigenous content into the product itself, a native voice, so to speak.

Other features of Shanghai commercial culture, to judge from what is said here, appear to be similar in character. In New York, William Leach has pointed out, Edward Bernays initiated a new kind of publicity campaign by advocating a more generalized appeal than that contained in conventional advertising. Instead of promoting particular velvet garments, for example, he undertook a year-long campaign to herald the qualities of velvet as material used in clothing, a campaign similar to that undertaken by the silk industry, as described by Carlton Benson. The promotional activities of Shanghai's dairy industry during the war with Japan, as described by Susan Glosser, also seem to have been similarly engineered to underscore the general virtues of milk and to stress its scientific modernity, much as Bernays had done with qualities of velvet in New York. In both instances there appears to have been more than a subliminal appeal to patriotic and national pride. Once again, *dubbing* would seem to describe the nature of the adaptation, since the strategy was imported but the voices were from the locality.

Some of the other features of Shanghai's commercial culture, to judge from the evidence provided here, seem to fall somewhere between *dubbing* and the *remake*. In a remake, a film is reset in the host culture, recast with local talent and rewritten in the language and cultural idiom of the market nation. The great success that Zhang Shankun obtained with his film epic, *Hua Mulan Joins the Army*, all while it being based on a traditional story, owes much of its success to the Western Show Biz style through which it was promoted, but the fact that Zhang was unable to repeat the success of this film in the movies he subsequently made indicates that there was more than publicity involved. The germ of success in this instance appears to have been the appeal of the plot—a young woman disguises herself as a man and joins the army—to the feelings of a Shanghai audience under Japanese occupation at the time of its release, as described by Poshek Fu.

The *shikumen* or row house seems to provide an incontestable example of a *remake*. The Western concept of row house development underwent almost complete refashioning at the hands of British and Chinese builders trying to capitalize on the influx of Chinese refugees into the settlement areas during the various crises of the late nineteenth century. The problem that the builders faced, it appears, was one of providing in Western settlement areas for working Chinese families with little experience of urban life. These families were used to detached houses in mainly rural areas that provided some communal space both indoors and out. Large scale real estate development itself was unknown in nineteenth-century China. The real estate market in the settlement areas was created and dominated by Westerners who saw the need for some sort of segregated arrangement for these local newcomers, but at the same time were looking to their profits. With these concerns in mind, they devised a speculative form of collective housing, a gated compound of row houses, whose external arrangements were Western but whose internal configuration drew on the traditional Chinese courtyard house. This kind of house, modified in various ways over the years, provided a flexible format for many different living arrangements, including subtenants and elements of extended families.

In the case of the *shikumen*, both the concepts of large-scale real estate development and of the row house were extracted from Western experience but the inside story, so to speak, was Shanghainese. The case of the *shikumen*, as it is described by Hanchao Lu, is of particular interest here because it once again illustrates the pervasiveness and flexibility of Western marketing ideas in situations far removed from the site or circumstances of their origination in New York or London.

There is more than marketing to international global commerce, but anyone who has traveled in Asia today quickly realizes the central place that the international marketing of corporate products has now assumed. These marketing strategies have taken root and succeeded in every kind of political and social situation. The ability of an industry as market sensitive as film to carry on successfully, even for a few years, when Shanghai was surrounded by an occupying Japanese army at war with China, is still further evidence of this resilience. Part of the film industry in France succeeded in carrying on in much the same way during the German occupation of Paris during World War 11. The ability of the milk industry not only to survive but to expand during the war with Japan is equally astonishing, especially considering the newness of milk as a consumer product in China. We now know the extent to which the banking industry in Switzerland carried on its dealings with the German government all while professing political neutrality. Clearly what appears to be an age characterized by the triumph of the product, as in the French concept of "Cocacolonization," is really a period in which corporations now exercise the kind of dominance in the market place once enjoyed by national governments. Japan, for example, now devotes much of its foreign policy to fighting off the incursions of international corporations.

It would be useful to examine more closely the circumstances that have made this kind of change in corporate behavior possible. Susan Glosser's account of the carefully framed courtesy in the correspondence between the Shanghai Dairy Association and Japanese authorities provides one clue. The language of business etiquette seems to provide a certain kind of immunity from politics and a partial shelter from war, revolution and other national contingencies. Corporations cloak themselves in this kind of formal discourse as a means overriding precisely the kinds of limitations imposed by international barriers of one kind or another. They do this, one suspects, for reasons similar to those that have led some corporations to establish headquarters very like embassies in countries where they do extensive business, their corporate logos illuminated at night over capital cities. Like the distinctive uniforms adopted by some service corporations, such as UPS, the corporate logo is an icon of a new kind of hegemony that has made the whole world into an international settlement of a somewhat different kind.

Contributors

Carlton Benson is Assistant Professor of History at Pacific Lutheran University

Wellington K.K. Chan is Professor of History at Occidental College

Sherman Cochran is Professor of History at Cornell University

Poshek Fu is Associate Professor of History at University of Illinois at Urbana-Champaign

Susan Glosser is Assistant Professor of History at Lewis & Clark College

Hanchao Lu is Associate Professor of History at Georgia Institute of Technology

William R. Taylor is Professor Emeritus of History at New York University

Carrie Waara is Assistant Professor at Castleton State College

Index

CORNELL EAST ASIA SERIES

104 Harold M. Tanner, *Strike Hard! Anti-Crime Campaigns and Chinese Criminal Justice, 1979-1985*

105 Brother Anthony of Taizé & Young-Moo Kim, trs., *Farmers' Dance: Poems by Shin Kyong-nim*

106 Susan Orpett Long, ed., *Lives in Motion: Composing Circles of Self and Community in Japan*

107 Peter J. Katzenstein, Natasha Hamilton-Hart, Kozo Kato, & Ming Yue, *Asian Regionalism*

108 Kenneth Alan Grossberg, *Japan's Renaissance: the Politics of the Muromachi Bakufu*

109 John W. Hall & Toyoda Takeshi, eds., *Japan in the Muromachi Age*

110 Kim Su-Young, Shin Kyong-Nim, Lee Si-Young; *Variations: Three Korean Poets*; Brother Anthony of Taizé & Young-Moo Kim, trs.

111 Samuel Leiter, *Frozen Moments: Writings on Kabuki, 1966-2001*

112 Pilwun Shih Wang & Sarah Wang, *Early One Spring: A Learning Guide to Accompany the Film Video February*

113 Thomas Conlan, *In Little Need of Divine Intervention: Scrolls of the Mongol Invasions of Japan*

114 Jane Kate Leonard & Robert Antony, eds., *Dragons, Tigers, and Dogs: Qing Crisis Management and the Boundaries of State Power in Late Imperial China*

115 Shu-ning Sciban & Fred Edwards, eds., *Dragonflies: Fiction by Chinese Women in the Twentieth Century*

116 David G. Goodman, ed., *The Return of the Gods: Japanese Drama and Culture in the 1960s*

117 Yang Hi Choe-Wall, *Vision of a Phoenix: The Poems of Hŏ Nansŏrhŏn*

118 Mae J. Smethurst, ed., *The Noh Ominameshi: A Flower Viewed from Many Directions*

119 Joseph A. Murphy, *Metaphorical Circuit: Negotiations Between Literature and Science in Twentieth-Century Japan*

Order online: www.einaudi.cornell.edu/eastasia/CEASbooks, or contact Cornell East Asia Series Distribution Center, 369 Pine Tree Rd., Ithaca, NY 14853-2820, USA; toll-free: 1-877-865-2432, fax 607-255-7534, ceas@cornell.edu